Fodor

Fodor

Language, Mind and Philosophy

M. J. Cain

Polity

The right of M. J. Cain to be identified as author of this work has been asserted in accordance with the Copyright, Designs and Patents Act 1988.

First published in 2002 by Polity Press in association with Blackwell Publishers Ltd

Editorial office:
Polity Press
65 Bridge Street
Cambridge CB2 1UR, UK

Marketing and production:
Blackwell Publishers Ltd
108 Cowley Road
Oxford OX4 1JF, UK

Published in the USA by
Blackwell Publishers Inc.
350 Main Street
Malden, MA 02148, USA

ISBN 0-7456-2472-3
ISBN 0-7456-2473-1 (pbk)

A catalogue record for this book is available from the British Library and has been applied for from the Library of Congress.

Typeset in $10\frac{1}{2}$ on 12 pt Palatino
by Best-set Typesetter Ltd., Hong Kong
Printed in Great Britain by TJ International Ltd., Padstow, Cornwall

This book is printed on acid-free paper.

Key Contemporary Thinkers

Published

Geoffrey Stokes, *Popper: Philosophy, Politics and Scientific Method*
Georgia Warnke, *Gadamer: Hermeneutics, Tradition and Reason*
James Williams, *Lyotard: Towards a Postmodern Philosophy*
Jonathan Wolff, *Robert Nozick: Property, Justice and the Minimal State*

Forthcoming

Maria Baghramian, *Hilary Putnam*
Sara Beardsworth, *Kristeva*
James Carey, *Innis and McLuhan*
Rosemary Cowan, *Cornell West: The Politics of Redemption*
George Crowder, *Isaiah Berlin: Liberty, Pluralism and Liberalism*
Thomas D'Andrea, *Alasdair MacIntyre*
Eric Dunning, *Norbert Elias*
Jocelyn Dunphy, *Paul Ricœur*
Matthew Elton, *Daniel Dennett*
Nigel Gibson, *Frantz Fanon*
Espen Hammer, *Stanley Cavell*
Keith Hart, *C. L. R. James*
Sarah Kay, *Žižek: A Critical Introduction*
Paul Kelly, *Ronald Dworkin*
Carl Levy, *Antonio Gramsci*
Moya Lloyd, *Judith Butler*
Dermot Moran, *Edmund Husserl*
Kari Palonen, *Quentin Skinner*
Steve Redhead, *Paul Virilio: Theorist for an Accelerated Culture*
Chris Rojek, *Stuart Hall and Cultural Studies*
Wes Sharrock and Rupert Read, *Kuhn*
Nicholas Walker, *Heidegger*

Contents

Acknowledgements

This work started life as a PhD thesis submitted to the University of St Andrews in 1997. I benefited from the supervision of Roger Squires and (whilst I was a visiting research student at Birkbeck College, London) that of Sarah Patterson and Barry Smith along with the comments of my examiners, Crispin Wright and Martin Davies. I have received valuable feedback on draft versions of the early chapters from Anna Hindley and members of classes that I taught at Birkbeck College and the University of Nottingham. The comments of two anonymous readers for Polity helped me to improve the clarity and organization of the text. I would like to take this opportunity to express my gratitude to all of these people.

Julie Reid has been a constant source of affection, support and encouragement. Without her companionship, completing this project would have been a much more stressful experience than it turned out to be. My greatest debt is to my parents, Bernard and Christine Cain. Without their unceasing support, my philosophical career would have ground to a halt several years ago. This book is dedicated to them.

1

The Fodorian Project

Introduction

Since the early 1960s Jerry Fodor has been engaged in developing a collection of distinct yet mutually reinforcing positions on a range of related issues and in doing so has set much of the agenda in the philosophy of mind and cognitive science. What binds together the various elements of Fodor's output is that they all count as engagements in a single project. In this chapter I will give an account of Fodor's project and a description and motivation of the commitments that underlie it.

Fodor has two basic commitments: one is to folk psychology and the other is to physicalism. These two commitments generate the task of providing a vindication of folk psychology within a physicalist framework. But what is folk psychology and what is physicalism? And why would anyone devote a career spanning several decades to the project of vindicating folk psychology within a physicalist framework? It is to these questions that I now turn.

Folk Psychology

Folk psychology (otherwise known as common-sense psychology) is a descriptive, explanatory and predictive practice that is central to human life. We engage in this practice whenever we interact with our fellows and we would be at sea in the social world without it. Folk psychology is bound up with a conception of the human individual according to which we are minded and engage in behaviour that is influenced by our mental states. Here are some examples of typical engagements in folk psychology.

- I hear Edgar utter the English sentence 'Fang is ferocious and if there is one thing that I don't like it's a ferocious dog'. I immediately jump to the conclusion that Edgar believes that Fang is ferocious and that, in all probability, he wants to avoid any contact with Fang.
- Whilst running with Edgar, I hear a gruff bark. Edgar gasps 'Oh no! It's Fang' and suddenly veers off the path and dives behind a nearby bush, where he remains cowering for some time. Later I am asked why Edgar behaved in such a strange manner. I answer by reporting that Edgar, believing Fang to be ferocious, wants to avoid Fang and that, having heard a gruff bark, he believed that Fang was in the vicinity.
- On being asked why I didn't follow Edgar's Fang-avoidance tactic, I point out that though I believe Fang to be ferocious and want to avoid close contact with him, I also believe that my running prowess is such that Fang has little chance of catching me.
- On another occasion I am running ahead of Edgar. I see Fang in the distance heading our way and predict that, shortly, Edgar will engage in hiding behaviour.
- I fear that Fang's menacing behaviour is going to put Edgar off running altogether. So, in order to keep my running companion, I devise a new route lying outside the beast's territory and tell Edgar about my plans and the Fang-free nature of the new route.

In the above examples I did various things: I described some of my own mental states by means of language; I came to a conclusion about the mental states of one of my fellows on the basis of seeing him behave in a particular way; I explained and predicted the behaviour of one of my fellows on the basis of the mental states that I took him to have; I engaged in behaviour (including linguistic behaviour) with a view to influencing the mental states and subsequent behaviour of one of my fellows. Such activity is the very stuff of folk psychology and it is difficult to see how I – or anyone else – could explain, predict and manipulate the behaviour of my fellow humans as effortlessly and effectively by any other means.

The mental states that figured in the above examples were beliefs and desires. Beliefs and desires (along with intentions, expectations, hopes, fears etc.) belong to an important category of mental states known collectively as the intentional states.[1] In this context 'intentional' is a technical term and does not mean what it means in everyday discourse. To describe an individual as having an intentional state is not to say that she deliberately has that state. Moreover, although intentions are a species of intentional state, not all intentional states are intentions.

Folk psychology is committed to the existence of a wide range of mental states and events that are to be distinguished from the intentional states. In addition to beliefs, desires and the like, folk psychologists routinely attribute perceptual experiences, sensations, feelings, emotions, moods, personality traits and so on to themselves and to their fellows. Hence, as far as folk psychology is concerned, the mental realm is populated by a heterogeneous collection of phenomena. However, it is arguable that the intentional states occupy a central role in folk-psychological practice so that it is only an exaggeration – as opposed to an outright misrepresentation – to describe folk psychology as being an intentional psychology.

Intentional states have the following important features, all of which are emphasized by Fodor. (See Fodor 1987, ch. 1.)

Intentional states have semantic properties; in particular, they have meaning or content and, correlatively, they can be about particular objects and possible states of affairs and they have truth or satisfaction conditions. Consider the state of believing that Fang is ferocious. It is central to the identity of this state that it has a particular meaning or content: namely, the content expressed by the English sentence 'Fang is ferocious'. Alternatively, one might say that it is central to the identity of this state that it is about Fang, that it represents him as being ferocious and that it is true if and only if Fang is ferocious. Folk psychology distinguishes between intentional states that differ in terms of their content. For example, the belief that Fang is ferocious is a different belief than the belief that Fang enjoys savaging joggers.[2]

Intentional states can be about objects and phenomena that do not exist. For example, it is possible to have beliefs about Santa Claus, ghosts, unicorns and phlogiston.

Just as one can believe that Fang is ferocious, one can desire that it be the case that Fang is ferocious, intend to make it the case that Fang is ferocious and so on. What distinguishes these intentional states is not their respective contents (for they all have the same content). Rather, what distinguishes them is the relation involved: believing that Fang is ferocious involves standing in the belief relation to the content expressed by the English sentence 'Fang is ferocious', whereas desiring that it be the case that Fang is ferocious involves standing in the desire relation to the same content. In short, whenever an individual has an intentional state, there is a relation and a content involved and folk psychology classifies or individuates intentional states in terms of both their content and the relation involved. Thus, when engaged in the folk-psychological practice of attributing an intentional state to one of our fellows, we will typically specify both a relation and a content ('I believe that Fang is ferocious', 'He wants it to be the case that Fang is impounded', 'She hopes that Fang does not spot her').

Intentional states are not causally inert; on the contrary, they are very much part of the causal fray. There are three distinct types of causal process in which intentional states figure prominently. First, intentional states are often caused by environmental factors impinging on an individual, as when a display of Fang's ferocious behaviour causes me to believe that Fang is ferocious. Second, intentional states often cause intentional states, as when my belief that Fang is ferocious causes me to want to avoid all contact with Fang. Third, intentional states often cause behaviour, as when Edgar's belief that Fang is in the vicinity causes him to crouch behind the nearest bush. Consequently, folk-psychological explanations of intentional states and behaviour are causal explanations. The manner in which intentional states causally interact with environmental impingements, other intentional states, and behaviour is not random and undisciplined; rather it is regular or law-governed. Hence, there exists a large battery of counterfactual and hypothetical supporting generalizations relating intentional states to one another, to environmental impingements and to behaviour.[3]

There is a systematic relationship between the causal powers of intentional states and their semantic properties; intentional states tend to cause intentional states and behaviour to which they are semantically related. Suppose that an individual faced by a snarling Fang wanted to scare Fang away and believed that the best way of doing this would be to start shrieking at the top of her voice. Then, typically, this belief and desire pair would interact to cause her to form the intention to start shrieking at the top of her voice and this intention would subsequently cause her to so behave. In this case, an intention and subsequent behaviour are caused by a belief and desire pair to which they are coherently related. This would not be the case were the intention and behaviour caused by a desire to see an aardvark and a belief that Kilimanjaro is the highest mountain in Africa. The process of reasoning constitutes another graphic case of this general kind. When a subject reasons, she will have a thought that causes her to have another thought that in turn causes her to have a third thought, and so on. Typically, the contents of the members of the resultant chain of thoughts will be related to one another in a way that mirrors the relationship between the propositions of a logically valid argument. As Fodor puts it, 'one of the most striking facts about the cognitive mind as commonsense belief/desire psychology conceives it [is] . . . the frequent similarity between trains of thoughts and *arguments*' (1987: 13).

A natural language such as English is productive in the respect that there are infinitely many distinct sentences of English that a competent speaker of that language is capable of constructing and understanding. A similar point can be made about intentional states: there are infinitely many distinct thoughts that a normal human subject is capable of having. Moreover, it is commonplace for an individual to form an intentional state that she has never had before. For example, the sentence 'a ferocious dog has never been seen swallowing a double-decker bus' is likely to cause most readers to entertain a thought that they have never had before. In thinking such a thought for the first time, an individual will typically deploy concepts that she has a prior grasp of but arrange them in a new way so as to express a content that she has never previously entertained.

The system of intentional states is systematic in the respect that any human subject capable of believing (or desiring, or intending, etc.) that object a stands in the relation R to object b (for any relation R and any objects a and b) is also capable of believing that b stands in the relation R to a. For example, any human subject capable of believing that the ferocious dog savaged the jogger is capable of believing that the jogger savaged the ferocious dog.

It is possible to believe that Mark Twain was the greatest American writer of the nineteenth century without believing that Sam Clemens was the greatest American writer of the nineteenth century despite the fact that Mark Twain and Sam Clemens were one and the same person. Similarly, it is possible to believe that water is wet without believing that H_2O is wet despite the fact that water and H_2O are one and the same substance. Put generally, it is possible to believe (or desire, or intend, etc.) that a is F without believing (or desiring, or intending, etc.) that b is F despite the fact that a = b. How is this possible? Because the belief that Mark Twain was the greatest American writer of the nineteenth century is a different belief from the belief that Sam Clemens was the greatest American writer of the nineteenth century and an individual can have either of these beliefs without being aware of the fact that Mark Twain and Sam Clemens were one and the same person. This fact has a linguistic consequence: within sentences that ascribe an intentional state to a subject, co-referential expressions are not generally interchangeable *salva veritate* (that is, without a change of truth value). For example, the sentence 'Edgar believes that Mark Twain was the greatest American writer of the nineteenth century' is true. But the sentence generated from that sentence by replacing the expression 'Mark Twain' with the co-referential expression 'Sam Clemens' is false. This feature of sentences that ascribe intentional states to individuals is known as their intensionality.[4]

Sensations such as pains, aches, itches and tickles have a qualitative character, as do experiences or feelings of joy, disappointment, frustration and the like. To use Thomas Nagel's (1974) memorable expression, there is something that it is like to have a sensation or a feeling and what it is like to have a sensation or a feeling of a particular type is different from what it is like to have a sensation or a feeling of any other type. Indeed, it seems plausible to say that sensations and feelings are at least partly individuated in terms of their qualitative character so that a subject's sensation isn't (for example) a pain or her feeling an experience of joy if it doesn't have the appropriate qualitative character. Matters are quite different with respect to intentional states for they do not have any distinctive qualitative character; for example, there is nothing in particular that it is like to believe that Fang is ferocious. That is not to say that experiences with a distinctive qualitative character are never associated with intentional states. It is perfectly possible for Fang's new neighbour to experience a sinking feeling when she comes to believe that Fang is ferocious. But such an experience would appear to be an effect of the acquisition of the belief rather than part of the belief itself, and someone else could acquire just the same belief whilst having a different resultant experience or whilst having no associated experience at all.

How do we engage in folk psychology? How do we so effortlessly and effectively construct intentional explanations and predictions of the intentional states and behaviour of our fellows? Fodor's answer invokes the idea that folk psychology is a theory akin to a scientific theory. (See Fodor 1987, ch. 1.) A scientific theory is a collection of sentences. These sentences contain terms that refer to observable phenomena. In addition, they contain terms that refer to unobservable entities postulated by the theorist in order to explain the observable phenomena that fall within the domain of the theory. Such terms are known as theoretical terms and familiar examples are 'gene', 'virus', 'electron', 'quark' etc. The sentences that constitute a theory specify generalizations concerning the relations (particularly the causal relations) that are taken to hold between the theoretical entities and observable phenomena referred to by the terms of the theory.

It is widely held that the core sentences of a scientific theory implicitly define the theoretical terms of the theory en masse (Lewis 1970). So, for example, the core sentences of genetic theory implicitly define the term 'gene' or, in other words, specify what it is to be a gene. Consequently, if the core sentences of a theory are largely false – in that the world doesn't contain a collection of entities whose causal relations to one another and to observable phenomena correspond to that described by those sentences – then the entities postulated by the theory have no existence.

Fodor takes folk psychology to be a theory in the respect that it consists of a large collection of sentences that assert the existence of a network of causal generalizations relating mental phenomena, environmental impingements and observable behaviour. The mental terms that appear in these sentences (for example, 'belief', 'desire' etc.) are theoretical terms that refer to unobservable phenomena postulated by the theory in order to explain observable behaviour.

The view that folk psychology is a theory, though not without its detractors,[5] is widely held in the philosophical community and has been dubbed the theory-theory (Morton 1980). An early and important expression of the theory-theory can be found in the work of Wilfred Sellars (1956). Another important element of the theory-theory is the idea that folk psychologists have knowledge of the generalizations that constitute the theory of folk psychology and that this knowledge is employed in the construction of folk-psychological explanations and predictions. At first appearances, this idea might sound somewhat implausible. After all, few of us would be able to specify more than a small number of banal psychological generalizations. However, consider the case of our linguistic capacities. Few speakers of English are able to specify any of the grammatical rules of that language. Nevertheless, their speech largely consists of grammatically correct sentences and they are pretty effective when it comes to the task of determining whether any given string of English words constitutes a grammatically correct sentence. How, one might ask, could speakers of English have such capacities unless there was some respect in which they knew the grammatical rules of their language? Chomsky has famously argued (see Chomsky 1986, for example) that the best explanation of such capacities is that speakers of natural languages have a form of unconscious knowledge of the grammar of the language that they speak. Such unconscious knowledge is known as tacit knowledge and is held to be encoded in the brain. Fodor thinks that an analogous claim holds with respect to folk psychology. The best explanation of our ability to explain and predict the behaviour of our fellows is that we have a tacit knowledge of a rich battery of causal generalizations relating intentional states to one another and to behaviour. Moreover, just as Chomsky holds that human subjects have an innate knowledge of universal principles of human language, Fodor hypothesizes that much of our folk-psychological knowledge is innate. (See e.g. Fodor 1978b.)

Fodor cites the following as a paradigmatic example of a folk-psychological generalization: 'If X wants P, and believes that not-P unless Q, then, ceteris paribus, X tries to bring it about that Q' (1987: 13). Another prominent example is this: if X intends to do P then, *ceteris paribus*, X will do P. Note that these generalizations quantify over intentional states and behaviours that are semantically related. This reflects the above described fact that the causal powers of intentional states tend to be coherently related to their content. In virtue of this feature of such generalizations, a typical folk-psychological explanation of a subject's having a particular intentional state or behaving in a particular way will appeal to intentional states that are semantically related to the target state or behaviour. Hence, such explanations are not merely causal explanations; in addition, they rationalize or make sense of the subject's intentional states and behaviour. For example, when I explain Edgar's jumping behind a bush in terms of his desire to hide from Fang and his belief that, in the circumstances, the best way to hide from Fang would be to jump behind the bush, I reveal Edgar's behaviour to be sensible or rational in the light of its intentional causes.

What are we to make of the fact that the phrase '*ceteris paribus*' appears in the above examples of folk-psychological generalizations? '*Ceteris paribus*' is a synonym of 'all else equal'. Hence, generalizations that contain *ceteris paribus* clauses are hedged or qualified rather than universal. Fodor accepts that folk-psychological generalizations invariably contain *ceteris paribus* clauses, but he denies that this tells against their explanatory or predictive value. (See Fodor 1991b.) For, it is typical of the special sciences (that is, the sciences other than physics) that their generalizations are hedged as is indicated by the geological generalization that a meandering river erodes its outer bank, *ceteris paribus*. I will have much more to say about *ceteris paribus* generalizations and how they can be of explanatory value in due course.

Fodor is an enthusiastic champion of folk psychology. For him we really do have beliefs, desires and the like, and these mental states have the properties that folk psychology takes them to have. Moreover, the generalizations of folk psychology are largely true.[6] This is not to say that folk psychology captures all the facts about our mental lives. No doubt there are mental states and generalizations concerning our mental lives that folk psychology is blind to. And folk psychology doesn't have the power to explain all of the mental phenomena with which we are acquainted. (For example, folk psychology does not seem to provide us with a particularly effective way of explaining perceptual illusion, mental illness, depression or intellectual ability.) However, when it comes to explaining and predicting everyday human behaviour, folk psychology has no peers. Here is a case of Fodor waxing lyrical.

> [Folk] psychology works so well it disappears. It's like those mythical Rolls Royce cars whose engines are sealed when they leave the factory; only it's better because they aren't mythical. Someone I don't know phones me at my office in New York from – as it might be – Arizona. 'Would you like to lecture here next Tuesday?' are the words he utters. 'Yes thank you. I'll be at your airport on the 3 p.m. flight' are the words that I reply. That's *all* that happens, but it's more than enough; the rest of the burden of predicting behaviour – of bridging the gap between utterances and actions – is routinely taken up by the theory. And the theory works so well that several days later . . . and several thousand miles away, there I am at the airport and there he is to meet me. Or if I *don't* turn up, it's less likely that the theory failed than that something went wrong with the airline. (1987: 3)

In characterizing folk psychology as a body of true causal generalizations that are of considerable explanatory and predictive power, that appeal to unobservable entities and that contain *ceteris paribus* clauses, Fodor is explicitly comparing folk psychology to a special science. Moreover, he is suggesting that a respectable scientific psychology would, at the very least, bear much in common with folk psychology.

Physicalism

Fodor's second basic commitment is to a metaphysical position known as physicalism. In a nutshell, physicalism is the doctrine that reality is ultimately physical in nature so that the sum totality of physical facts determines the sum totality of facts. But what does that mean? What is the physical and in what respect are physical facts supposed to determine all other facts? A good way of approaching these questions involves reflecting on the structure of science.

There are many distinct sciences including physics, chemistry, biology, geology, neurophysiology and (perhaps) psychology. Each science has its own particular domain of enquiry and, therefore, is concerned with explaining a distinctive range of phenomena. To this end, each science will appeal to a range of objects, states, events and processes that are described and classified in terms of their possession of a distinctive range of properties. Hence, each science has its own proprietary vocabulary. For example, physics talks of atoms, fields, quarks, photons and the like, but not of living organisms, genes, viruses or (biological) reproduction. And just as biology doesn't talk of atoms, fields, quarks and photons, geology doesn't talk of living organisms, genes, viruses or reproduction.[7]

The sciences other than physics are known as the special sciences. It would appear that there is a respect in which all special science phenomena inhabit the physical domain, that is, the domain of physics. Consider the one pound coin located in my pocket. It is identical to, or constituted by, a particular physical object, an object that is nothing more than a collection of physical particles standing in certain physical relations to one another. Hence, the coin can be described in physical terms, that is, in terms of such physical properties as its mass, its micro-physical structure and the like. Such a description would constitute a more basic or fundamental description of the coin's nature than one that talked of its monetary value or its purchasing power. The latter description would specify some of the higher-level properties of the coin. There is nothing special about my coin; all coins are physical objects. But not vice versa, for there are plenty of physical objects that are not identical to, or do not constitute, a coin. Consequently, a complete description of the nature of the world at the physical level would provide a specification of the fundamental nature of all the coins that exist. Moreover, it would specify the fundamental nature of a domain of objects that was much wider than the domain of coins but one that the domain of coins belongs to or inhabits.

What is true of coins would also appear to be true of biological phenomena. Each and every biological object, state, event or process (be it a living organism, a gene, a viral infection, a mating or whatever) would appear to be identical to, or constituted by, a physical object, state, event or process. Hence, anything that is biological will also have a physical description but not vice versa (as there are plenty of physical things that are not identical to, or do not constitute, anything biological). And a physical description of, say, a living organism will constitute a more basic or fundamental description of that thing than would a biological description. Whenever a biological event causes some other biological event, a physical event that is identical to, or constitutes, the biological cause will set off a causal process that eventuates in a physical event that is identical to, or constitutes, the biological effect. The course that this physical causal process follows will be determined by the laws of physics. Hence, biological causal processes and any biological causal generalizations or laws that there are will be underpinned by the laws of physics.

This point about biology can be generalized to all of the special sciences: each and every special science object, state, event or process is identical to, or constituted by, a physical object, state, event or process; special science causal processes and laws are underpinned by physical causal processes and the laws of physics; and a complete physics would provide the most basic and general description of the scientific domain.[8]

What is the relationship between physical properties, on the one hand, and special science properties, on the other? Given that special science phenomena inhabit the physical world and that that world is at bottom governed by the laws of physics, if there are any special science laws then there must be a systematic and disciplined relationship between physical and special science properties. In the absence of such a relationship, the behaviour of phenomena at the special science level would be entirely random, in which case the special sciences would not be sciences at all.[9]

We can distinguish between two types of disciplined and systematic relationship that might hold between physical and special science properties, both of which would appear to enable physical laws to underpin higher-level special science laws. First, special science properties might be identical to physical properties so that any true statement expressing an identity relationship between a particular special science property and some physical property will lay bare the ultimate nature or essence of that property. There would appear to be examples of such a relationship: water is H_2O, that is, the property of being (a sample of) water is identical to the property of being a collection of H_2O molecules, and it is often claimed that heat is mean kinetic energy. However, it would appear that such examples of property identity are thin on the ground. Consider an example from outside the scientific realm. It is difficult to envisage a non-physical can-opener; each and every can-opener is a physical thing of some description. However, the property of being a can-opener cannot be identified with any physical property for the simple reason that the class of can-openers constitutes a physically heterogeneous bunch. (Think of how widely can-openers can differ in terms of their shape and size, what they are made of, their principles of operation, and the like.) Suppose that the human species had been particularly unadventurous when it came to developing the can-opener so that all can-openers were made out of the same material to the same design. It would then be true that all the can-openers that existed were physically alike so that the property of being a can-opener was coextensive with a particular (perhaps conjunctive) physical property. However, it would not be true that the property of being a can-opener was identical to that physical property; the fact that these properties were coextensive would be a mere accident.

What is true of can-openers is true of many special science phenomena. It is difficult to envisage how anything could be a heart or a mountain (to pick just two examples) without being a physical thing. But notice how physically different the heart of a frog is from the heart of a human and how much mountains can vary in terms of their shape, size, mass and micro-physical constitution. Moreover, had the world been such that all actual existing hearts were physically similar, one could still coherently imagine the discovery or evolution of a heart that bore no physical similarity to all the other hearts that had previously existed or been known about. What these reflections suggest is that the property of being a heart and that of being a mountain, though perfectly respectable special science properties, cannot be identified with any physical property. In this respect, these properties are hardly atypical special science properties.

The second type of disciplined relationship that might exist between special science and physical properties is that of supervenience: special science properties might supervene upon physical properties. Supervenience is a relationship that holds between distinct families of properties and is somewhat weaker than that of identity.[10] Consider another example from outside the scientific realm. Fang is unpleasant. But why, one might ask, is Fang unpleasant? This question is ambiguous. On the one hand, it could be a question about the causal origins of Fang's being unpleasant. On this reading, the question would be answered by an appeal to the nature of Fang's upbringing, his history or his genetic make-up. On the other hand, it might be a question concerning what it is about Fang in virtue of which he merits the description 'is unpleasant'. This is not a causal question; rather, it is a question as to which lower-level or more basic properties of Fang are responsible for his being unpleasant. It is a question that is answered by describing the way in which Fang typically behaves; by pointing out his tendency to chase runners, snarl at other dogs, drool and dribble whilst eating and so on. These behavioural properties are such that if you have them you thereby have the property of being unpleasant. In short, these properties are capable of generating and sustaining the property of being unpleasant so that having them is sufficient for having the property of being unpleasant. However, it is not necessary to behave as Fang does in order to be unpleasant. Edgar is thoroughly unpleasant despite the fact that he doesn't chase people, never snarls and has impeccable table manners. Why then, in the non-causal sense, is Edgar unpleasant? What is it about Edgar in virtue of which he can be described as being unpleasant? Again, the answer has to do with how Edgar behaves, but in his case it is a different collection of behavioural properties that generates and sustains his unpleasantness. Edgar has a tendency to ignore strangers, boorishly monopolize conversation and ridicule those who express views that he does not share. That is why he is unpleasant. Hence, there are different collections of behavioural properties that are equally capable of generating the property of being unpleasant. In order to be unpleasant, two individuals need not have the same behavioural properties, but if they have the same behavioural properties then if one is unpleasant so must be the other.

The relationship that the property of being unpleasant bears to lower-level behavioural properties of the sort had by Fang and Edgar is one of supervenience. Put generally, supervenience is a relation of non-causal determination holding between distinct families of properties. B properties supervene upon A properties if and only if the A properties that an object has fix or determine its B properties. If B properties supervene upon A properties then two objects that agree with respect to their A properties will thereby have just the same B properties. However, as in the above example, it is possible for objects to share a B property without sharing any A properties.

There is a distinction between different types of supervenience relation. For example, there is a distinction between weak supervenience and strong supervenience. If A properties weakly supervene upon B properties then any two objects inhabiting the same possible world that agree in their B properties will thereby agree in their A properties. The existence of such a relation is consistent with the possibility of two objects that inhabit different possible worlds agreeing in their B properties yet having different A properties. If A properties strongly supervene on B properties then any two objects that agree in their B properties will thereby agree in their A properties regardless of whether or not they inhabit the same possible world. In what follows I will talk about supervenience in general and will ignore the question of what specific type of supervenience relation (for example, strong, weak or whatever) must hold between mental and physical properties for physicalism to be true.

Having described the relations of identity and supervenience, we can give a general account of the structure of science in the following terms. Physics is the most basic and general science. Special science phenomena are physical in the respect that each and every special science object, state, event and process is identical to, or constituted by, some physical phenomenon. Special science properties are either identical to or supervene upon physical properties. And the laws of physics underpin all the special science laws. This account of the structure of science, though not mandatory, is certainly the received view in the philosophical community and is endorsed by Fodor.

We are now in a position to characterize physicalism. Physicalism is the view that reality in general – and not just the scientific domain – is at bottom physical in nature so that all properties that are genuinely instantiated ultimately supervene upon physical properties in such a way that the sum totality of physical facts determines the sum totality of facts. It is important to appreciate that the physicalist need not hold that all real properties are scientifically respectable or that science is the only source of knowledge. For, there can be properties that ultimately supervene upon the physical yet do not figure in any laws. The scientist will have no interest in such properties or the facts involving their instantiation. Consider the property of having a degree. This is a perfectly real property that many people have. This property features in a whole battery of rough-and-ready generalizations (people with degrees tend to be of higher than average intelligence; people with degrees tend to earn more than those who have no academic qualifications; people with degrees tend to be over the age of 5), but such generalizations don't have the status of scientific laws. Consequently, the property of having a degree is not one that any science cares about and knowledge of the geographical and social background, the economic well-being and the leisure activities of those people who have degrees does not count as scientific knowledge despite the fact that such knowledge may well be very interesting and important. Moreover, degrees are not physical things; there is no physical thing that can be identified with my degree despite the fact that we talk about degrees as if they were objects (although there is a physical thing that can be identified with my degree certificate). None of this need pose any great problem for the physicalist. For the physicalist might argue that it is physical things (namely human individuals) that have degrees and that they have them in virtue of facts about their history and facts concerning certain social institutions and practices, facts that ultimately hold in virtue of how the world is at the physical level. Therefore, physicalism, though bound up with a healthy respect for science and a commitment to the primacy of physics and the physical, is not a crudely scientistic position.

In developing an account of the nature of physicalism I have freely written of physical properties, facts and phenomena. But how, one might ask, are we to understand the term 'physical'? It has been objected that those who call themselves 'physicalists' face major problems when it comes to formulating their position in such a way that it comes out as both plausible and non-trivial (see Crane and Mellor 1990). An easy answer would be to say that physical properties, facts and phenomena are the kind that the science of physics cares about; the kind that are referred to in the statements of the laws of physics and that are appealed to in the descriptions, explanations and predictions proffered by physicists. No doubt, there are many physical properties and phenomena that contemporary physics is ignorant of. And, I dare say, some of the properties and phenomena that contemporary physicists appeal to are as real as phlogiston and caloric fluid. So, perhaps it would be more accurate to characterize physical properties and phenomena as those that would be recognized by some future true and complete science that was a direct descendant of contemporary physics. Of course, this characterization of physical properties is a little vague until an account is given of the descendancy relation that it appeals to. I am not going to attempt to provide such an account as, for the purposes at hand, it should be clear enough what it is to be a physical property and there is no reason to believe that the required account could not be given.

Physicalism and the Mental

Physicalism implies that human individuals are physically constituted and that they inhabit a world that is, at bottom, physical in nature. Therefore, if we really have mental states then those states must be states of a complex physical system. Moreover, mental properties must either be identical to or supervene upon physical properties so that the mental states that an individual has will be a product of her physical nature and/or the physical relations that she bears to external physical phenomena.

How, one might ask, can the mental be related to the physical in this kind of way? One might ask a similar question about biological or geological phenomena, but such a question doesn't appear to be quite as pressing. No doubt the details are very complicated, but it is not an affront to common sense to assert that biological and geological phenomena are physically constituted and that if something has any biological or geological properties then, ultimately, it has those properties in virtue of the way the world is at the physical level. However, matters are somewhat different with respect to the mental. An important class of mental states, namely the intentional states, have a number of salient characteristics that make it difficult to see how the truth of physicalism could be consistent with the existence of such states. To recap, here are just three of those characteristics. Intentional states have content; they represent particular objects and states of affairs and sometimes represent objects that do not exist and states of affairs that do not hold. Intentional states have causal powers that cohere with their content so that causal processes involving intentional states are typically rational. A human subject is capable of having infinitely many content-distinct intentional states. How, one might reasonably ask, could a finite physical system (in virtue of its physical nature and/or its physical relations to other physical phenomena) have states that have content, be capable of having infinitely many such states and be rational to boot? Throughout the ages, many philosophers have had strong intuitions to the effect that this question has no positive answer: a mere physical system could not have intentional states. Therefore, the physicalist is faced with a dilemma. Grasping the first horn of this dilemma involves denying the reality of the mental; we do not have beliefs, desires and the like and so we do not instantiate mental properties. Grasping the second horn of the dilemma involves constructing a physicalist theory of mind that shows how a physical system could have intentional states and have such states in virtue of its physical nature and/or physical relations to other physical phenomena. As we have seen, Fodor is an enthusiast of folk psychology and is therefore committed to grasping the second horn of the physicalist dilemma. Indeed, constructing a physicalist account of how we could be minded in the way that folk psychology conceives us to be is the central task of Fodor's philosophical project. In other words, his basic aim has been to vindicate folk psychology within the framework of a physicalist world-view. And given that he conceives of folk psychology as being very much like a scientific theory, he has thereby been engaged in the project of showing how there could be a respectable scientific psychology that is – at the very least – a close relation of folk psychology.

Are mental realists forced to be physicalists? Is there any mileage in the view that mental phenomena are perfectly real yet do not inhabit the physical domain? Physicalists typically appeal to causal considerations when objecting to such a view. A good example of such an argument runs as follows. Mental phenomena often have physical effects, as when a desire for ice-cream along with a belief that there is ice-cream in the freezer causes an individual to open the freezer door and reach inside. Whenever an individual acts, a physical event involving the movement of the individual's body takes place, and if intentional states were not capable of causing such physical events then there would be little point in having a mind. If intentional states did not inhabit the physical realm then it would be a mystery as to how they could cause actions. But there would be no mystery were intentional states physical. Moreover, it is a principle of physics that the physical world is causally closed, that is, that every physical event has a physical cause that is sufficient to determine its occurrence (or determine the probability of its occurring). If intentional states were not physical then every action would have two independent causes sufficient to determine its occurrence. On the one hand, it would have a physical cause, and on the other, it would have a mental cause. In other words, actions would be systematically overdetermined. But is it plausible that actions are systematically overdetermined? To paraphrase Steven Schiffer (1987), surely God is not such a bad engineer.

Indeed, the idea that actions are systematically overdetermined strikes me as being close to incoherent. It is part of the nature of causation that if A is the cause of B then had A not happened, all else equal, neither would have B. Therefore, for a mental state to be the cause of an action it would have to be the case that if the subject had not had that mental state then, all else equal, she would not have executed the action in question. But if actions are systematically overdetermined then putative mental causes will never satisfy this condition for the simple reason that had a subject not had the mental state that apparently causes her action then she would still have so acted as the result of one of her physical states. This argument applies equally to putative physical causes of actions. Therefore, the overdetermination thesis implies that neither mental states nor physical states are causes of our actions. In short, mental states had better inhabit the physical realm if they are to be the causes of our actions.

A response open to the anti-physicalist would be to deny the principle of the causal closure of the physical realm so that a physical event need not have a sufficient physical cause thereby freeing the way for actions to have sufficient mental causes. In addition, it might be pointed out that the principle of the causal closure of the physical realm is not a law of physics and is therefore hardly sacrosanct. The problem with this line of thought is that it is difficult to see how there could be any laws of physics if the principle did not hold. Suppose that it is a putative law of physics that whenever an event of physical type P occurs (perhaps in certain physically specifiable circumstances) it causes an event of physical type P* to occur. If non-physical events are capable of causing physical events that themselves have no physical cause then what is to stop such a non-physical event from intervening when an event of type P occurs so preventing the occurrence an event of type P*? In principle, such an interference would be perfectly possible and, clearly, could not be ruled out by the laws of physics. Thus, it would be a mere accident that Ps generally caused P*s rather than a law. To avoid denying that there are any laws of physics, the anti-physicalist is forced to postulate the existence of mechanisms that prevent the interference of non-physical phenomena whenever the antecedent of a physical law is satisfied. An example of such a mechanism would be a psychophysical law to the effect that whenever a P occurred it had an effect in the mental realm that (given the laws operative in that domain) prevented the occurrence of any mental event of a type that was capable of blocking the occurrence of an event of type P^*. In short then, if one rejects the principle of the causal closure of the physical domain, one is forced either to deny that there are any physical laws or to commit oneself to the existence of a battery of psychophysical laws. Neither of these options strikes me as very attractive.[11]

Conclusion

In this chapter I have given an account of the nature of folk psychology as conceived by Fodor along with an account of the metaphysical doctrine of physicalism. Fodor is a great champion of folk psychology. For him, the entities that it postulates are real and the generalizations that it takes to hold are largely true and are of considerable explanatory and predictive power. Fodor is also a physicalist. Thus, he faces the problem of squaring his enthusiasm for folk psychology with his physicalism. In other words, he faces the problem of explaining in physicalist terms how we could be as folk psychology represents us as being; that is, of explaining in physicalist terms how we could have intentional states that are governed by the generalizations of folk psychology. Solving this problem, and so vindicating folk psychology within a physicalist framework, has been Fodor's major philosophical project.

2

Philosophical and Scientific Background

Introduction

In chapter 1 I characterized Fodor's central ambition as being that of vindicating folk psychology within a physicalist framework. The core of Fodor's attempted vindication of folk psychology is a theory of intentional states and processes according to which intentional states are computational relations to sentences of a language of thought and intentional processes are computational processes involving the manipulation of such sentences. Call this theory the computational theory of mind (CTM for short). In order to gain a full understanding of CTM and Fodor's motivations for holding it, it is important to be aware of a series of important developments that took place in scientific psychology and the philosophy of mind in the second half of the twentieth century. In this chapter I will give a detailed account of these historical developments and Fodor's role in them.

Psychology and Philosophy

The historical developments that we are concerned with in this chapter can be summarized in the following terms. From the early years of the twentieth century into the 1960s, behaviourism constituted the dominant approach in scientific psychology in the English-speaking world. With the birth and development of cognitive psychology and cognitive science in the 1960s, this behaviourist dominance was challenged and behaviourism gradually fell into disrepute. As a result of this 'cognitive revolution' psychologists came to operate with a quite different conception of the research agenda of their discipline. They came to see their central concern as being that of explaining intentionally characterized cognitive capacities and held that in order to explain such capacities, it is necessary to appeal to internal representational states and processes. In addition, the cognitive revolution marked the birth of cognitive science, an interdisciplinary study of the mind to which cognitive psychologists, artificial intelligence (AI) researchers, theoretical linguists, neuroscientists and philosophers contribute. In the philosophy of mind the same historical period witnessed the rise of functionalism, a theory concerning the nature of mental states. Despite taking place in different disciplines, the similarity between these developments is striking. For both the cognitive psychologist and the functionalist share a conception of the human mind according to which there is an important class of mental phenomena (i) that are intentional; (ii) that causally mediate the links between sensory stimulation and behaviour; and (iii) that are neurophysiologically realized yet do not have an essence that resides at the neural or physical level.

What explains this development of a shared conception of the human mind amongst practitioners of separate disciplines during the same historical period? Part of the answer lies in the pioneering work in mathematical logic and the theory of computability of such figures as Alan Turing and the subsequent development of the digital computer. A computer is a mechanical device that manipulates symbols; a computer takes symbols as input and, by means of the application of symbol manipulating rules, produces symbols as output. If the symbols-manipulated by a computer are given an appropriate interpretation then the computer can be used to solve complex information-processing problems. Hence, once the symbols that it manipulates are interpreted, a computer would appear to have precisely the kind of reasoning and problem-solving capacities that are characteristic of minded subjects. It was hardly surprising that theorists interested in the mind (be they psychologists or philosophers) should come to be gripped by the idea that mental phenomena are in important respects analogous to computational phenomena. As we shall see, this idea played a significant role in motivating both the cognitive revolution and the rise of functionalism.

However, the previous paragraph describes only part of the story. Over the past four decades there has been an increasingly close

relationship between the philosophy of mind and scientific psychology and this fact goes a long way towards explaining similarities between the general outlook of philosophers of mind, on the
one hand, and scientific psychologists, on the other. What is the
nature of this relationship? It would be naive to think of philosophers of mind and psychologists as being engaged in a genuinely
collaborative enterprise. It is true that some of the figures who have
most influenced the development of scientific psychology were
philosophically highly sophisticated (here I have Noam Chomsky
and David Marr in mind). However, it is fair to say that most
working psychologists have little interest in overtly philosophical
issues and only a limited familiarity with the philosophical literature. In saying this, I am not denying the reality of cognitive science.
It is just that the research methods and discoveries of linguists,
neuroscientists and AI researchers are of more direct relevance (and
are thus of greater interest) to the psychologist than are the products of philosophical research. Despite this fact, philosophers of
mind have become increasingly interested in scientific psychology.
Answers to traditional philosophical questions about the mind have
be-come increasingly informed and influenced by work in scientific
psychology and that work has itself raised a battery of new
philosophical questions.

  In the middle years of the twentieth century most philosophers
held that there was a fundamental distinction between philosophy
and science. As they saw it, philosophy was concerned with conceptual questions, questions as to the nature of our concepts and
the relationships between them[1] that could be answered from the
armchair by means of a reflection on the everyday usage of the
words that express the concepts in question and the criteria governing that usage. For example, questions such as 'what is it to have
a belief?', 'what is it to be in pain?' and 'what is it to understand
the meaning of a word?' are to be answered by reflecting on our
actual usage of the words 'belief', 'pain' and 'understand' and the
criteria that competent speakers of English employ when deciding
whether such words are applicable in a given situation. The idea
that scientific psychology could shed any light on these questions
would have been regarded as absurd, a case of confusing a conceptual question for an empirical question. In so far as most
mid-century philosophers of mind were interested in scientific
psychology, it was to reveal that the theories and explanations proffered by its practitioners were conceptually confused.[2]

In the late 1950s and early 1960s philosophy took a 'naturalistic turn'. That is, philosophers (particularly those based in the United States) came to be convinced that there is no fundamental divide between philosophy and science.[3] In the philosophy of mind, naturalism manifests itself in the view that it is misguided to attempt to answer traditional philosophical questions in a state of indifference to, and ignorance of, developments in scientific psychology. Consequently, over the last four decades most of the prominent attempts to solve the mind–body problem, construct a theory of the nature of intentional states and settle the question as to whether we have innate knowledge (to pick just three examples) have in some significant way been influenced by work in scientific psychology. As we shall see, Fodor is a prominent member of this naturalist tradition.

Quite apart from the naturalistic turn, there is another reason why philosophers of mind have become increasingly interested in scientific psychology. Since the cognitive revolution psychology has flourished, becoming an increasingly prominent feature of the intellectual landscape. This success raises a whole battery of questions of interest to the philosopher, questions such as the following. What is the nature of psychological explanation and what role does content play in such explanations? What relationship does psychology bear to sciences such as physics and neuroscience? How are psychological states to be individuated? Do developments in psychology serve to undermine our folk conception of ourselves as rational agents who act out of their beliefs and desires? Moreover, like any science, psychology rests on a body of theoretical assumptions and this raises questions about the legitimacy of those assumptions. For example, it would appear to be a fundamental assumption of psychology that some of the internal states that underlie and facilitate perception and cognition have content. But how could such internal states have the contents that psychologists routinely attribute to them? In effect, much of contemporary philosophy of mind can be represented as a branch of the philosophy of science: it investigates fundamental and foundational questions that are raised by psychological theory and practice. In so far as philosophy has a genuine contribution to make to cognitive science, I think that it is in answering such questions and in doing so providing an account of the foundations of cognitive science. For these are precisely the kind of question that require rigorous logical reflection and analysis by empirically informed thinkers rather than further empirical investigation.

Psychological Behaviourism and the Cognitive Revolution

From the early years of the twentieth century to the 1960s scientific psychology (at least in the English-speaking world) was dominated by an approach known as behaviourism. Behaviourism was born of a desire to make psychology an objective and respectable scientific enterprise. With this aim in mind, behaviourists explicitly eschewed mentalist psychology, that is, any psychology whose theories and explanations appeal to inner mental phenomena. For the behaviourist, the primary concern of psychology is to control and predict observable behaviour.

Behaviourism came to fruition in the work of the Harvard-based psychologist B. F. Skinner. Skinner's early work focused on the conditioning of simple animals such as rats and pigeons. In a typical Skinnerian experiment, a rat is placed in a box with a bar attached to one of its internal walls. The box is set up in such a way that whenever the bar is pressed a food pellet is released. Initially, the rat might press the bar as a random episode. However, the dispersal of a food pellet as a result of the random bar-pressing behaviour will have an effect on the subsequent behaviour of the rat. For it will reinforce that behaviour, that is, increase the likelihood that the rat will respond to similar situations in the future by engaging in bar-pressing behaviour. If the dispersal of a food pellet is made conditional on the presence of some other factor (for example, the flashing of a light) then the rat will be conditioned to press the bar only when that factor is present (for example, only when the light flashes). Similarly, if the dispersal of the food pellet is made conditional on the bar being pressed with a particular and specific force, then the rat will be conditioned to press the bar with just that force when placed in the box. On the basis of such experiments, Skinner concluded that the behaviour of simple creatures is governed by a law dubbed (following Thorndike) the Law of Effect. According to the Law of Effect, the behaviour of a creature is determined by its current stimulus and its history of reinforcement. Consequently, the way that a creature behaves in response to any given stimulus can be conditioned by means of reinforcement and its behaviour at any point in time can be predicted on the basis of a knowledge of the current stimulus and the creature's history of reinforcement.

Skinner came to believe that human behaviour is governed by the Law of Effect. Hence human behaviour, though much more complex and intricate than that of simple animals, can be controlled and predicted by analogous means. In a famous study of verbal behaviour Skinner (1957) constructed a behaviourist theory of language-learning: learning a language is a process whereby the language learner is conditioned – by means of reinforcement – to execute specific behavioural responses to specific stimuli. So, for example, learning the English word 'dog' is a matter of being conditioned to utter the word 'dog' when confronted by a dog.

It is important to realize that the behaviourist operates with a quite austere understanding of the term 'behaviour'. In everyday contexts, we typically describe and classify human behaviour in implicitly intentional terms. For example, I do not describe Edgar's behaviour in terms of the physical movements that he makes. Rather, I say that he is hiding from Fang. What makes Edgar's behaviour so describable is not so much its physical nature. For someone could make just the same bodily movements as Edgar without it being the case that they were hiding from Fang and someone could be hiding from Fang even though the movements that they make bear little resemblance to those executed by Edgar. What makes Edgar's behaviour a case of hiding from Fang has partly to do with his intentions or what he has in mind: his intention in moving as he does is to prevent Fang from seeing him, what he has in mind in so moving is to make himself invisible to Fang.

Given the behaviourists' opposition to mentalist psychology, they do not describe and classify behaviour in implicitly intentional terms. Rather, they describe and classify behaviour in physical terms or in terms of its immediate non-intentional effects (as when Skinner describes the rat's behaviour as being that of pressing a bar). Hence, the term 'behaviour' as used by the behaviourist should be understood in a narrow technical sense and should not be confused with its folk-psychological homonym.

Why, one might ask, were the behaviourists so opposed to mentalist psychology, that is, to any psychology that constructs theories and explanations that appeal to inner mental phenomena (be they beliefs, desires and thought processes or the more exotic postulates of psychoanalytic theory)? After all, it is natural to think that mental phenomena are perfectly real, play an important role in determining how we behave and mediate such causal connections as there are between external stimuli and behavioural responses. And one might think that if any science should be concerned with such phenomena it is psychology. Several behaviourist objections to mentalist psychology can be isolated.[4]

First, mental phenomena, unlike behaviour and external stimuli, are not publicly observable. The unobservable nature of mental phenomena is not in and of itself a problem as many perfectly respectable scientific theories postulate unobservable phenomena. However, in the case of mentalist psychology, appeals to the unobservable are not constrained by observable data as is evidenced by the ease with which mentalist explanations can be constructed. Moreover, disputes between advocates of competing mentalist theories cannot be settled by appeal to observable data (for example, behavioural data). In these respects, mentalist explanations differ from scientific theories that appeal to unobservable phenomena. Consequently, mentalist psychology lacks any trace of objectivity and is therefore thoroughly unscientific. (This kind of criticism echoes Popper's 1962 attack on Freudian psychology.)

Second, many mentalist theories effectively postulate a homunculus or little man residing in the mind of the subject. The problem with such explanations is that they get us nowhere. If we attempt to explain the behaviour of a subject by appeal to an inner homunculus then the behaviour of the homunculus will in turn require explanation. If we attempt to explain the behaviour of the homunculus by positing a homunculus in his mind, then we are faced with a need to explain the behaviour of the second homunculus and an infinite regress looms. Suppose, on the other hand, that we can explain the behaviour of the homunculus without postulating a further army of little men. Then we could use the same tactic to explain the behaviour of the subject who is our primary concern and thus avoid the need to postulate a homunculus in the first place.

Third, a common form of mentalist explanation has no explanatory power at all as its instances merely redescribe the phenomena that they purport to explain rather than specify their cause, as when one explains the fact that an individual smokes a great deal by saying that they have a smoking habit.

Fourth, one possible objection to mentalist psychology is based upon the idea that mental phenomena do not exist; that they are as real as ghosts and phlogiston. Behaviourists have tended to vacillate between this idea and the idea that mental phenomena can be identified with brain states (and, thus, are perfectly real). In either case, though, mental phenomena have no legitimate role to play in the explanation, prediction or control of behaviour. Suppose that mental phenomena are not real. Then, clearly, mentalist explanations of behaviour will be systematically false and it will not be possible to predict a creature's behaviour by appeal to its mental states or control its behaviour by manipulating its mental states. Suppose, on the other hand, that mental states are states of the brain. Then an explanation of a creature's behaviour that appealed only to its mental states would be incomplete for it requires to be explained why the creature was in the mental state in question. Such an explanation must appeal to the external causes of the mental states. Given that there is a lawful relation between external stimuli and mental states, on the one hand, and mental states and behaviour, on the other, there exists a lawful relation between external stimuli and behaviour. Consequently, explanations and predictions of behaviour can be constructed that appeal only to external stimuli and make no reference to mental states, and a creature's behaviour can be controlled by manipulating the external stimuli that it is subject to. In short, even if mental states exist, they have no role in the explanation, prediction or control of behaviour thereby making mentalist psychology redundant.

In the 1960s the influence of behaviourism waned as psychology underwent a cognitive revolution. Two major reasons for the decline of behaviourism can be isolated. First, it was subject to powerful criticisms that questioned the applicability of its approach to human subjects.[5] One of the central insights of the critics of behaviourism is that human behaviour is stimulus-independent. That is, how a human subject behaves in response to any given stimulus will depend not so much on the nature of the stimulus and her history of reinforcement, but upon which mental states she is in at the time of stimulation. Second, the development of the digital computer and the rise of artificial intelligence suggested a view of the mind and a mentalist approach to its study rich with possibility and not as vulnerable to the behaviourist objections as earlier manifestations of mentalism.

With the rise of cognitive psychology, psychologists came to adopt a conception of the human individual and the aims of psychology that sharply contrasted with that held by the behaviourists before them. Fodor was an early champion of the cognitive revolution and did much to publicize the cognitivist cause within the philosophical community during the 1960s. That he adopted this role should be of no surprise given the details of the early stages of his academic career, which Fodor has described in the following terms:

> I was trained as a philosopher at Princeton. My first academic job was at MIT, about 1960, when all the Chomsky stuff was starting.

There was a lot of linguistics around there, which I picked up a little. Then I spent a year visiting the University of Illinois, where I was involved in a program of Charles Osgood's. I had a position in a research program he was running. I talked a lot with graduate students about psychology, and so I got involved in doing some experiments. For fairly fortuitous reasons, I picked up some information about philosophy, linguistics and psychology. Since a lot of it seemed to bear on the same set of problems, I have worked back and forth between those fields ever since. (Baumgartner and Payr 1995: 85)

Of particular importance in this connection are his first book, *Psychological Explanation* (published in 1968), and a collection of philosophical and linguistic articles entitled *The Structure of Language* that he co-edited with Jerrold Katz (published in 1964).

In the remainder of this section I will give a brief description of the basic assumptions of cognitive psychology and of the nature of the theories and explanations that its champions attempt to construct. As this description applies to cognitive science in general, from this point I will use the terms 'cognitive science', 'cognitivism' and the 'cognitive approach' rather than the more specific 'cognitive psychology'. The central aim of cognitive science is to account for our cognitive capacities. Prominent examples of such capacities include our capacities to perceive objects and features of the external world; remember and recall past events; understand the utterances of our fellows and express our own thoughts by means of language; solve problems and reason generally; categorize objects; recognize acquaintances; coordinate our behaviour in such a way as to fulfil our goals. These capacities are intentional capacities in the respect that exercising any one of them involves having intentional states. How are these capacities to be explained? The cognitive scientist's answer is that they are to be explained by uncovering and describing the mental processing that underlies them and takes place whenever they are exercised. Hence, cognitive science is unashamedly mentalist.

The cognitive revolution was partly inspired by the development of the digital computer and early successes in artificial intelligence (the project of programming computers to execute tasks that require intelligence when performed by humans). Put simply, a computer is a device that mechanically manipulates symbols by means of the application of symbol-manipulating rules. If the symbols manipulated by a computer are given an interpretation or attributed content then by appropriately programming the computer, it can be used to process information and solve complex information-processing problems. A pocket calculator is a familiar example of a computer; we interpret the symbols that such a machine manipulates as representing numbers and mathematical functions and so use it to solve arithmetical problems. In other words, an appropriately programmed and interpreted computer engages in an activity that very much resembles cognition. Given this, it would hardly have been surprising had psychologists entertained the idea that cognition may well be a form of computation. Indeed, the core idea of early cognitive science was that the mind is a computer (or an ensemble of interlinked computers) and that mental states and processes are computational. However, the symbols that are manipulated by the mind are seen as differing from the symbols manipulated by manufactured computers in an important respect. For their meaning is not the product of any act of interest-relative interpretation. Consequently, in order to explain a particular cognitive capacity, it is necessary to uncover and describe the underlying computational processing that takes place within the mind whenever that capacity is exercised.

How does the cognitivist conceive of the relationship between the mind and the brain? My computer is a physical object in the respect that it is either identical to, or composed of, a particular physical object; namely, the physical object that is located on the top of my desk. Similarly, every computational process that it executes is a particular physical process that takes place within that physical object. In short, computers and computational processes can be physically embodied. However, computational phenomena are multiply realizable in that they can be physically embodied in many different ways. For example, a machine composed of cogs and pulleys could be built to run the very same word-processing program that is run on my desktop computer. In this respect computers are like can-openers and other familiar household implements. It is difficult to imagine a non-physical can-opener but can-openers vary a great deal in their physical properties. According to the cognitivist, the mind is a computer that is housed within the brain; in other words, the mind and mental processes are neurally embodied. Hence, the computational processing that is described in the course of accounting for our cognitive capacities is conceived of as being executed by or within the brain. However, in principle, that very processing could be executed by a system that was physically very different from the brain. (Fodor gives an account of the cognitivist's conception of the relationship between the mind and the brain in Fodor 1968b, ch. 3.)

How does cognitive science bear up to the behaviourist objections to mentalist psychology described above? It would appear that those objections have little force. Computational processes are such that they can be executed by a mechanical device and the computational capacities of any physical system can ultimately be explained in physical terms (just as the computational capacities of a pocket calculator or a desktop computer can be explained in physical terms). Consequently, to regard the mind as being a physically embodied computer housed in the brain hardly amounts to the postulation of an inner homunculus. Moreover, to account for the ability of a computer to solve a certain complex information-processing problem in computational terms (say, by describing the program that it runs) is far more illuminating than saying that a person smokes a large number of cigarettes because they have a smoking habit. Hence, to account for an individual's cognitive capacities in computational terms escapes the charge of vacuity.

Suppose that a computer scientist discovered a machine that had the capacity to solve a complex information-processing problem and she wished to explain this capacity in computational terms. Constructing a plausible explanation would hardly be an easy task but could be done by reflecting on the nature of the information-processing problem in question. She could decide between competing accounts on the basis of the extent to which they were consistent with observable data concerning the relative time taken by the machine to solve particular instances of the target problem, the circumstances in which the machine made mistakes and so on. In short, she could adopt a procedure analogous to the standard scientific procedure for constructing and evaluating explanations of observable phenomena by appeal to unobservable phenomena. Finally, the charge that appeals to mental phenomena are superfluous has no force if, as the cognitivist thinks, human behaviour is stimulus-independent.

Thus far my account of the cognitivist approach to the study of the mind has been abstract and schematic. To make it more concrete, it will be helpful to look at a particular cognitivist account of a cognitive capacity, namely, David Marr's (1982) hugely influential theory of vision. This theory has been widely discussed in the philosophical literature and Fodor makes favourable references to it in Fodor (1983).

We have the capacity to discover facts about the world by means of vision; facts such as the shape, size, colour, surface markings and motion of objects in our immediate environment. How do we do this? How is this capacity to be explained? Marr held that underlying this visual capacity is a computer or information-processing system housed within the brain. The system in question is the visual module and Marr's theory is an attempt to describe its workings and in doing so go some way towards explaining our visual capacities. He argues that a complete account of the workings of the visual module will comprise three distinct levels: these being the computational theory, the theory of representation and algorithm and the theory of hardware implementation.

The computational theory concentrates on the semantic and intentional details of the visual module's activity. Its task is to specify the information-processing problem solved by the visual module, and the semantic and intentional details of how it solves this problem. In order to construct an adequate computational theory one must do the following. First, the information that the visual module takes as input and the information that it generates as output must be indicated. Second, the visual module doesn't generate output from input in one fell swoop. Rather it makes a series of information-processing steps. Consequently, these information-processing sub-steps and the intermediary information that they generate must be described. Third, the visual module generates information from information by applying mathematical operations or computing mathematical functions, just as I work out the current balance of my bank account from information about its previous state and intervening banking transactions by means of such mathematical operations as addition and subtraction. Consequently, the mathematical operations executed by the visual module (in other words, the mathematical functions that it computes) must be described in precise mathematical terms. Fourth, the appropriateness of the information that the visual module generates and the mathematical operations that it employs must be indicated. Such questions as 'why are that information and those operations relevant to the task at hand?' and 'how do they facilitate the solution of the information-processing problem that it is the visual module's function to solve?' must be answered. The appropriateness of the intermediary information generated, on the one hand, and the mathematical operations by means of which it is generated, on the other, are closely interlinked. What makes a piece of intermediary information relevant is that it is information from which further relevant information can be generated by the mathematical means available to the visual module. And what makes a particular mathematical operation relevant is that it can be employed to generate relevant information from information that the module already has at its disposal. The appropriateness of such information and operations depends crucially on general facts about the world, facts that Marr calls physical constraints. An example of such a physical constraint is that changes in the intensity of light falling on the retina are caused by, and correspond to, such objective features of the external world as boundaries between objects, edges of objects, changes in colour, changes in surface texture, surface contours and suchlike. Another example is that physical objects are rigid, not changing their shape and size from one moment to the next. The visual module takes advantage of these constraints with assumptions corresponding to them being hard-wired into it. Were these constraints not to hold, the visual module would not be able to generate the information that it in fact generates by means of the mathematical operations that it employs, or what information it did succeed in generating would be of little use or relevance. For example, were it not the case that such features as object edges, boundaries between objects and the like caused and corresponded to sudden changes in light intensity falling on the retina, then there would be little point in the visual module's constructing a representation of the location of sudden intensity changes on the retinal image; such a representation would not contain information from which the shape of the objects impinging on the subject's visual apparatus could be derived. Consequently, the physical constraints that the visual system takes advantage of must be described.

The computational theory does not tell us which language the visual module employs to encode the information that it processes, or what mechanical procedures or rules it applies in manipulating the symbols of that language. One and the same computational theory could be implemented in several different ways at the level of mechanical symbol manipulation, just as the mathematical function of addition could be computed by applying one body of rules or procedures to arabic numerals, or another body of rules or procedures to binary symbols. The theory of representation and algorithm spells out such lower-level details of the visual module's mechanical symbol-manipulating activity.

Both the very information-processing and the very mechanical symbol-manipulating activity that the visual module engages in could be implemented in many different ways at the physical level.

Reflecting the fact that computational phenomena are multiply realizable at the physical level, the details of how that activity is implemented in the brain are not specified by either the computational theory or the theory of representation and algorithm. Rather, the theory of hardware implementation does that.

So we know what the goal of Marr's research is, but what are the details of the theory that he offers? How does he describe the workings of the visual module? Marr's theory is far from complete; in particular, the neural details are somewhat limited and sketchy. However, he has much to offer by way of a computational theory. The outlines of that computational theory can be described in the following manner. When we open our eyes to the world, light waves reflected off objects in the immediate environment are focused onto the retina. The intensity of the light falling on the retina will vary from point to point as a result of such factors as differences in the source and strength of illumination across the viewed scene, differences in colour, texture, orientation and other properties of the various surfaces off which light is reflected and so on. The retina is a transducer. In response to the light falling upon it the retina generates a two-dimensional array, each value of which represents the intensity of light falling on the corresponding point of the retina. This two-dimensional array is known as the grey coding. The visual module takes as input pairs of grey codings. As output, the module produces object-centred 3-D representations that indicate the shape, size, colour and motion of whatever objects are in the subject's field of view. This representation can then be employed by other cognitive modules to perform such tasks as object recognition and classification. Hence, the information-processing problem solved by the visual module is that of generating object-centred 3-D representations from pairs of grey codings.

This information-processing problem is solved in three distinct stages. In the first stage the primal sketch is constructed. In the second stage the $2\frac{1}{2}$-D representation is constructed. And in the third the object-centred 3-D representation is constructed. In greater detail, these stages can be described as follows.

The construction of the primal sketch. As noted above, changes in light-intensity values across the retinal image tend to be caused by, and correspond to, such objective features of the viewed scene as boundaries between objects, object edges, changes in surface texture, changes in colour, surface contours and the like. Consequently, such changes in intensity value are potentially a very rich source of the kind of information that the visual module seeks to extract. Hence, it makes sense to represent explicitly the presence and location of significant changes in intensity on the retinal image. This is what the primal sketch does. But how is the primal sketch constructed? To detect intensity changes at a particular scale, a mathematical operator is applied to groups of neighbouring values of the grey codings to generate another two-dimensional array, each value of which represents the gradient of the gradient of intensity at the corresponding point of the retina at the scale in question. Where a positive value in such an array lies next to a negative value, the point between them is known as a zero crossing. Zero crossings correspond to intensity changes. Different-sized operators are applied to the grey codings in this manner to detect intensity changes at different scales; small operators will detect small-scale local changes, whereas larger ones will reveal the presence of more gradual, larger-scale changes. The results of applying these different-sized operators are combined to produce a representation that represents the presence and location of zero crossings that show up at more than one scale. This is the raw primal sketch in which groups of adjacent zero crossings are represented as edge segments and blobs. Computations are then performed on the raw primal sketch to produce the full primal sketch which represents the global pattern of intensity changes. (For example, locally similar items are clustered to form higher-level units, and boundaries between different regions are detected and explicitly represented.)

The construction of the $2\frac{1}{2}$-D sketch.   The second stage of the visual process involves the construction of the $2\frac{1}{2}$-D sketch, a representation that represents the relative distance from the subject of each point on the viewed surfaces together with their orientation relative to the subject. This representation is generated from the primal sketch by means of the execution of several modular processes. These processes include stereopsis and the extraction of depth information from motion information. Both stereopsis and the generation of motion information involve the comparison of distinct representations (primal sketches) and the computation of the displacement of corresponding elements of the representations so compared (where elements of distinct representations correspond with one another if and only if they are caused by and represent the same feature of the objective world). In order for such a comparison process to be performed, a matching process that pairs off corresponding elements of the respective representations must first be executed. This matching process relies upon the three following assumptions. First, that an element of a representation has at most one element of any distinct representation corresponding to it. Second, that elements of distinct representations correspond to one another only if they are similar. And third, that displacements are small and vary smoothly. As a result of making these three assumptions, the matching process pairs an element of a representation with at most one element of any distinct representation, pairs elements of distinct representations only if they are similar, and pairs elements only if they occupy similar positions in their respective representations. That such a matching process is successful, and thus facilitates the subsequent extraction of depth and motion information, is a product of the fact that the assumptions that it relies upon are true, or correspond to real facts about the world.

The construction of the 3-D representation. In the final stage of the visual process, computational operations are applied to the primal sketch and the $2\frac{1}{2}$-D sketch in order to generate an object-centred 3-D representation of the objects in the viewed scene, a representation that is such as to facilitate object recognition and classification. The 3-D representation represents objects as generalized cones or ensembles of generalized cones, and thus relies on the assumption that our world is populated by objects that have such shapes. The details of how this final representation is constructed are complicated, but once again the utilization of motion information plays an important role. Generally speaking, if the motion of two neighbouring features of a primal sketch that are separated by a zero crossing differs over time, then they will lie on different surfaces, for if they lay on the same surface their respective motions would be equivalent. This constraint enables the visual module to determine which zero crossings correspond to object edges (as opposed to, say, changes in colour or surface texture) and thus helps in the construction of the 3-D representation.

That completes my account of Marr's theory of vision and, with it, of the cognitive revolution and the cognitivist approach to the study of the mind.

Philosophical Behaviourism

During the historical period that witnessed the cognitive revolution in psychology, parallel developments took place in the philosophy of mind. The developments in question involved the rise of functionalism at the expense of both philosophical behaviourism and the type identity theory. Once again, Fodor was at the forefront of these developments during the early stages of his career. (Hilary Putnam is the figure most closely identified with the rise of functionalism in the 1960s. As a graduate student at Princeton in the late 1950s Fodor was a student of Putnam's.) In Fodor (1968b) he both champions the functionalist cause and argues against philosophical behaviourism and the type identity theory. In the remaining sections of this chapter I will give an account of these philosophical developments.

Philosophical behaviourism is a theory concerning the nature of mental states that was particularly influential in the middle years of the twentieth century. It is a doctrine that was explicitly championed by logical positivists such as Carnap and Hempel and is at least gestured towards in the writings of Wittgenstein. However, it is most closely associated with the English philosopher Gilbert Ryle.[6]

What is philosophical behaviourism? As we shall see, philosophical behaviourism is not to be confused with psychological behaviourism. A particularly bold and straightforward version of behaviourism can be expressed in the following terms. Consider the state of being water-soluble. There is an intimate link between being water-soluble and the behaviour of dissolving when submerged in water. However, an object can be water-soluble even though it has never dissolved. For, solubility is a dispositional state and an object can be disposed to behave in a particular way in certain circumstances even though it has never manifested that disposition (as it has never been in the relevant circumstances). To be water-soluble *just is* to be disposed to dissolve when submerged in water and for an object X to be so disposed *just is* for the following conditional statement to be true of it: if X were submerged in water then X would dissolve. It is important to realize that the water-solubility of an object cannot be identified with any of its internal states or properties, even the internal state that is causally responsible for its dissolving when submerged in water. Hence, to say that the sugar cube dissolved when placed in water because it was water-soluble is not to provide an illuminating causal explanation of its dissolving. Rather, it is to say something elliptical for the statement: the sugar cube dissolved when submerged in water because it is true of it that if it was submerged in water then it would dissolve.

According to behaviourism, mental states are analogous to the state of being water-soluble in that to have a particular mental state (for example, the belief that dogs are ferocious) *just is* to be disposed to behave in specific ways in certain circumstances. Consequently, mental states are not internal states that cause behaviour (internal states either of the brain or of a non-physical mental substance) and explanations of an individual's behaviour that appeal to her mental states are not causal explanations.

Specifying what it is to be water-soluble is a straightforward matter as the nature of solubility can be cashed out by means of a single conditional statement. However, mental states are far more complicated. A given mental state will manifest itself in different behavioural episodes in different circumstances. Consider the state of believing that dogs are ferocious. Suppose that Edgar has this belief. Were he confronted by an untethered dog then this belief would manifest itself in fleeing behaviour. Alternatively, were he confronted by a tethered dog he would not flee but would behave in such a way as to keep a safe distance between himself and the dog. And so on. In short, in order to cash out what it is to believe that dogs are ferocious, one must specify a whole battery of conditional statements. In other words, mental states are multi-tracked behavioural dispositions. Each distinct type of mental state is a distinct multi-tracked behavioural disposition so that, for example, the collection of conditional statements that cash out what it is to believe that dogs are ferocious will differ from the collection that cash out what it is to believe that giraffes have long necks.

It is one thing to argue that mental states are multi-tracked dispositions and quite another to provide a fully worked out behaviourist account of what it is to be in a particular mental state. To be acceptable, any such account must characterize both behaviour and circumstances in non-mental (and in particular, in non-intentional) terms. For example, it is no good to say that part of what it is to believe that dogs are ferocious is to be disposed to engage in hiding behaviour in the circumstances where a dog is approaching one. As we saw earlier, what makes a behavioural episode an instance of hiding behaviour is not so much its physical nature but the intentions of the individual who so behaves. Consequently, a behaviourist account of what it is to believe that dogs are ferocious that makes reference to hiding behaviour is a circular account for it characterizes what it is to have the belief in question in mental terms. Such an account would be no better than one according to which part of what it was to have the belief is to be disposed to want to be elsewhere when confronted by a dog. As a matter of fact, the behaviourist literature is notably lacking in remotely plausible non-circular behaviourist characterizations of any of our mental states.

What arguments did the behaviourists give for their position? Perhaps the most influential argument for behaviourism rested on an appeal to the criteria or methods that we employ in determining whether or not a given mental concept applies to an individual. For example, when determining whether an individual can be said to believe that dogs are ferocious, we typically observe and reflect upon how they behave in various circumstances (for example, how they behave when confronted by a dog). Similarly, when justifying or evaluating the attribution of a mental state to an individual, we do so by appeal to facts concerning how they were observed to behave in various circumstances. (For example, I might attempt to justify my claim that Edgar believes that dogs are ferocious by pointing out that on numerous occasions I have seen him flee or tremble when confronted by a dog.) This is taken to imply an important fact about our mental concepts. The fact in question is this. Mental concepts are not concepts of inner states (be they states of the brain or of a non-physical substance). Rather, they are dispositional concepts. For example, the concept of believing that dogs are ferocious is the concept of a particular multi-tracked behavioural disposition. From such facts about our concepts, it follows that mental states just are behavioural dispositions.

The chain of reasoning described in the preceding paragraph has a distinctly Wittgensteinian air about it and is utilized by both Ryle and Malcolm. Moreover, it echoes the verification principle of the logical positivists according to which the meaning of a sentence is its method of verification. But how convincing is it? The main problem with the argument is that the means by which we determine the applicability of our mental concepts are perfectly consistent with an alternative and conflicting account of those concepts and, therefore, of the nature of mental states. Suppose that our mental concepts were the concepts of internal states that stand in a rich network of causal relations to one another, to external stimuli and to behaviour. Moreover, suppose that ordinary individuals have a tacit knowledge of this rich network of causal relations. In other words, suppose that the account of folk psychology that I attributed to Fodor in chapter 1 is true. Then a consideration of observable behaviour would play an important role in determining the mental states of other people (and, thus, the applicability of mental concepts) and we would justify and evaluate particular attributions of mental states to our fellows by appeal to how we observed them to behave in various circumstances. Consequently, one can accept much of what the behaviourist claims concerning how we go about determining the applicability of our mental concepts and how we justify and evaluate attributions of mental states, without endorsing the behaviourist account of mental concepts and states. Hence, the behaviourist argument is inconclusive. (See Fodor and Chihara 1965 for a detailed critique of Wittgenstein-inspired arguments for behaviourism of the type that I have been considering. Fodor and Chihara explicitly compare mental concepts with the theoretical concepts that figure in scientific theories and explanations.)

An important idea running through the writings of Wittgenstein and Ryle is that explanations of cognitive capacities (or an exercise of such a capacity) that appeal to inner mental processes are either circular or lead to infinite regress and are therefore explanatorily bankrupt. This line of thought echoes one of the psychological behaviourist's objections to mentalist psychology described in the preceding section and can be brought out by means of an example taken from Wittgenstein's *The Blue Book*. Suppose that I am standing in a field filled with flowers of various colours. I am told to fetch a yellow flower, an order that I successfully execute. How did I manage to obey the order? One very appealing explanation runs along the following lines. I called up a mental image of yellow that I compared with the flowers before me. When I found a match between this mental image and a flower, I picked that flower. Wittgenstein argues that the problem with this explanation is that the mental process of calling up an image of yellow resembles the episode that it is invoked to explain far too closely. If it requires to be explained how I managed to select a yellow flower (as opposed to, say, a red one) then it also requires to be explained how I managed to select a mental image of yellow (as opposed to, say, a mental image of red). As it stands, the explanation attempts to explain the exercise of an ability by appeal to an act that constitutes an exercise of the very same ability. For this reason, the explanation is unsatisfactorily circular. Suppose we attempt to explain how I managed to call up a mental image of yellow by appealing to a prior act of calling up a mental image, an image that I used to enable me to select successfully an image of yellow. Then, once again, we have a circular explanation as it requires to be explained how I managed to select the relevant mental image. If a third mental image is invoked an infinite regress of images (or acts of calling up images) looms. In order to avoid circularity or an infinite regress, it is necessary to explain an act of calling up a mental image without any reference to a prior act of calling up an image. But if this could be done, a parallel explanation of the act of picking a yellow flower could be constructed that made no reference to mental images. For Wittgenstein, all explanations that appeal to inner mental processes are explanatorily bankrupt in this kind of way.[7]

This objection to explanations of intelligent acts that appeal to inner mental processes provided an important motivation for behaviourism. For if the postulation of inner mental phenomena cannot adequately explain our intelligent acts and the capacities that they manifest, then the motivation for thinking that such phenomena must lie behind and cause those acts evaporates.

With the development of the computer and the rise of cognitive science, the influence of this objection waned. Computers manipulate symbols and in doing so process information and solve information-processing problems. However, the computational capacities and activity of a computer can ultimately be explained in mechanical terms. The mental processes that cognitive scientists postulate in order to account for our cognitive capacities and the intelligent acts that manifest those capacities are conceived of as being computational processes. Hence, it is far from clear that cognitive scientific explanations must be either circular or lead to infinite regress. (For Fodor's development and expression of such objections to traditional arguments for behaviourism, see Fodor 1968a, chs 1 and 2, 1975, introduction.)

Behaviourism declined in popularity partly because of the perceived inadequacies of the central arguments for the position that I have described. But it was also undermined by a number of objections developed by philosophers in the late 1950s and early 1960s. It is to these objections that I now turn. First, suppose that Edgar believes that dogs are ferocious and is confronted by Fang. Will he begin to tremble or engage in fleeing behaviour? If he does not see Fang or believes that Fang is some other kind of creature then he may well not flee or tremble. Alternatively, he may well see Fang and believe him to be a dog but also believe that the best way to deal with a ferocious dog is to remain perfectly still, in which case he will remain perfectly still. In general, how a mental state manifests itself in behaviour in any given circumstance will depend on the subject's other mental states. (This is just another way of making the point that behaviour is stimulus-independent.) A consequence of this fact is that any conditional statement that a behaviourist appeals to in characterizing what it is to have a particular mental state will be false. Therefore, whatever type of mental state one cares to consider, there is no hope of constructing a true behaviourist analysis of what it is to be in that mental state. (Important early expressions of this objection can be found in Geach 1957 and Chisholm 1957.)

Second, according to the behaviourist, there is nothing contingent about the way that our mental states manifest themselves in behaviour. For example, an advocate of a behaviourist view of the nature of pain would argue that there is a conceptually necessary connection between being in pain and crying or moaning and groaning. For to be in pain *just is* to behave, or be disposed to behave, in such a way. But, surely, one can coherently conceive of individuals (perhaps members of different cultures or different species) who are not remotely disposed to manifest their pain by crying or moaning and groaning. In other words, one can conceive of pain manifesting itself in a wide variety of different ways across a range of culturally or biologically distinct groups. What this suggests is that any link between human pain and crying (or moaning and groaning) is contingent rather than necessary and that, therefore, behaviourism *vis-à-vis* pain is an untenable position. Surely the point generalizes: the way that any type of mental state manifests itself in the behaviour of a particular individual is contingent rather than necessary. (This line of argument is associated with Putnam 1965.)

Third, on pain of circularity, any behaviourist account of the nature of a particular type of mental state must characterize the behaviour that it appeals to in non-intentional terms. For example, it won't do to say that part of what it is to want a gin and tonic is that if one were in a pub one would go to the bar and order a gin and tonic. But it is unlikely that any mental state is associated with a specific type of non-intentionally characterized behaviour. Suppose that it is generally true that whenever an individual wants a G & T they engage in G & T seeking behaviour. Obviously it won't do to say that what it is to want a G & T is to engage, or be disposed to engage in, G & T seeking behaviour. But, it might be thought, all the behaviourist need do is characterize G & T seeking behaviour in non-intentional terms. However, that is not going to be possible as instances of that type of behaviour need have nothing in common that can be characterized in non-intentional terms and a particular instance of that type of behaviour can be non-intentionally identical to an instance of behaviour that doesn't belong to that type.

Fourth, it is commonplace for an individual to engage in behaviour for which she has several reasons whilst only one of those reasons constitutes *the* reason why she so behaves. Consider an example. Edgar is sitting in a pub in the company of some people he finds very boring. He wants a brief respite from their company. He subsequently rises from his seat and goes to the bar and thereby fulfils his desire. However, although his desire constituted *a* reason for going to the bar it was not *the* reason for his so acting. For, he also wanted a drink and it was this desire that constituted *the* reason why he acted as he did. What makes the desire for a drink *the* reason why Edgar acted as he did as opposed to merely being *a* reason? An appealing answer is that the desire for a drink caused Edgar to go to the bar whereas the desire for a brief respite from a group of bores did not. Put generally, the idea is that what makes a reason *the* reason is that it caused the behaviour that it motivates. (This line of thought is closely associated with Donald Davidson 1963.) The behaviourist denies that mental states cause behaviour and so has great difficulties accounting for the distinction between a mental state's being *a* reason and being *the* reason for a particular behavioural episode. The worry is that behaviourism implies that there could be no such distinction and is therefore inconsistent with a perfectly familiar feature of our mental and behavioural life.

What is the relationship between philosophical behaviourism and its psychological namesake? They should be sharply distinguished. Philosophical behaviourism is a theory of the nature of mental states that seeks to deny neither the reality of such states nor the legitimacy and importance of explanations of human behaviour that appeal to them. Psychological behaviourists, on the other hand, are hostile to the practice of explaining behaviour by appeal to mental states and tend either to deny the reality of such states or to identify them with states of the brain that mediate the causal links between external stimuli and behaviour.

The Type Identity Theory

The decline in the popularity of philosophical behaviourism in the early 1960s coincided with the rise to prominence of an alternative theory, namely, the type identity theory.[8] Advocates of the type identity theory argued that types of mental states are identical to types of brain states, or, alternatively, that mental properties are identical to neural properties. Such identity relationships were held to be analogous to such familiar identity relationships as those holding between water and H_2O and heat and mean kinetic energy. For example, water just is H_2O (or the property of being water just is the property of being composed of H_2O molecules) and the statement of this identity relationship lays bare the very nature or essence of water. Thus, with respect to any particular type of mental state M, the answers to such questions as 'what is M?', 'what is it to be in M?' and 'what do all creatures that are in M have in common in virtue of which they are in M?' will appeal to a particular type of neural state or neural property. They will be of the form: 'M is a particular type of brain state, namely N', 'to be in M is to be in N' and 'what all creatures that are in M have in common in virtue of which they are in M is that they are in N'. The identity theorists held that the identity relationships holding between mental types or properties and neural types or properties are contingent and so can be discovered only by means of empirical investigation. Hence, it is a task for the scientist – rather than the philosopher – to lay bare the nature of our mental states. This explains why the identity theorists were reluctant to postulate specific identity relations. As a matter of fact, influenced by a then popular theory about pain, they tended to restrict themselves to the hypothesis that pain is C-fibre firing,[9] remaining silent with respect to most other mental types.

The type identity theory is to be distinguished from the token identity theory. A token of a particular type is a concrete particular that belongs to that type. For example, Fang is a token of the type *ferocious dog* and Vinnie is a distinct token of that same type. Similarly, my belief that Fang is ferocious is a token of the type *belief that Fang is ferocious* and Edgar's belief that Fang is ferocious is a distinct token of the same mental state type. According to the token identity theory, every token of a given mental state type will be identical to a token physical state (for example, a token brain state). But the tokens of that mental type will not all belong to the same physical type; from the physical point of view, the tokens of that mental type will constitute a heterogeneous collection. Thus, although each and every mental state token will be a physical state token, the nature or essence of our mental states cannot be expressed in physical terms.[10] This is in contrast to the type identity theory as that theory implies not only that each mental state token is identical to some physical state token but also that the tokens of any given mental state type will all belong to the same physical state type. Hence, the essence of any given mental state type can be expressed in physical terms.

The type identity theory contrasts with philosophical behaviourism in representing mental state tokens as being internal states of the brain and thus as being capable of entering into causal relations with stimulations of the sense organs, bodily behaviour and other mental states. Indeed, causal considerations constituted an important motivation for the type identity theory. For, whatever the behaviourists said, it seems intuitively obvious that mental states are very much part of the causal fray. However, everything that science tells us about the human body indicates that the brain plays a fundamentally important role in causing us to behave in the way that we do and in mediating the causal relations between sensory stimulations and behaviour. The type identity theory explains how there could be mental causation despite the fact that brain states occupy the very causal roles that we naturally conceive mental states as occupying.

A second historically important motivation for the type identity theory is bound up with a commitment to the scientific view of the world and a particular conception of the nature of science. Many type identity theorists held that one of the major achievements of science is to discover identity relationships holding between higher-level phenomena and lower-level phenomena and thereby uncover the nature or essence of the former by reducing them to the latter. Familiar examples of such discoveries include the identification of water with H_2O and heat with mean kinetic energy. Such discoveries in turn enable scientists to account for higher-level laws and regularities (for example, the law that at normal atmospheric pressure water boils at 100°C) by appeal to lower-level laws. For, such higher-level laws will hold in virtue of the identity relations between the properties that figure in them and lower-level properties, along with the laws governing those lower-level properties. Consequently, higher-level laws reduce to lower-level laws in that they can be deduced from, and explained in terms of, lower-level laws and inter-level identity relationships. Thus, for example, one of the major achievements of science has been to reduce the laws of thermodynamics to those of classical mechanics and so explain the former in terms of the latter.

Identity theorists tended (at least implicitly) to operate with the following conception of the relationship between the sciences. Science has a hierarchical structure with physics being the most basic and general science. The special sciences are less general than physics in that whereas the laws of physics govern everything in the scientific realm, the laws of any given special science govern only a sub-component of that realm (recall the account of science that I sketched in chapter 1). The phenomena and laws that are the concern of any given special science will ultimately reduce to those of physics in the manner in which thermodynamics reduces to classical mechanics. In the case of high-level special sciences, this reduction will run via a reduction to a lower-level special science, which in turn reduces to a special science at a yet lower level, and so on. Thus, assuming that psychology is a science, it will reduce to neurophysiology, a science that reduces to biochemistry, a science that reduces to chemistry, a science that reduces to physics. One implication of this reductionist view of science is that in principle the special sciences can be dispensed with without any loss of explanatory and predictive power. For, once physics is complete, everything in the scientific realm can be explained and predicted without any recourse to the special sciences. In effect, our concern with the special sciences is a manifestation of our limitations as physicists.

It is easy to appreciate how an endorsement of the above conception of science motivates the type identity theory. For if mental states cause behaviour and figure in laws that facilitate the explanation and prediction of behaviour, then one would expect mental states to be related to lower-level phenomena in a way that is typical of special science phenomena. In short, one would expect mental state types to be identical to the types of some lower-level science and the obvious candidate for such a lower-level science is neurophysiology. To reject the type identity theory would involve adopting an anti-scientific stance, something that no self-respecting twentieth-century philosopher should do. For it would involve either rejecting an assumption that underlies the scientific endeavour (that is, that all the special sciences ultimately reduce to physics) or placing the mental outside the scientific realm and thus implying that there is an important aspect of reality that science can shed no light upon.

The type identity theory's dominance was short-lived as it was subjected to a battery of powerful and influential objections. Perhaps the most important criticism came from Putnam (1967). Putnam accused the type identity theory of being chauvinistic in that it denied the mentality of systems (be they earthly creatures, extraterrestrials or inorganic machines) physically unlike humans. For example, if pain is identical to C-fibre firing, then a system that didn't have C-fibres would not be capable of being in pain. Put generally, the type identity theory implies that only systems that have brains that are very similar to the human brain are capable of sharing any aspect of our mental life (be that having a pain, wanting a drink, believing that danger is afoot or whatever). But, Putnam pointed out, this consequence of the type identity theory is highly implausible. After all, we are confident that many non-human animals share aspects of our mental lives (for example, feel pain, have beliefs and desires and so on) even though their central nervous systems are quite different from ours. Similarly, we can coherently imagine a system with, say, a silicon-based chemistry, that was capable of thought and feeling. Such considerations led Putnam to suggest that mental properties are multiply realizable; that is, any given type of mental state can be realized or physically embodied in a huge variety of different ways. Thus, that which binds together the tokens of a given mental type does not reside at the physical level. This idea that mental properties are multiply realizable paved the way to the development of functionalism.

For our purposes, the most interesting attack on the type identity theory comes from Fodor. In his classic paper 'Special Sciences' (1974) Fodor presents a devastating critique of the above-described conception of the structure of science and thereby undermines a major motivation for the type identity theory. His reasoning can be described in the following terms. Rather than being the norm, inter-level identity relations are thin on the ground. There are many perfectly respectable special sciences that frame generalizations of considerable explanatory and predictive value featuring types of phenomena whose tokens clearly don't have a shared physical essence. Consider the case of economics. A monetary exchange is an important type of economic phenomenon and there are laws of economics concerning monetary exchanges, for example, Gresham's law. No doubt each and every monetary exchange is a physical event, but it is wildly implausible to claim that that economic type can be identified with any physical type. For, in physical terms, the class of monetary exchanges is a wildly heterogeneous one: 'Some monetary exchanges involve strings of wampum. Some monetary exchanges involve dollar bills. And some involve signing one's name to a check' (p. 134). Consequently, the economic property of being a monetary exchange cannot be identified with any physical property and Gresham's law does not reduce to any law of physics.

Fodor thinks that the case of economics is typical of the special sciences: special science types are not generally identical to lower-level types and special science laws do not reduce to those of lower-level sciences. That is not to deny that physics is the most general and basic of the sciences or that special science laws are underpinned by lower-level laws. For special science tokens are identical to or constituted by physical tokens and special science properties supervene on physical properties. Thus, the special sciences cross-classify physical phenomena and their laws cross-cut one another. A consequence of all this is that the special sciences are autonomous in the respect that each special science is concerned with a distinctive aspect of reality and has the capacity to capture generalizations (and thus explain and predict certain types of phenomena) that all other sciences (including physics) are blind to. Thus, even when physics is complete, each of the special sciences will have something important and distinctive to tell us. To see this consider the following example. A particular English lake is inhabited by members of a wide range of distinct species of animals, plants and micro-organisms. A small population of pike occupy the top of the food pyramid in this particular environmental niche and their diet is largely made up of smaller fish such as perch and trout. If the pike population underwent a sudden decline (say, as a result of a pike-specific disease or the actions of the local gamekeeper) there would be a sudden increase in the size of the population of smaller fish which the pike normally prey upon. Thus, one can explain and predict population changes at one level in the food pyramid by appeal to population changes at higher levels. For example, one can explain why the trout population exploded by appeal to a decline in the population of the pike that preyed upon them. Now consider a stretch of the African savannah where a population of lions occupy the top of the food pyramid and prey upon antelope. A sudden decline in the lion population would result in a sudden increase in the antelope population. It is clear that such an event is analogous to a rise in the trout population of the English lake as a result of the decline in pike population. For both chains of events are cases where a population decline at one level in the food pyramid causes an explosion in the population of creatures at a lower level. Both these chains of events are subsumed by a single law of the population dynamics of complex ecological systems, a law that has considerable explanatory and predictive power. This law will invoke such phenomena as population changes, relations of predation between distinct biological species and so on. A rough-and-ready expression of this law might take the following form: In any environmental niche, a sudden decline in a population of predators will cause a subsequent explosion in the population of creatures upon which those predators prey, *ceteris paribus*. The crucial point is that this law does not reduce to any law of physics. For, in physical terms, distinct environmental niches bear little in common, a point that is also true of population changes, predators and acts of preying. Thus, there is a law of considerable explanatory and predictive power that physics is totally blind to. As a result of this, physics, though it is capable of explaining and predicting an explosion in the trout population of a lake *qua* physical event, is not capable of predicting and explaining that event *qua* population explosion of a colony of animals occupying a particular role in a food pyramid.

Functionalism

The final episode to be described in this brief history of recent philosophy of mind is the rise of functionalism. Functionalism superseded behaviourism and the type identity theory, being born of the perceived weaknesses of those two theories. It is arguably the case that functionalism is still the most widely held philosophical theory of the nature of mental phenomena. Fodor was an early champion of functionalism who stressed its close relationship to the view of the mind central to the cognitivist approach in psychology. (See Fodor 1968b.) According to functionalism, mental types are functional types; that is, what the tokens of any distinct mental type have in common in virtue of which they belong to that type is the functional or causal role that they play.[11] Although our concern is with intentional states rather than phenomenal states, and although functionalism is probably a more plausible theory of the former than it is of the latter, it will be helpful to consider a functionalist theory of pain. Pain plays a distinctive causal role in our internal economy. This causal role is captured by specifying generalizations such as these: pain is caused by bodily damage; pain causes worry; pain causes moaning, groaning and crying behaviour; and so on. According to the functionalist, occupying this causal role is not a contingent feature of pain. Rather, it is part of the nature of pain that it occupies this causal role or bears these causal relations to bodily stimulations, other mental states and behaviour. Thus, pain just is that state that occupies a particular causal role in a rich network of bodily stimulations, mental states and types of behaviour and to be in pain is to token an internal state that occupies the pain role. Generalized, the functionalist view is that each distinct type of mental state plays a particular causal role that is central to its identity and that to token a state of a given mental type is to token an internal state that plays the appropriate causal role in one's internal economy.

Most functionalists are physicalists in the respect that they regard minded systems (human beings, for example) as being complex physical systems and hold that the token states that occupy mental state roles are internal physical states of such systems (brain states in the case of humans). Thus, the functionalist differs from the behaviourist in regarding mental states as having causal powers and tokening a mental state as involving tokening an internal physical state that has the appropriate causal powers. The functionalist is therefore readily able to account for the fact that the manner in which a token mental state manifests itself in behaviour is sensitive to other facts about the mind of the subject. For mental states causally interact with one another and the distinctive causal role of any given type of mental state is partly a matter of the effects that it causes in conjunction with other types of mental state.

A fundamental feature of functionalism is that it represents mental states as being multiply realizable at the physical level. That is, for any given type of mental state M, although the M role will be occupied by internal physical states of complex physical systems, the particular physical state which occupies the role in one system may vary considerably from that which occupies the role in another system. For example, the pain role may be occupied by C-fibre firings in humans, a quite different state in octopuses and yet another state in a Martian with a silicon-based chemistry. Thus, functionalism sharply contrasts with the type identity theory and is not prone to the particular charges of chauvinism that undermined that theory. Moreover, functionalism is a theory that is particularly amenable to someone who is enthusiastic about the scientific status of psychology and endorses the account of the structure of science that Fodor gives in 'Special Sciences' (1974).

We are now in a position to see how functionalism coheres with the view of the mind that underlay the cognitive revolution in psychology. According to champions of the cognitive revolution, the mind is a neurophysiologically embodied computer. Hence, mental states and processes are causally efficacious phenomena that take place within the brain. However, as computers and computational states and processes are multiply realizable, the essence of mental phenomena does not reside at the physical level and a system could share our mentality whilst being physically very different from us. Clearly, this conception of the mind echoes that of the functionalist. Indeed, many functionalists (Putnam being the most prominent) were inspired by work in the theory of computability and by the development of the digital computer and explicitly compared mental states with the states of Turing machines.[12] In short, functionalism would appear to be particularly well suited to being the philosophy of mind of the cognitive scientist.

Conclusion

The early stages of Fodor's career coincided with the cognitive revolution and the rise of functionalism and he was an important champion of both of these developments, a champion who, moreover, stressed their continuity. In 1964 he co-edited and contributed to a collection of philosophical papers discussing philosophical issues arising out of Chomsky's work in theoretical linguistics and so manifested an interest in the empirical study of language and linguistic processing (Fodor and Katz 1964). In *Psychological Explanation* (1968b) Fodor launched a thoroughgoing attack on psychological behaviourism, philosophical behaviourism and the type identity theory and vigorously argued in favour of functionalism and mentalist psychology. In addition to his philosophical work, throughout the 1960s and early 1970s Fodor actively engaged in empirical work in psycholinguistics within the Chomskian framework (see Fodor *et al.* 1974 for an overview).[13] The development and presentation of the computational theory of mind in the mid-1970s constituted a natural extension of this early work in that that theory has a distinctive functionalist element and is explicitly inspired by theories of cognitive processing prominent in the cognitive science of that period.

With a firm grasp of the historical and theoretical background, we are now in a position to turn our attention directly to the computational theory of mind.

3

The Computational Theory of Mind

Introduction

The central plank of Fodor's attempt to construct a physicalist vindication of folk psychology is a theory of intentional states and processes. According to this theory intentional states are computational relations to mental representations and intentional processes are processes involving the manipulation of mental representations by means of computation. These mental representations belong to a language, namely the language of thought (LOT for short).[1] I shall call this theory the computational theory of mind (CTM for short).[2] In this chapter I will give a detailed account of CTM and Fodor's motivations for holding it, and in doing so will discuss the question of Fodor's conception of the relationship between LOT and natural language and the extent to which he thinks that LOT is an innate language.

Intentional States

Fodor's CTM can be split into two components: a theory of intentional states and a theory of intentional processes. In this section I shall focus on the first of these components. What then has CTM to say about the nature of intentional states, that is, beliefs, desires and the like? CTM was first explicitly advanced by Fodor in *The Language of Thought* (1975) and recapitulated with the emphasis being placed on intentional states – as opposed to intentional processes –

in 'Propositional Attitudes' (1978c). CTM is a contemporary version of an age-old theory of the mind known as the representational theory of mind (RTM), a theory that was particularly prominent in the seventeenth and eighteenth centuries.[3] The basic claim of RTM is that intentional states are relations to mental representations. Thus, for example, believing that Fang is ferocious involves standing in the belief relation to a mental representation that has the content *Fang is ferocious*. As their name suggests, mental representations are meaningful symbols that reside within the mind. Hence, they are the mental analogues of spoken and written sentences, maps, pictures and the like. For Fodor, the mental representations involved in the tokening of intentional states are more like linguistic symbols (for example, the words and sentences of a natural language such as English) than they are like such analogue representations as maps and pictures. In fact, mental representations belong to a non-natural language known as the language of thought (LOT). Hence, believing that Fang is ferocious involves tokening a sentence in one's mind that is the analogue of the English sentence 'Fang is ferocious' rather than, say, tokening an image of a dog of Fang's appearance behaving in a ferocious manner.

What is involved in describing mental representations as belonging to a language? To answer this question it will be helpful to consider some of the salient features of natural languages such as English. There are infinitely many distinct sentences of English, each of which is a complex symbolic structure ultimately made up of simple symbols – that is, words of English – combined in a particular way. English has finitely many words, these words constituting the vocabulary of that language, and finitely many grammatical or syntactic rules that are employed in combining words to make complex structures such as phrases and sentences. The syntactic rules determine which combinations of words of English count as legitimate sentences and which do not. For example, the syntactic rules entail that 'the ferocious dog chased the frightened runner' is a legitimate sentence whereas 'the chased dog ferocious runner frightened the' is not. How do such rules work? Words belong to syntactic categories. Examples of such syntactic categories include: noun, verb, adjective, determiner and so on. The rules appeal to such syntactic categories and each rule in effect says that words belonging to certain syntactic categories can be combined in a particular way to create a more complex symbol structure. For example, Pinker (1994) cites the following as syntactic rules of English:

- 'A noun phrase consists of an optional determiner, followed by any number of adjectives followed by a noun' (p. 98); 'the ferocious dog' is an example of a product of the application of this rule.
- 'A verb phrase consists of a verb followed by a noun phrase' (p. 98); 'chased the frightened runner' is an example of a product of the application of this rule.
- 'A sentence consists of a noun phrase followed by a verb phrase' (p. 98); 'the ferocious dog chased the frightened runner' is an example of a product of the application of this rule.

Each distinct sentence of English has a particular syntactic structure and specifying this structure involves breaking the sentence down into its component parts and indicating how those parts were put together by means of the application of syntactic rules of English. For example, in the case of the sentence 'the ferocious dog chased the frightened runner' such an analysis might go as follows. The sentence consists of a noun phrase ('the ferocious dog') followed by a verb phrase ('chased the frightened runner'). The noun phrase consists of a determiner ('the'), followed by an adjective ('ferocious'), followed by a noun ('dog'). The verb phrase consists of a verb ('chased') followed by a noun phrase ('the frightened runner') that can in turn be analysed into its constituent words. Hence, all of the above rules are employed in the course of constructing this sentence and are to be appealed to in specifying its syntactic structure.

English has finitely many words and finitely many syntactic rules yet there are infinitely many distinct sentences of English. How can that be so? The syntactic rules of English are recursive, that is, they can be applied over and over again so that the rules employed in the construction of a given sentence S can be employed to construct a more complex sentence in which S is embedded. For example, for every sentence S, there is a sentence of the form 'it is true that S'. Hence the rules of English allow one to construct the sentences 'Fang is ferocious', 'it is true that Fang is ferocious', 'it is true that it is true that Fang is ferocious', 'it is true that it is true that it is true that Fang is ferocious' and so on. Reflecting the fact that there are infinitely many distinct sentences of English, English speakers routinely produce sentences they have never produced before and hear and understand sentences they have never encountered before. Therefore, as linguists say, language is both productive and creative.

When one talks about the syntactic rules of English, the syntactic categories to which its words belong and the syntactic structure of its sentences, one remains silent about the semantics of English. Yet words and sentences are meaningful and so the question arises as to the nature of the relationship between syntax and semantics. Syntax and semantics are distinct but the syntactic properties of sentences play a systematic and disciplined role in influencing their meaning. For the meaning of any sentence is exhaustively determined by the meaning of its component words and its syntactic structure. In other words, English has a combinatorial syntax and semantics. Consequently, just as there are infinitely many distinct sentences of English, there are infinitely many meanings that English is capable of expressing.

The words and sentences of English can be physically embodied or encoded, for example, by means of sounds (as in the case of spoken sentences) or marks on paper (as in the case of written sentences). Yet word and sentence types cannot be identified with physical types as word and sentence types are multiply realizable at the physical level. For example, my last utterance of the sentence 'Fang is ferocious' is physically very different from the ink mark that encoded that sentence the last time I wrote it on paper. Moreover, in physical terms, your utterances of the sentence 'Fang is ferocious' may well differ from mine, reflecting differences in our respective vocal pitches, accents, speeds of speech and the like.

For Fodor, LOT is very much like English. There are finitely many simple symbols or words of LOT and syntactic rules for combining those words to form sentences. Yet there are infinitely many distinct sentences of LOT. The meaning of any given sentence of LOT is determined by the meanings of its constituent words and its syntactic structure as LOT has a combinatorial syntax and semantics. LOT has a rich expressive power. Indeed, it is capable of expressing any meaning that English is capable of expressing. This follows from the fact that understanding a sentence of English involves tokening a belief about the meaning of that sentence. As tokening a belief involves tokening a symbol of LOT that has the appropriate meaning, for every sentence of language that we are capable of understanding, there must be a sentence of LOT that has just the same meaning.

In virtue of his physicalism, Fodor thinks that LOT is physically embodied in the respect that token sentences of LOT are either identical to or constituted by states of the brain.[4] For example, I believe that Fang is ferocious and thus token the LOT analogue of the

English sentence 'Fang is ferocious'. This LOT sentence will be identical to a particular state of my brain and for every distinct intentional state that I have there will be a distinct state of my brain that encodes the relevant sentence of LOT. However, as in the case of English, the words and sentences of LOT are multiply realizable at the physical level.

At this point it would be relevant to describe how Fodor envisages the sentences of LOT as being encoded in the brain. Suppose that I token LOT sentence S, a sentence consisting of a number of words arranged into a particular syntactic structure. This token of S will be identical to a particular complex state of my brain. Each constituent word of the token of S will be identical to a distinct component part of this physical state. Moreover, this physical state will have an internal structure (that is, its parts will have particular physical relations to one another) that corresponds to and encodes the syntactic structure of S. Now suppose I token another sentence of LOT (call it S*) that, like S, contains a particular word W. This token of S* will also be identical to a complex state of my brain and it will have a component part that is identical to a token of W. This physical component will belong to the same physical type as the component that encodes W in the token of S. In short, there will be a physical similarity between these tokens of S and S*, a similarity that corresponds to the word that the two sentences have in common. In general, within any given individual, tokens of sentences that share words will be similar at the physical level in that, corresponding to the shared word, they will each have a component part of the same physical type. A parallel point can be made of tokens of sentences that are similar in terms of their syntactic structure,[5] for, corresponding to a similarity in their syntactic structure, there will be a similarity between their respective internal physical structures.

Specifying how LOT is encoded in the brain of a given individual involves specifying a function that maps physical states of the brain that the subject is capable of tokening onto symbols of LOT. When one specifies such a function one describes the physical form that any given symbol of LOT takes when it is tokened in the individual in question. Reflecting the point made in the previous paragraph, this function is such that symbolically similar sentences of LOT have mapped onto them physically similar brain states. Following Pylyshyn (1984) let us call this function the instantiation function. As the symbols of LOT are multiply realizable, the instantiation function that specifies how LOT is physically encoded in one individual might not apply to another despite the fact that that individual thinks in the same LOT. Indeed, it is in principle possible for the manner in which LOT is encoded in a particular individual to change over time.

Despite the fact that Fodor conceives of LOT as having much in common with natural languages such as English, he resists the idea that LOT is a natural language for the following reasons. First, he thinks that having a non-natural LOT is a prerequisite for learning a natural language. Learning a natural language involves acquiring knowledge of the meanings of the words of that language. For Fodor, such learning is a matter of constructing and confirming hypotheses that represent the meaning of the words of the target language. So, for example, learning the English word 'dog' involves constructing and confirming a hypothesis of the form: 'x is a "dog" if and only if x is a G'. In order to construct such hypotheses it is necessary that the language learner has a representational system at her disposal; otherwise, she would not be able to frame any hypotheses concerning the meaning of the target natural language words. Therefore, assuming that we do not have innate knowledge of the vocabulary of any natural language, we must have a non-natural language at our disposal in order to learn the first natural language that we acquire. In other words, unless one conceives of LOT as being a non-natural language then it is a complete mystery how human individuals ever manage to learn their first natural language. (See Fodor 1975, ch. 2.)

Second, intentional states have determinate contents and this fact is inconsistent with LOT's being a natural language. Many sentences of English are ambiguous. For example, an utterance of 'Fang chased the runner with a stick' could mean either that Fang has the stick or that the runner has the stick. If English was the medium of thought then whenever an individual tokened this sentence in forming a belief, there would be no fact of the matter as to whether she believed that it was Fang that had the stick or that it was the runner who had the stick. Given that such ambiguity is rife within natural languages, the implication of the claim that LOT is a natural language is that many of our intentional states have ambiguous contents. But, thinks Fodor, this implication is unacceptable as our intentional states typically have quite determinate contents and this is a fact that it is incumbent upon a theory of mind to explain. Similarly, if LOT is a natural language then it becomes a mystery how individuals disambiguate ambiguous sentences that they hear or read and how there can be a determinate fact of the matter as to what an individual meant when she uttered an ambiguous sentence. For Fodor, disambiguating a sentence is a matter of representing the speaker or writer's intended meaning by tokening an unambiguous sentence of LOT. And a speaker or writer's intended meaning is a matter of which particular unambiguous sentence of LOT lies behind her production of the ambiguous natural language sentence. (See Fodor 1998b, ch. 6.)

What is Fodor's conception of the relationship between LOT and the natural languages that we master? For Fodor, it is in principle possible for an individual to have intentional states and be capable of reasoning despite the fact that they do not possess a natural language such as English, German or whatever. Indeed, many animals and pre-verbal infants engage in thought without having mastery of a natural language and, as we saw above, learning a natural language involves a good deal of thinking. For those individuals who have mastery of a natural language, that language is not the medium of their thinking. Rather, it is a system that they employ in order to communicate their intentional states to their fellows or represent their intentional states to themselves. For many years Fodor sympathized with the idea that the meaning of natural language symbols is derived from the content of our intentional states and, thus, from the contents of the symbols of LOT.[6] On this view, for example, the meaning of a natural language symbol on my lips is determined by the content of the intentional state that I routinely use it to express or, alternatively, by the meaning of the LOT symbol that I associate it with. However, more recently Fodor has suggested that natural language symbols might not actually have semantic properties. On this view, although we use natural language symbols to communicate our intentional states, those symbols, unlike the intentional states that underlie their use, are meaningless. (Fodor expresses this view in Fodor 1998b, ch. 6, in the course of responding to the charge levelled by Carruthers 1996 that the Gricean programme of reducing natural language meaning to mental meaning has failed.) In sum, Fodor holds the view that thought, although it involves the deployment of a linguistic system, is prior to, and independent of, natural language.[7]

Why, it might be asked, should we think that having intentional states involves tokening symbols of a language as opposed to such analogue representations as pictures or images? For most pre-twentieth-century advocates of RTM conceived of mental representations as being imagistic in nature and there is considerable introspective evidence that thinking involves the deployment of images. It should be pointed out that Fodor has never denied the reality of mental images or that some thought processes involve the manipulation of such images.[8] (See Fodor 1975, ch. 4, 1981c and 2000, introduction.) However, he rejects the idea that mental representations are generally imagistic in nature for the following reasons. First, intentional states typically have contents that are precise and specific and in this respect differ considerably from images. For example, it is possible to believe that Fang is black in colour whilst remaining neutral on such issues as Fang's size, his tail length, his ear shape and so on. For the only property that the belief in question represents Fang as having is that of being black. But suppose one attempted to represent the fact that Fang is black by means of an image. It is difficult to see how such an image, being an image of Fang, could succeed in representing the target fact without also representing Fang as having a whole host of other appearance properties. Thus, if believing that Fang is black involved entertaining an image of Fang, then it is a complete mystery how one could have this belief without having any beliefs about Fang's size, shape and so on. Similarly, it would be a mystery as to how there could be a difference between believing that Fang is black and believing that he is, say, large or has long pointed ears. Second, many familiar intentional states have contents that are unamenable to imagistic expression. For example, how would one go about saying by means of an image that philosophy is hard, that Jerry Fodor is one of the most widely discussed philosophers of mind of recent years or that there are infinitely many sentences of English? Third, images are inherently ambiguous. Part of the traditional attraction of images is that, unlike linguistic representations, their meaning does not appear to depend on how they are understood, used or interpreted by intelligent agents. For an image means what it means in virtue of the natural relation of resemblance that it bears to the item that it represents. For example, an image of Fang is about Fang in virtue of resembling Fang. This characteristic of images implies that in claiming that thinking involves entertaining mental images one doesn't thereby postulate an infinite regress of homunculi in the mind that are needed in order to fix the meanings of the images by their acts of interpretation and understanding. However, this line of reasoning doesn't stand up to rigorous examination. Many images can be used to represent quite distinct and, indeed, incompatible states of affairs. To borrow an example from Wittgenstein, consider an image representing an old man climbing an incline. This image could just as effectively be used to represent an old man sliding down an incline. The image equally resembles each of these distinct events and in so far as it represents one, rather than the other, that is in virtue of how it is used or understood. In short, resemblance alone is not sufficient to bestow determinate contents on images.

Fodor presents these objections to imagistic versions of RTM in Fodor (1975, ch. 4). All of them echo points made by Wittgenstein (1953), a fact that Fodor refers to. Thus, Fodor's line on mental images constitutes one of the few issues upon which he agrees with Wittgenstein.

I have characterized Fodor as holding that intentional states are computational relations to mental representations. Thus far I have focused upon his conception of the nature of the mental representations involved in tokening intentional states. But how are we to understand the notion of a computational relation? It is to this question that I now turn.

Just as one can believe that Fang is ferocious, one can desire, intend, hope, fear or expect that Fang is ferocious. The difference between believing that Fang is ferocious and desiring that Fang is ferocious (or, more generally, between believing that P and desiring that P) is not a matter of a difference in the content of the LOT symbol involved in tokening these respective intentional states. For the two states have identical contents and tokening either of them may well involve tokening one and the same LOT sentence. Rather, the difference has to do with the intentional state relation involved. Believing that P involves standing in the belief relation to an LOT sentence that means *P*, whereas desiring that P involves standing in the desire relation to an LOT sentence that means *P*. The difference between the belief relation and the desire relation is a functional – that is to say, a causal – difference. Suppose that I token a sentence of LOT (call this token S). Whether or not I stand in the belief relation or the desire relation or some other intentional state relation to S (and thus, whether S serves to express the content of a belief, a desire or whatever) depends upon the functional role that S plays within my internal economy. This functional role is a matter of the nature of the generalizations concerning how S is processed by the mental mechanisms that manipulate or process symbols of LOT.[9] If I stand in the belief relation to S then the generalizations concerning how S is processed by the mechanisms within my mind will be characteristic of the belief relation and will differ from the generalizations that would have held were I in the desire relation to S. In short, then, the distinct species of intentional state relations are distinct species of functional relations to sentences of LOT and which intentional state relation an individual bears to an LOT sentence that she tokens is a matter of the functional role that that sentence plays in her internal economy. In addition, Fodor thinks that the mind is a computer; that is, he thinks that mental mechanisms manipulate sentences of LOT by means of computation. Consequently, the functional role of a sentence token of LOT is a matter of its functional role within a computational system so that distinct species of intentional state relations can be characterized as distinct species of computational relations.

With his talk of belief boxes, desire boxes and so on, Steven Schiffer (1987) has invented a helpful metaphor. Employing this metaphor, Fodor's theory of intentional states can be characterized in the following terms. To believe that P is to token a sentence of LOT that has the content P and that is located in one's belief box. To desire that P is to token a sentence of the same type in one's desire box. And so on for all the other species of intentional state relations. The mind is a computer that is programmed to process sentences stored in the belief box in a manner characteristic of sentences stored in the belief box. Such processing involves a computational mechanism taking a sentence of LOT as input and generating a sentence of LOT as output, a sentence that is placed in some box or other. Thus, a sentence of a given type that is stored in the belief box will be processed by the mechanisms that have access to it in a way that is quite different from that in which a sentence of the same type stored in the desire box would be processed by the mechanisms that have access to it.

Specifying the functional role corresponding to each distinct type of intentional state relation would be an extremely complicated business. Accordingly, Fodor offers little by way of details of the precise nature of the belief relation, the desire relation and so on. However, the basic way in which beliefs differ from desires in terms of their functional role can be brought out by means of a simple example. Consider a belief of the form: the best way to make it the case that P is to do Q. Suppose that I token such a belief and that, in addition, I token a desire to make it the case that P. All else equal, this belief–desire pair will interact to cause a tokening of an intention to do Q and subsequent engagement in Q behaviour. In this respect, the belief that the best way to make it the case that P is to do Q differs in its functional role from that of the corresponding desire. For suppose that I desire, but do not believe, that the best way to make it the case that P is to do Q. Then this desire is hardly going to interact with my desire to make it the case that P to cause an intention to do Q and subsequent engagement in Q behaviour. This difference between the functional role of the belief that the best way to make it the case that P is to do Q and the corresponding desire is a manifestation of the general difference in functional role between beliefs and desires.

A qualification of my account of Fodor's position is needed. I have implied that according to Fodor, for every intentional state that an individual has there is a corresponding sentence of LOT tokened in her brain. There is an obvious objection to such a thesis. Each of us has infinitely many distinct intentional states. For example, I believe that 2 is greater than 1, that 3 is greater than 1, that 4 is greater than 1, and so on. If each of these beliefs is physically encoded in my brain then, given that my brain is of finite dimensions, it would not be possible to fit them all in.[10] Fodor's response is to concede that some of our intentional states are dispositional and having a dispositional intentional state is a matter of being disposed to token an appropriate sentence of LOT rather than actually tokening it. For example, few of us have a token of the LOT analogue of '694,732 is greater than 1' stored in our belief box. Nevertheless, we do have sentences in our belief box that express arithmetic facts and from which we are disposed to infer that 694,732 is greater than 1 and in doing so token the appropriate sentence of LOT. (See Fodor 1987, ch. 1.)

Intentional Processes

Intentional processes are causal processes that intentional states figure in. A familiar example of such a process is one where a desire for a cup of coffee interacts with a belief that the easiest way to procure a cup of coffee would be to go to the Boulevard Café and causes an intention to go to the Boulevard Café. Thus far, I have focused my attention on Fodor's account of the nature of intentional states and have only alluded to his closely related theory of the nature of intentional processes. It is now time to make his account of intentional processes explicit.

According to Fodor the mind is a computer housed in the brain. Hence, intentional processes are computational processes; that is, they are processes involving the disciplined manipulation of sentences of LOT by means of computation. But what is a computer? A computer is a system that takes syntactically structured symbols as input and produces syntactically structured symbols as output by means of the application of symbol-manipulating rules. In the course of engaging in such activity, a computer does such things as retrieve symbols from its memory, write symbols and place them in its memory, compare symbols, delete symbols and so on. The symbols that are so manipulated have semantic properties and the processes executed by a computer are typically semantically or logically coherent in the respect that a computer's output usually 'makes sense' given its input and the information stored in its memory. Nevertheless, computers are mechanical devices that have no understanding of the meaning of the symbols that they manipulate. On the contrary, they are sensitive only to the syntactic properties of symbols. Hence, computers are, to borrow Dennett's phrase, syntactic engines driving semantic engines.

To say that a computer manipulates symbols by means of the application of symbol-manipulating rules is to say no more than that there are syntactic generalizations governing its input–output behaviour. Consider an example. I have built a computer that takes as input pairs of sentences of English and produces single sentences of English as output. The function of this machine is to generate the immediate logical consequences of sentences that it is fed as input. I have built the machine in such a way that whenever it is fed a sentence of English that has the syntactic form 'if A then B' along with a sentence of the form 'A', it produces a sentence of the form 'B' as output. So, for example, if it is fed 'if Fang is a dog then Fang is ferocious' and 'Fang is a dog' it will produce 'Fang is ferocious' as output. In virtue of this generalization concerning the machine's input–output behaviour, it can be described as applying the following rule: whenever given input that has the form 'if A then B, A' produce 'B' as output. This rule need not be explicitly represented by means of a symbol stored in the computer's memory. Nor, needless to say, need it be understood by the computer.

Computers can be physically instantiated in the respect that it is possible to create physical systems that are computers in virtue of the fact that they manipulate syntactically structured symbols by means of the application of symbol-manipulating rules. The machine described in the previous paragraph is an example of such a physical system, as is the iMac that I used to write this book, and, if Fodor is right, the human brain. Explaining how such a physical system executes the computational processes that it does ultimately involves descending to the physical level. Constructing such an explanation requires specifying how the symbols that the system manipulates are physically encoded and describing the internal physical transactions that mediate the causal links between the physical states that encode input symbols and those that encode output symbols. Computers are multiply realizable at the physical level in the respect that two distinct physical systems might be computationally equivalent (in that they manipulate symbols of one and the same language by means of the application of one and the same body of rules) whilst being physically divergent. Hence, computational states and processes cannot be type identified with or reduced to physical states and processes. (Fodor gives the most complete expression of his understanding of the nature of computation in Fodor 1980.)

With the above account of the nature of computation in hand, it is easy to understand Fodor's account of intentional processes. According to that theory, whenever an intentional process takes place, a computational mechanism embodied in the brain takes a sentence (or a number of sentences) of LOT as input and generates a sentence (or a number of sentences) of LOT as output, a sentence that it deposits in the belief box, the desire box or some other box. Given the meaning of the sentences of LOT and the rules that these mechanisms apply to those symbols, intentional processes are generally logically coherent. Thus, the logical coherence of intentional processes can be explained by describing LOT, specifying the meanings of its constituent symbols and highlighting the rules that are applied to such symbols.

It should be clear how Fodor's CTM fits into the historical developments described in chapter 2. On the one hand, CTM closely resembles the conception of the mind held by champions of the cognitive revolution. On the other hand, CTM is inconsistent with philosophical behaviourism and the type identity theory and bears considerable affinities to functionalism as, according to CTM, intentional states are causally efficacious internal states that are multiply realizable and intentional state relations are functional relations. However, it is important to note that Fodor's CTM is not a version of functionalism. Hence, although functionalism paved the way for CTM, Fodor's endorsement of CTM constitutes an abandonment of his earlier commitment to functionalism. This is because, as we shall see in chapter 5, although he holds that intentional state relations are functional relations, Fodor is opposed to functionalist theories of content. As a consequence of this, he rejects the functionalist view that the essence of the difference between beliefs that have different contents is a functional one.

Fodor's Arguments for CTM

Fodor has three major arguments for CTM. We have already encountered the first of these arguments: CTM enables us to explain first language acquisition, a phenomenon that would otherwise be utterly mysterious. The second argument is that CTM has independent support from cognitive science; hence, judged by purely scientific criteria, his theory is the best hypothesis that we have of the nature and workings of the cognitive mind. This line of thought is pushed particularly hard in *The Language of Thought* (1975) where he argues that all currently plausible psychological theories of decision-making, concept-learning and perception are committed to CTM. This reflects his official view that there is no fundamental divide between the philosophy of mind and the scientific study of cognition: empirical investigation is relevant to philosophers of mind as the questions that interest them cannot be answered by means of conceptual analysis or a priori reflection alone. There are a couple of problems with this argument. First, since the publication of *The Language of Thought* in 1975 an account of the workings of the cognitive mind very much at odds with CTM has been developed and has gained a considerable number of advocates within the cognitive science community. The account in question is connectionism. I shall discuss connectionism and Fodor's attempt to defend CTM against the connectionist challenge in chapter 4. Second, in 1983 Fodor published *The Modularity of Mind*, a hugely important psychological study of the architecture of the mind. In that work he made a distinction between input systems and the central system. Unlike the input systems, the central system is primarily concerned with belief fixation and is the domain of beliefs, desires and all the other familiar intentional states. Fodor claims that cognitive science has shed little light on the workings of the central system; all its achievements relate to the study of the input systems. (See chapter 7 for further details.) An implication of this would appear to be that there is little scientific evidence in support of CTM as a theory of central cognition, that is, as a theory of the nature of beliefs, desires etc. and the intentional processes in which they figure. Whatever version of CTM underlies the best cognitive scientific theories, it is not a theory concerning the intentional states and processes that are familiar from the perspective of folk psychology.

Fodor's third argument for CTM is that it explains many of the familiar properties of intentional states and processes described in chapter 1, something that no other theory can do. (This line of argument is particularly prominent in Fodor 1978c, 1985a and 1987, appendix.) Here is how Fodor envisages CTM as explaining such properties. First, intentional states have causal powers and they routinely enter into causal relations with stimulations of the sensory organs, bodily behaviour and other intentional states. According to CTM, intentional state tokens are identical to (or constituted by) brain state tokens and brain states are inherently well suited to enter into causal relations. Second, the causal powers of intentional states are systematically related to their contents in such a way that intentional processes are typically logically coherent. According to CTM the mind is a physically embodied computer and intentional processes are computational processes. As it is possible to build and program computers that engage in logically coherent processing activity and explain such activity in mechanistic terms, this element of CTM accounts for the logical coherence of intentional processes. Third, the system of intentional states is productive in the respect that there are infinitely many distinct intentional states that a normal human individual is capable of tokening. According to CTM, tokening an intentional state involves tokening a sentence of LOT. LOT is a language that has a combinatorial syntax and semantics so that there are infinitely many distinct sentences of LOT and infinitely many distinct contents that it is capable of expressing. Hence, productivity is no surprise. Fourth, the system of intentional states is systematic in the respect that any individual capable of thinking that object a stands in the relation R to object b (aRb for short) is also able to think that b stands in relation R to b (bRa for short). As the sentences of LOT are syntactically structured, thinking aRb involves tokening a sentence that contains distinct words that refer to, respectively, a, R and b. A consequence of this is that thinking that bRa involves deploying the very same resources as those that are deployed in thinking aRb so it is no surprise that an individual who has the capacity to think the former thought also has the capacity to think the latter. Fifth, CTM can account for the fact that an individual can think (that is, believe, desire or whatever) that a is F without thinking that b is F despite the fact that a and b are one and the same object and, therefore, that sentences that ascribe intentional states to individuals have the property of intensionality. For an individual to believe that Mark Twain was born in

Missouri they must have the LOT analogue of the sentence 'Mark Twain was born in Missouri' in their belief box. Even though Sam Clemens and Mark Twain are one and the same person, tokening the LOT analogue of 'Sam Clemens was born in Missouri' is not sufficient for believing that Mark Twain was born in Missouri as that sentence is not the sentence that one must token in order to have the belief in question. In general, according to CTM, it is due to the fact that tokening an intentional state involves tokening a sentence of LOT that an individual can think that a is F without thereby thinking that b is F despite the fact that a and b are one and the same object.

CTM is a physicalist theory and its ability to explain all of the above features of our intentional states and processes reveals why it should be described as the centrepiece of Fodor's attempt to construct a physicalist vindication of folk psychology. However, there is one salient feature of our intentional states that CTM does not in itself explain. Intentional states have content; they would hardly be intentional states if they didn't. But CTM doesn't account for the content of our intentional states. For example, it doesn't tell us in virtue of what my belief that Fang is ferocious has that content rather than some other content or no content at all. Due to this limi-tation, Fodor supplements CTM with a theory of content, that is, a theory that specifies the physicalist determinants of the contents of the symbols of LOT. This theory of content is the subject of chapter 5.

Concept Nativism

To what extent does Fodor conceive of LOT as being an innate language? There is an alternative way of putting this question: to what extent is Fodor committed to the idea that our conceptual repertoires are innate? That the question can be phrased in this alternative way is a product of the fact that for Fodor having a concept is a matter of having a symbol in one's LOT that has the appropriate content. For example, having the concept DOG is a matter of having a symbol in one's LOT that expresses the property of being a dog. Radical concept nativism is the view that all or most of the concepts that we grasp and deploy in thought are innate. For many years Fodor was a radical concept nativist but in his recent work he has attempted to backtrack. In this section I examine the reasons why Fodor once endorsed radical concept nativism and in the next section I will consider his attempt to move away from this position.

What exactly is nativism? A nativist with respect to a particular body of knowledge or battery of concepts holds that that knowledge or those concepts are innate. But what is it for something to be innate? An item will be innate if it is present at birth. However, it is important to appreciate that an item can be innate even if it is not present at birth and even if certain quite specific experiences are necessary in order to acquire it. Suppose that human individuals are built in such a way that (or have a genetic make-up such that) certain specific experiences automatically cause us to acquire a particular item. In addition, suppose that this process of acquisition is not one of learning. Then the item in question will be triggered by those specific experiences. Roughly speaking, for an item to be innate is for it to be either present at birth or to be such that its acquisition is automatically triggered by certain experiences rather than learned on the basis of those experiences. This raises a question about the nature of learning: what is it for an item to be learned rather than merely triggered? As Fodor puts it in 'The Present Status of the Innateness Controversy' (1981b), learning is a rational-causal process whereas triggering is a brute-causal process. When one learns a concept there is an intentional description of the acquisition process that reveals the acquisition of the concept to be rationally related to the experiences that gave rise to it or to 'make sense' in the light of those experiences. For example, suppose that you read a philosophical account of the nature of nativism and, fully understanding that account, you acquire the concept NATIVISM. Then there will be an intentional description of the acquisition process that reveals it to be rational. This description will talk about your reading and understanding a piece of meaningful text, forming particular related beliefs, and so on. In such a case you will have learned the concept NATIVISM. In contrast consider the case where you acquire the concept as a result of being hit over the head with a saucepan. In this case there will be no intentional description of the acquisition process that reveals that process to be rational and the concept will not have been acquired by means of learning. In fact, Fodor has a quite specific understanding of the nature of concept-learning that coheres with the account of language-learning that we have already encountered. On this account, concept-learning is a process of hypothesis-testing and confirmation. Consider his account of learning the concept FLURG. Something is a flurg if and only if it is a green triangle. Suppose that you are in a situation where you are shown cards with geometrical figures printed upon them and are invited to say whether or not the figure printed on each card is a flurg. For each judgement you make you are told whether or not you are correct. You begin by formulating a speculative hypothesis of the form 'x is a flurg if and only if x is a G'. You modify this hypothesis when it is disconfirmed by your experiences; that is, when you are informed that your judgement about a particular card is mistaken. As a result of this process of hypothesis modification, you ultimately formulate the hypothesis 'x is a flurg if and only if x is a green triangle'. When this hypothesis is confirmed a number of times you are confident to endorse it as the correct hypothesis concerning what a flurg is. In this way you learn the concept FLURG as your acquisition of this concept is rationally related to the experiences that gave rise to it.

There are two related arguments that nativists often present for their view that a particular body of knowledge or battery of concepts is innate. The first appeals to universality. Suppose that certain knowledge or concepts are universal in the respect that all human individuals acquire them by a particular age regardless of their social and cultural background, intellectual ability or the specifics of their learning experiences. Then, so the argument goes, the best explanation for this universality is that the knowledge or concepts are innate. For, if they were learned one would expect them to be unevenly distributed across the population in the manner in which abstruse philosophical knowledge and concepts are unevenly distributed. The second argument is the poverty of stimulus argument. Suppose that human individuals routinely acquired certain knowledge or concepts despite the fact that their experiences were far too limited for them to have learned the knowledge or concepts in question from their experiences. Then, so the argument goes, as the knowledge or concepts outstrip experience they cannot have been learned and so must be innate.

Chomsky has famously presented such arguments in favour of the thesis that we have innate knowledge of Universal Grammar.[11] They also have considerable plausibility when applied to folk psychology.[12] Moreover, one might – with equal plausibility – advance these arguments with respect to many of the concepts that are fundamental to human life and without a grasp of which a human individual could hardly prosper. The concepts I have in mind include the following: CAUSE, TRUTH, KNOWLEDGE, EXPLANATION, BELIEF, DESIRE, FEAR and PAIN.

Clearly natural languages are not entirely innate as in acquiring a language one has to learn the meaning of its words. It is natural to think that in learning a language one learns a whole battery of new concepts. For, example, that in learning the meaning of 'proton' one learns the concept PROTON, a concept that one didn't previously have. However, Fodor presents an account of language-learning that undermines this assumption. This is the account of language-learning that we have already encountered according to which learning the meanings of the words of a language is a matter of hypothesis-testing and confirmation and involves utilizing LOT in order to frame the relevant hypotheses. On this account, to learn the meaning of a word one must have a symbol in one's LOT that has the equivalent meaning, otherwise one would not be able to frame the relevant hypothesis. In 'The Present Status of the Innateness Controversy' (1981b) Fodor expresses what is essentially the same argument explicitly in terms of concept acquisition. As we saw in the case of the concept FLURG, learning a concept involves testing and confirming hypotheses and in order to test and confirm the correct hypothesis one must already grasp the target concept. To learn the concept FLURG one must have the concept GREEN TRIAN-GLE, but as something is a flurg if and only if it is a green triangle, these putatively distinct concepts are one and the same concept. In effect, it is not possible to learn a new concept so all our concepts must be innate.

There is an obvious line of response to this argument for radical concept nativism that can be expressed as follows. We have an innate stock of basic concepts that we can use to define non-basic concepts outside that stock. Learning a concept involves constructing a definition in terms of basic concepts and in doing so acquiring a new concept. In the case of Fodor's example, learning the concept FLURG involves constructing a definition utilizing the basic concepts GREEN and TRIANGLE. As the concept FLURG cannot be identified with either of these basic concepts, there is an important respect in which one does learn a new concept when one confirms the hypothesis that flurgs are green triangles. Therefore, the concept FLURG is not innate.[13]

Fodor flirted with this attempt to escape the clutches of radical concept nativism in *The Language of Thought* (1975). However, by the time of 'The Present Status of the Innateness Controversy' (1981b) he had come to see it as a hopeless move for the simple reason that very few of the concepts corresponding to the words of English[14] can be defined. FLURG is therefore atypical. This line of thought is also prominent in *Concepts* (see 1998a, chs 3 and 4). Why does Fodor think that few lexical concepts are definable or that, in other words, few lexical concepts have necessary and sufficient conditions for their application? Despite the exertion of considerable energy by philosophers and linguists, there are few lexical concepts that have been given plausible definitions. Typically, whenever a philosopher or linguist produces a definition of a target concept, one of her colleagues presents a compelling counter-example. From the repeated failure of attempts to produce such definitions, Fodor induces the conclusion that most lexical concepts are indefinable. The upshot of this is that most lexical concepts – for example, HOUSE, ELEPHANT, PROTON, CARBURETTOR – are innate.

Another possible response to Fodor's argument for radical concept nativism involves questioning his account of concept-learning. The argument I have in mind runs thus. Learning a concept is not a matter of constructing a definition. For concepts are prototypes. Hence, learning a concept is a matter of constructing a prototype out of more basic concepts and doing this doesn't require one to have the target concept before the learning period begins. Nor does the possibility of such learning fall foul of the fact that most lexical concepts are not definable, for prototypes, though they are structured representations, are not definitions. (Carruthers 1992, ch. 7.)

Fodor responds to this line of thought by rejecting the claim that concepts are prototypes, but before examining this response it will be helpful to describe the theory that concepts are prototypes in a little more detail.[15] A prototype is a complex mental representation that, rather than specifying necessary and sufficient conditions, specifies the characteristics that any item falling within its extension is likely to have. For example, on this view the concept DOG is a complex representation that specifies properties that dogs generally have, properties that something is likely to have if it is a dog. Examples of such properties might be those of having four legs, having fur, having a tendency to bark and so on. Thus, the DOG prototype constitutes a description of a prototypical or stereotypical dog and grasping the concept DOG is a matter of having this description encoded in one's head. A prototype also includes a similarity metric so that, for example, determining whether an item x falls within the extension of DOG involves employing a similarity metric in order to determine whether x resembles the prototypical dog to a sufficient extent. A Labrador or a golden retriever would be a serious candidate for a prototypical dog but, presumably, a Great Dane or a Pekinese would not be. That an individual would categorize a Pekinese, but not a Siamese cat, as a DOG reflects the fact that employment of the similarity metric generates the result that the former, but not the latter, is sufficiently similar to the prototypical dog to fall within the extension of the concept DOG.

Fodor's critique of the prototype theory,[16] though prominent in his recent work, echoes points that he made in 'The Present Status of the Innateness Controversy' (1981b). His argument runs as follows. Concepts are compositional in the respect that the content of a complex concept is determined by the content of its constituent concepts and the manner in which they are combined. Generally speaking, prototypes don't compose; that is, the prototypes of complex concepts are not generally determined by the prototypes of their constituents. Therefore, as concepts have a salient property that prototypes do not, concepts cannot be prototypes. There are two reasons why prototypes don't compose. First, infinitely many concepts don't have prototypes. As he points out in 'The Present State of the Innateness Controversy', although there are prototypical cities and prototypical grandmothers, 'there are surely no pro-totypical *American cities situated on the East coast just a little south of Tennessee* [and] . . . there are surely no prototypical properties of *grandmothers most of whose children are married to dentists*' (1981b: 296–7). In *Concepts* (1998a) he makes essentially the same point, this time focusing on Boolean concepts, that is complex concepts that contain such logical operators as 'and', 'not' and 'or'. Boolean con-cepts do not have prototypes as can be seen by examining the concept NOT A CAT. A bagel would be a clear-cut instance of this concept as would a Tuesday and an eraser. But bagels, Tuesdays and erasers have nothing in common apart from their being non-cats. Bagels, unlike Tuesdays and erasers, tend to be edible; Tuesdays, unlike bagels and erasers, follow Mondays; and erasers, unlike bagels and Tuesdays, tend to be made of rubber. Therefore, there is no collection of properties that could figure in the prototype for NOT A CAT. (Fodor 1998a, ch. 5.)

Fodor's second reason for concluding that prototypes don't compose is that the prototypes of many complex concepts that plau-sibly have prototypes bear little relation to the prototypes of their component concepts. A goldfish is neither a prototypical PET nor a prototypical FISH (a dog would be an example of a prototypical PET and a trout an example of a prototypical FISH). Nevertheless, a gold-fish is a prototypical PET FISH. Thus the prototype for the complex concept PET FISH will refer to properties (for example, those of living in a bowl, being less than 10 cm in length, and so on) that do not figure in either of the prototypes of its constituent concepts. And properties will figure in the prototypes of the constituent concepts that do not figure in the prototype of the complex (for example, having fur in the case of PET, and being cherished by anglers in the case of FISH). Therefore, the prototype of PET FISH is not determined by the prototypes of its component concepts; in other words, such cases suggest that prototypes do not generally compose. Fodor points out that any advocate of the prototype theory who makes a technical attempt to get round this problem is barking up the wrong tree. This is because what counts as a prototypical instance of a complex concept depends upon contingent facts about the world that are independent of what count as prototypical instances of its component concepts. (Fodor 1998a, ch. 5; Fodor and LePore 1994.)

A response that might be made by advocates of the prototype theory to the compositionality objection is to argue that it is only simple concepts that are prototypes. I suspect that Fodor would reply that anyone who makes this move is thereby left with a theory of concepts that has nothing to say about the nature of concepts; some theory of concepts!

Before closing this section I will briefly describe a way of avoiding radical concept nativism whilst accepting the power of Fodor's attack on the idea that lexical concepts are definable and that concepts are prototypes. The line of thought that I have in mind involves endorsing a particular model of concept acquisition and runs as follows. Assume that having a particular concept involves having a symbol in one's LOT whose tokening is caused by and only by instances of the property expressed by the concept. So, for example, having the concept AARDVARK involves having a symbol in one's LOT that is caused by and only by aardvarks. Thus, acquiring a particular concept involves establishing the appropriate mind–world causal relations. Now consider the following model of concept acquisition. We have a stock of innate basic concepts and innate mechanisms to construct prototypes out of such concepts. These prototypes are associated with symbols of LOT and serve to mediate whatever causal relations those symbols bear to worldly properties. Consider a child who is attempting to learn the concept AARDVARK, a concept that does not belong to her innate repertoire of concepts. In the course of learning this concept, in-head mechanisms construct a prototype utilizing concepts that the child already has (for example, concepts such as GREY, QUADRUPED, LEATHERY and so on). This prototype is associated with the child's LOT symbol AARDVARK and serves to specify the properties that, on the basis of her experiences, she regards the prototypical aardvark as having. Most importantly, the prototype mediates whatever causal relations her symbol AARDVARK bears to the external world. The child has succeeded in learning the concept AARDVARK when the prototype associated with her LOT symbol AARDVARK is such that aardvarks, and only aardvarks, cause her to token that symbol. Thus, on this model of concept acquisition, the construction of prototypes out of innate concepts plays an important role in the learning of concepts that are not innate. However, such prototypes are not to be identified with concepts. For the property expressed by any given symbol of LOT doesn't depend directly on the specific nature of the associated prototype. Rather, it depends upon the nature of causal relations that the symbol bears to the external world, causal relations that are, as a matter of contingent fact, mediated by a prototype.

Whether or not the model of concept acquisition sketched in the preceding paragraph is true is an empirical matter. If it is true, then not all our lexical concepts need be innate even if lexical concepts are not definable and even if they are not prototypes. Thus, the model offers a way of resisting Fodor's one-time claim that all our concepts are innate without endorsing the view that concepts are definable or that concepts are prototypes.

Fodor's Attempt to Retreat from Radical Concept Nativism

In *Concepts* (1998a) Fodor attempts to retreat from the radical concept nativist position that he held throughout the 1970s and 1980s. In this section I will examine this attempted retreat. His attention focuses upon concepts that are neither natural kinds nor logico-mathematical concepts. He argues that many, if not all, such concepts are not innate.

Central to Fodor's change of position is an account of the nature of the properties expressed by the target concepts. The example that he focuses upon is that of the concept DOORKNOB. He advances a metaphysical account of the nature of doorknobhood that has the implication that the concept DOORKNOB is not innate. He approaches the issue by describing a problem that faces the nativist. This is the problem of accounting for the doorknob–DOORKNOB effect or solving the d–D problem. What is this problem? If concepts are triggered rather than learned, then why is it the case that we typically acquire them as a result of experiences of items that fall under them? For example, why do human individuals typically acquire the concept DOORKNOB as a result of experiences of or inter-actions with doorknobs? If concepts are triggered then why isn't it the case that interactions with giraffes or whipped cream trigger the concept DOORKNOB? The fact that we typically acquire the concept DOORKNOB as a result of interactions with doorknobs suggests that learning is involved as doorknobs constitute the best source of evidence about doorknobs. In short, the d–d effect undermines the idea that concepts are triggered rather than learned. Fodor attempts to solve the d–d problem by constructing an independently plausible account of the nature of the property of being a doorknob. Here is how that account runs. Doorknobhood is like redness in being an appearance property. Whether or not an object is red depends upon the effects that it has on us; to be red just is to be an object that would cause a normal human individual to have a certain type of visual experience were she to be confronted by it. Thus, what all red things have in common in virtue of which they are red is the power to have a particular effect on us. It is metaphysically necessary that red things look red to us (that is, cause us to have the 'red' experi-ence) in the respect that there is no possible world where there are red objects that do not look red to us in that world. In short, redness is a mind-dependent property. Fodor thinks that something similar is true of doorknobhood. Whether or not an object is a doorknob depends upon how it strikes us. We have the kinds of minds that are such as to respond to objects that satisfy the doorknob proto-type by tokening DOORKNOB. That doorknobs affect us in this way makes them doorknobs. Thus, Fodor would appear to be saying that to be a doorknob just is to be an object that affects us in the way in which objects that satisfy the doorknob prototype typically do (that is, by causing a tokening of DOORKNOB).[17] However, he quickly shifts his account to one that identifies the crucial effect that doorknobs have on us as that of causing us to acquire the concept DOORKNOB. For example, he writes, 'what doorknobs have in common qua doorknobs *is being the kind of thing that our kinds of mind (do or would) look to from experience with instances of the doorknob stereo-type*' (1998a: 137). And 'what makes something a doorknob is just: being the kind of thing from experience with which our kind of mind readily acquires the concept DOORKNOB' (ibid.). As justifica-tion of this account of doorknobhood, Fodor argues that none of the alternatives are remotely plausible: one cannot define what it is to be a doorknob in terms of more basic properties and doorknobs do not share a common hidden essence.

How does this account of doorknobhood help solve the d–D problem? If to be a doorknob just is to be the kind of thing that interaction with it would cause us to acquire the concept DOORKNOB, then it is metaphysically necessary that interaction with doorknobs causes us to acquire the concept DOORKNOB. In other words, there is no possible world where there are doorknobs that do not have this effect on us. Consequently, the d–D effect is metaphysically necessary. Therefore, we do not need an explanation of why the d–D effect holds that appeals to a process of learning. As Fodor puts it: 'if being a *doorknob* is a property that's *constituted* by how things strike us, then the intrinsic connection between the content of DOORKNOB and the content of our doorknob-experiences is metaphysically necessary, hence not a fact that a cognitivist theory of concept acquisition is required in order to explain'.[18]

From all this, Fodor concludes that the concept DOORKNOB is not innate. If this concept is acquired by means of hypothesis-testing and confirmation then it follows that it is innate. For, one cannot frame the relevant hypothesis unless one already has the concept DOORKNOB. But as Fodor's account of the nature of the property of being a doorknob allows us to account for the d–D effect without recourse to the hypothesis-testing and confirmation model, the nativist implications of that model are avoided. As this argument generalizes to all concepts that express mind-dependent properties, no such concepts are innate. In short, Fodor avoids radical concept nativism by resisting the account of the nature of concept acquisition that implies such a nativist position.

One might object that this argument only applies to concepts that express mind-dependent properties so that Fodor is still committed to a nativist view with respect to natural kind concepts such as WATER. A consequence of this is that, as many of our concepts are natural kind concepts, Fodor hasn't managed to make a substantial retreat from radical concept nativism. However, Fodor goes on to consider natural kind concepts and, drawing upon similarities that they bear to such concepts as DOORKNOB, concludes that they too are not innate. To see how this argument goes consider the concept WATER.

In addition to sharing a common hidden essence, all samples of water share certain superficial properties and it is nomologically necessary that they do so. That is, water has a characteristic collection of appearance properties; water looks, tastes, smells and feels a particular way to human individuals. Children and scientifically unsophisticated adults generally apply the concept WATER to samples of water on the basis of the appearance properties of those samples rather than on the basis of determining that those samples have a particular hidden essential property. Applying the concept WATER on this latter basis is a highly sophisticated accomplishment that human individuals develop long after they have acquired the concept WATER. But how is the concept WATER acquired? According to Fodor, we humans have the kind of mind such that anything that has the appearance properties that water typically has strikes us in a particular way; that is, causes us to token WATER or to acquire the concept WATER. That we respond in this way is, from the psychological perspective, a brute fact about us that is not mediated by any process of hypothesis-testing and confirmation. Hence, there is a significant parallel between the process of acquiring the concept WATER and that of acquiring the concept DOORKNOB; in neither case is the acquisition process such as to require the prior possession of the target concept. Of course there is a crucial difference between these two concepts. All those items that we are disposed to apply WATER to in virtue of their appearance properties share a common hidden essence. However, the items that we are disposed to apply the concept DOORKNOB to have no such common hidden essence. On the contrary, all they have in common is that we are disposed to respond to them by tokening DOORKNOB. It is because of this difference that WATER is a natural kind concept whereas DOORKNOB is not.

In the course of our intellectual development we learn that water has a hidden essence (and, in particular, that it is H_2O). We also learn how to determine whether or not any given item has the requisite essential property to fall under the concept WATER. Or, alternatively, we come to adopt the policy of deferring to those experts who are able to make such determinations when it comes to questions of whether or not something falls under the concept WATER. Fodor characterizes this development as one of moving from having a concept of a natural kind to having a concept of a natural kind as such. Children, along with all adults prior to the chemical revolution of the eighteenth century, have the concept WATER in the first respect but not in the second respect. However, most educated contemporary adults have the concept WATER in the second respect. Fodor suggests that the development from having WATER as a concept of a natural kind to having WATER as a concept of a natural kind as such is not a matter of acquiring a new concept. Rather, it is a matter of becoming disposed to apply WATER to samples of water on the basis of their essence rather than on the basis of their non-essential appearance properties. Thus, as the concept WATER as possessed by children is not innate then neither is the concept WATER as possessed by adults. In sum, as this argument generalizes to all natural kind concepts, Fodor concludes that neither natural kind concepts nor concepts expressing mind-dependent properties are innate.

Does Fodor's argument work, that is, does he succeed in escaping the clutches of extreme concept nativism? I think that there are three reasons for scepticism. First, as I hinted above, there is a crucial ambiguity in Fodor's account of the nature of the property of being a doorknob. Initially he seems to be suggesting that the effect that doorknobs have on us in virtue of which they are doorknobs is that they cause us to token DOORKNOB. Subsequently, however, his view is that the crucial effect is that of causing us to acquire the concept DOORKNOB. There is a distinction between these two accounts and Fodor needs the latter for his argument to have a hope of going through. To see this, consider the property of being chic. This is a mind-dependent property if anything is: to be chic just is to be seen as such by a non-negligible proportion of those individuals who care about such things or are widely deemed to be authorities on such matters. Nevertheless, it doesn't follow from this that we have the kind of mind that automatically acquires the concept CHIC on being presented with a chic individual. Most of us require a great deal of education in order to acquire the concept CHIC; without such an education we are not remotely disposed to token CHIC in response to chic individuals. The same probably holds of officially recognized authorities on matters of chicness. It is likely that such education involves the acquisition of a whole collection of beliefs and thus that a cognitivist account of the acquisition of the concept CHIC holds true. But that is entirely consistent with the mind-dependence of the property of being chic; for, if the education process undergone by the experts on matters chic didn't dispose them to token CHIC in response to, say, Jacqueline Kennedy, then Jacqueline Kennedy would not have been chic. With respect to CHIC, then, Fodor's argument doesn't work, for the property of being chic isn't mind-dependent in the right kind of way: it just isn't metaphysically necessary that we have the kind of mind such that we automatically acquire the concept CHIC as a result of experiences of chic people. If the property of being a doorknob is mind-dependent in the respect analogous to that in which that of being chic is, then it won't be metaphysically necessary that interactions with doorknobs cause us to acquire the concept DOORKNOB. For it could be the case that the human mind is such that children need to acquire a substantial body of knowledge about doorknobs in order to become disposed to token DOORKNOB in response to doorknobs and so bring their reactions to doorknobs into line with that of the general populace.

The consequence of all this is that Fodor needs to justify his second account of the precise way in which the property of being a doorknob is mind-dependent. However, he offers no such justification. For the record, the first account strikes me as having greater intuitive plausibility.

Second, as Cowie (1999) points out, even if Fodor's account of the nature of the property of being a doorknob is correct, it is far from clear that his anti-nativist argument works. Here is how Cowie reasons. Even if Fodor is correct in what he says about the property of being a doorknob, it is still legitimate to ask the question 'why do doorknobs affect our kinds of minds in the way that they do?' To ask this question is to enquire about the mechanisms that underlie the fact that we respond to doorknobs in the way that we do (that is, by acquiring the concept DOORKNOB). Consider the property of being a sleep inducer. To be a sleep inducer just is to be something that would cause a human individual to fall asleep were they to ingest it. But why do sleep inducers cause us to fall asleep? This is a perfectly legitimate question that is not satisfactorily answered by saying that it is metaphysically necessary that sleep inducers cause us to fall asleep when we ingest them. With respect to the question about the effects that doorknobs have on us, the mechanistic story might be a cognitivist one for all that Fodor establishes. In short, Fodor's account of the nature of doorknobhood is consistent with the truth of a cognitivist story about the acquisition of the concept DOORKNOB.

It would appear that Fodor anticipates Cowie's objection in chapter 6 of *Concepts* (1998a). For he concedes that he has not fatally undermined nativism. However, he suggests, it is possible that the mechanism underlying the d–d effect might not have a psychological or intentional description. (This is a possibility that he takes very seriously.) In other words, from the point of view of psychology, the d–d effect might be a brute inexplicable fact. If the mechanism doesn't have an intentional description, then any cognitivist account of how we acquire the concept DOORKNOB will be false with the implication that that concept is innate. My third and final objection to Fodor's attempted retreat from nativism suggests a way of answering Fodor's response to the kind of charge made by Cowie.

The answer that it suggests is that if the mechanism underlying the d–d effect has no intentional description then the concept DOOR-KNOB is thereby innate. I will now turn to that third objection.

There is something a little odd about Fodor's argument for it is far from clear why his solution to the d–d problem should be taken as providing an escape route from radical concept nativism. For if we have the kind of mind that is such that we automatically acquire the concept DOORKNOB as a result of interactions with doorknobs, and do so without the mediation of intentional mechanisms, doesn't it follow that DOORKNOB is innate? It would certainly seem to do so if we understand concept nativism as Fodor does in 'The Present Status of the Innateness Controversy' (1981b). Recall that in that paper he characterizes learning as a rational-causal process and distinguishes it from triggering, which is a brute-causal process. Radical nativism is the view that we acquire our concepts by means of a brute-causal process rather than a rational-causal process of learning. In *Concepts* (1998a) Fodor portrays the process of acquiring such concepts as DOORKNOB as a brute-causal process. So, whatever he says, rather than distancing himself from radical concept nativism, Fodor would appear to have reaffirmed his commitment to that doctrine. Why doesn't he realize this? One possibility is that he has been misled by the dialectical situation. The standard argument for radical concept nativism has it that any concept that we acquire by means of hypothesis-testing and confirmation must already belong to our conceptual repertoire. In short, the argument is that the hypothesis-testing and confirmation model of concept acquisition implies that all our concepts are innate. Hence, Fodor appears to think that he can avoid the conclusion of this argument if he can vindicate a non-cognitivist account of concept acquisition. But that is a mistake as the nativist has no wish to endorse the view that hypothesis-testing and confirmation is the means by which we acquire our concepts. The nativist's point is that given that learning involves hypothesis-testing and confirmation, it is not possible to acquire a concept by means of learning as one would need to have the target concept already in order to frame the relevant hypothesis. Hence, concept acquisition must be a brute-causal process.

Cowie has an alternative explanation. She argues that Fodor has changed his view of what it is for a concept to be innate. For he has come to endorse the view that if a concept is acquired by means of a brute-causal process, that is, by means of a mechanism that doesn't have an intentional characterization, then it is not innate. However, whatever the truth value of this diagnosis, it seems fair to say that in its essentials, Fodor's position has changed in name only. Moreover, his new understanding of the term 'innate' would seem to be somewhat perverse as it implies that many of our concepts are neither innate nor acquired by means of learning.

A version of the third objection would appear to undermine Fodor's reflections on the acquisition of natural kind concepts. For suppose that he is right when he suggests that we have the kind of mind that is such that we automatically respond to experiences of stuff that has the superficial properties of water by acquiring the concept WATER or by tokening WATER. And suppose that our so responding is not mediated by any process of hypothesis-testing and confirmation. Then it would appear to follow that the concept WATER is innate. In sum, then, there are reasons for scepticism with respect to the success of Fodor's attempt to retreat from radical concept nativism.

Conclusion

In this chapter I have given a detailed account of CTM and Fodor's arguments for that theory and indicated how it is supposed to explain (in physicalist terms) some of the most salient features of intentional states and processes as viewed from the perspective of folk psychology. I have also addressed the question of the extent to which Fodor conceives of LOT as being an innate language and, thus, the extent to which he is committed to radical concept nativism. In the next chapter I will examine some of the most interesting and important challenges to CTM that have been generated by the philosophical and cognitive science communities and consider the way in which the Fodorian might respond to these challenges.

4

Challenges to the Computational Theory of Mind

Introduction

The discussion of the previous chapter suggests that we should take CTM very seriously indeed. But are there any convincing arguments that serve to undermine that theory? There are several widely known and much discussed objections to CTM that have been raised over the last few decades. For example, it has been claimed that CTM cannot account for common sense and the learning of skills and is sunk by the frame problem (Dreyfus 1979; Dreyfus and Dreyfus 1987), that CTM is fatally undermined by Gödel's incompleteness theorem (Lucas 1964; Penrose 1989) and that CTM is inconsistent with the pervasive manner in which moods affect cognitive processing (Haugeland 1978).[1] However, I do not propose to discuss these objections. Rather, my attention will focus upon four substantial challenges to CTM all of which are prominent in the contemporary philosophical and cognitive science literature. The first three of these challenges emanate from the work of, respectively, the philosophers Donald Davidson, Daniel Dennett and John Searle. The fourth challenge is that presented by connectionism, an alternative to CTM that has won many followers within the cognitive science community. In this chapter I will describe these four challenges and discuss the manner in which Fodor might respond to them.

Davidson and Dennett

Donald Davidson and Daniel Dennett have each made a substantial contribution to the philosophy of mind. There are important similarities between their views and they both advance a theory of intentional states and of the nature of folk psychology that stands in stark contrast to Fodor's CTM and thereby constitutes an important challenge to that theory. In this section I will give an account of Davidson and Dennett's views, describe the respects in which they constitute a challenge to CTM and discuss some of the lines of defence open to the Fodorian.

Let's start with Davidson.[2] Davidson recognizes the centrality of folk psychology to human life; for him, we routinely and effortlessly attribute intentional states to our fellows in order to make sense of and explain their behaviour and episodes in their mental life. He regards this enterprise of attributing intentional states as being one of interpretation. Thus, when I attribute beliefs, desires, intentions and the like to one of my fellows I interpret her on the basis of observable evidence concerning her behaviour (including her linguistic behaviour), and the nature of the external events impinging upon her. The practice of constructing such interpretations is governed by certain principles, the most prominent being the Principle of Charity. These principles enjoin the interpreter to attribute to a subject beliefs that are largely true, beliefs that are about their immediate external cause, beliefs that cohere with one another so as to constitute a consistent battery of beliefs, desires that it is rational to have, and beliefs and desires the possession of which make the subject's actions rational. Such principles are often described as normative in that they enjoin the interpreter to attribute to any individual whom she aims to interpret beliefs and desires that they ought to have and that reveal their actions to be rational. In addition, the principles are holistic in the respect that they rule out the attribution of intentional states on a one-by-one basis without consideration of what other intentional states one regards the subject that one seeks to interpret as holding and of how one regards her as acting. For example, to attribute a belief to a subject without consideration of what else one takes her to believe is to run the risk of attributing inconsistent beliefs to her. Similarly, when attributing a belief to a subject in order to explain a particular action, one must take into account the desires that one regards her as having so that the action is seen to be rational in the light of that belief and those desires. And vice versa; that is, desire attributions are constrained by the beliefs that one regards the subject as holding. Indeed, when determining the nature of a subject's actions one must take into account the beliefs and desires that one regards her as holding. A failure to do this would involve running the risk of interpreting the subject in such a way that her actions made no sense given the beliefs and desires attributed to her and thus violating the demands of the principles of interpretation.

A related point is that Davidson is committed to semantic holism. For him, any meaningful item (for example, a belief or a word) belongs to a system of meaningful items and gets its identity from its place in that system. With respect to beliefs, the idea is that, for example, one can't have beliefs involving the concept DOG without having beliefs involving the concept ANIMAL, in particular, perhaps, without having the belief that dogs are animals. Consequently, one cannot legitimately attribute to a subject the belief that Fang is ferocious without (at least implicitly) attributing to her the belief that dogs are animals or attribute to her the former belief if one regards her as not holding the latter.

It is of crucial importance to get clear on the status that these principles of interpretation have in Davidson's eyes. Davidson describes them as a priori in the respect that they are part and parcel of our concept of the intentional. In other words, to regard an individual as having intentional states is to regard her as having an intentional mental life that accords with the principles of interpretation. Thus, it makes no sense to talk of an individual having intentional states yet being systematically irrational (in the sense that most of her beliefs are false, she has an incoherent system of beliefs and routinely acts in a manner that is not coherently related to her beliefs and desires). Similarly, Davidson describes the principles as being constitutive of the intentional. That is to say, part of what it is to attribute intentional states to an individual is to attribute states on the basis of the kind of consideration enjoined by the principles (that is, on the basis of considerations to do with truth, consistency and so on). Consequently, to attribute intentional states without any concern for such considerations of rationality is no more to attribute an intentional state genuinely than to reposition a chess piece on a board without consideration of, or concern for, the rules of chess is to make a genuine move in a game of chess.

A consequence of all this is that the principles are not to be seen as capturing empirical generalizations or as constituting rules of thumb that we just happen to employ in order to divine the intentional states of our fellows. For empirical generalizations are by their nature contingent so that if the principles captured empirical generalizations it would be possible for an individual to have intentional states and yet be systematically irrational. And if the principles were rules of thumb, it would be possible for an individual to abandon them and attribute intentional states to her fellows by some other means that involved no concern for considerations of rationality.

Davidson is committed to the thesis of the anomalousness of the intentional. That is, there are no strict psychophysical laws linking the intentional to the physical (be they causal laws relating intentional states to physical events or bridge laws identifying intentional properties with physical properties) nor strict psychological laws concerning the interactions between distinct types of intentional states and actions. Davidson's reasons for thinking that there are no such laws has to do with the principles of interpretation described above. Suppose that it was a psychophysical law that whenever an individual tokened a physical state of type P she tokened an intentional state of type I. Then it would be possible to attribute the state I to an individual solely on the basis of evidence that she tokened P. In other words, it would be possible to attribute I without any concern for considerations of rationality. But to do this would not be to attribute an intentional state at all for it is constitutive of the practice of intentional state attribution that such attributions are governed by considerations of rationality. In short, the very nature of the concept of the intentional and the practice of attributing intentional states is inconsistent with the existence of psychophysical laws. As Davidson puts it:

> There are no strict psychophysical laws because of the disparate commitments of the mental and physical schemes. . . . It is a feature of the mental that the attribution of mental phenomena must be responsible to the background of reasons, beliefs and intentions of the individual. There cannot be tight connections between the realms if each is to retain allegiance to its proper source of evidence. (1970: 222)

With respect to strict psychological laws the considerations follow a similar course. Suppose it were a strict psychological law that whenever an individual tokened intentional state I she tokened intentional state I*. Then it would be possible to attribute I* to an individual solely on the grounds that she tokened I and without any consideration of the rationality of tokening I* given what else she believes, desires and so on. But, once again, to do this is not to attribute an intentional state at all. Therefore, the nature of the concept of the intentional and the practice of attributing intentional states is inconsistent with the existence of strict psychological laws.

Davidson's claim that there are no strict psychophysical laws serves as a premise in an argument for a physicalist token identity theory with respect to the intentional. Here is how that argument goes. The intentional and the physical causally interact with one another as when a belief and desire pair cause an action and as when an event in the external world causes someone to believe that that event took place. Every causal chain is subsumed by a strict law. Hence, whenever an event causes some other event, the cause will satisfy some description (call it D) and the effect some other description (call it D*) such that it is a strict law that whenever an event satisfying D takes place it causes an event satisfying D*. The strict laws subsuming causal interactions between intentional and physical events cannot be psychophysical as there are no such laws. Therefore, they must be physical laws. But an intentional state could not figure in a causal interaction subsumed by a physical law unless it satisfied a relevant physical description. But to satisfy a physical description just is to be a physical event. Therefore, although intentional types or properties cannot be identified with physical types or properties, each and every intentional state token is identical to some physical state token. Davidson labels his version of the token identity theory anomalous monism.

How do Davidson's views of the intentional relate to Fodor's CTM? Like Fodor, Davidson explicitly commits himself to physicalism, rejects behaviourism, objects to the identification of intentional types with physical types, views intentional states as being part of the causal fray and accepts that intentional states can figure in causal explanations of actions and the tokening of intentional states. However, underlying these agreements are differences so extensive that Davidson's views threaten not only to challenge CTM but to undermine the viability of the Fodorian project. To see this consider the following. First, Davidson draws a sharp distinction between folk psychology and science. For him, the nature of the intentional and the principles that govern the attribution of intentional states places a huge chasm between folk psychology and physics and implies that the relationship that the former bears to the latter is not that typical of the relationship that special sciences such as chemistry and biology bear to physics. Moreover, Davidson would appear to be committed to the idea that the nature of the intentional precludes the possibility of a scientific intentional psychology. Therefore, Davidson implies that Fodor is deeply confused in viewing folk psychology as being akin to a science, in championing the scientific status of a psychology closely related to folk psychology and in regarding the intentional as being related to the physical in broadly the same kind of way in which the chemical, the biological and so on are related to the physical. A second and related point is that for Davidson it makes no sense to turn to science in order to shed light on the nature of intentional states. The chasm between the intentional and the physical is such that questions about the nature of intentional states and of how a physical system is capable of tokening intentional states cannot be answered by appeal to the properties and phenomena that populate the theories developed by physicists and their colleagues working in the special sciences. But as Fodor's ambition is to answer such questions about the intentional by appeal to scientifically respectable lower-level properties and phenomena, the implication is that his project is profoundly misguided. Third, Davidson is committed to semantic holism. Fodor, on the other hand, is deeply opposed to holism as he thinks that it has unpalatable consequences and undermines the viability of a scientific intentional psychology. Thus, he has attempted to undermine holism, defend an atomist alternative and account for the content of our intentional states in atomistic terms.

There is little direct engagement with Davidson in Fodor's output. One exception occurs in chapter 1 of *Psychosemantics* (1987) where Fodor accepts that there are no strict psychological laws but points out that this does not impugn the scientific status of psychology as special science laws are in general *ceteris paribus* laws. In the course of describing, explaining and predicting phenomena within their domain of enquiry, special scientists make a whole load of assumptions or, as Fodor puts it, operative idealizations, concerning the nature and behaviour of the inhabitants of that domain. Making such assumptions facilitates the discovery and expression of manageable, unwieldy generalizations of considerable explanatory and predictive power. Fodor's favourite example of a *ceteris paribus* law comes from geology. The universal, unqualified generalization that a meandering river erodes its outer bank is clearly false. If the water in a meandering river freezes, or a concrete wall is built along its outside bank, or the tiny abrasive particles in its water are removed, or if the world comes to an end then it will not erode its outer bank. The occurrence of such an event constitutes an extra-geological interference with the smooth running of the geological realm. When such an event occurs, the operative assumptions or idealizations of geology fail to hold. Geologists do not offer such false unqualified generalizations; rather, their generalizations are hedged, featuring *ceteris paribus* clauses. Thus, for example, it is a generalization of geology that *ceteris paribus* a meandering river erodes its outer bank. When she proffers this generalization, the geologist is in effect saying 'something like "A meandering river erodes its outside bank in any nomologically possible world where the operative idealizations of geology are satisfied"' (Fodor 1987: 5).

Clearly, there are many distinct event types the tokening of which would result in a failure of the operative idealizations of geology to be satisfied. Hence, it would be difficult, if not impossible, to cash out the *ceteris paribus* clause of the above generalization. Moreover, the *ceteris paribus* clause could not be cashed out in geological terms given that the interfering events are non-geological. As Fodor puts the point:

> it simply isn't true that we can, even in principle, specify the conditions under which – say – geological generalizations hold *so long as we stick to the vocabulary of geology*. Or, to put it less in the formal mode, the causes of the exceptions to *geological* generalizations are, quite typically, not themselves geological events. . . . Exceptions to the generalizations of a special science are typically *inexplicable* from the point of view of (that is, in the vocabulary of) that science. (1987: 5–6)

In general then, special science generalizations feature ineliminable *ceteris paribus* clauses so that the *ceteris paribus* generalizations of the special sciences are not merely provisional staging posts on the journey to specification of strict laws. Thus, Davidson was mistaken when he argued (in Davidson 1970) that *ceteris paribus* clauses are ineliminable from psychological generalizations whereas *ceteris paribus* generalizations proffered by special scientists can in principle be sharpened and refined so as to generate strict laws.

In more recent work Davidson would appear to accept the prominence of unrefinable *ceteris paribus* generalizations in the special sciences but insists that intentional psychology cannot be assimilated to the special sciences due to the role that considerations of rationality have in the attribution of intentional states. (See Davidson 1987.)[3]

That completes my account of the Davidsonian challenge to Fodor. Before addressing the question of whether that challenge is decisive I will turn my attention to the work of Daniel Dennett.

Daniel Dennett has championed a theory of intentional states that bears significant similarities to Davidson's position. In particular, Dennett regards the practice of attributing intentional states as involving considerations of rationality and as being governed by normative principles, and the nature and role of such considerations and principles are reflected in his account of what it is to have intentional states. Nevertheless, there are some important differences between their respective views. First, Dennett is interested in cognitive science and is explicitly committed to its legitimacy as a science. Moreover, he thinks that cognitive science can go a considerable way towards accounting for our status as systems that have intentional states. Second, he does not wish to endorse the token identity theory. For him, intentional state tokens cannot be identified with physical state tokens such as internal states of the brain. Third, unlike Davidson, Dennett holds that a system without language could have intentional states.

Dennett's theory of intentional states can be characterized as follows.[4] There are various stances that one might adopt when attempting to predict the behaviour of a particular physical system such as a human individual, an animal or a machine. One such stance is the physical stance. Adopting the physical stance involves predicting the behaviour of a system on the basis of knowledge of its internal physical states, the nature of the physical events impinging upon it and the laws of physics. Most of the time we do not have the requisite knowledge to adopt the physical stance with respect to the systems whose behaviour we aim to predict. This is particularly true with respect to human beings. Another stance is the intentional stance. Adopting the intentional stance towards a system involves attributing to it the beliefs that it *'ought to have,* given its perceptual capacities, its epistemic needs, and its biography' along with the desires that it *'ought to have* given its biological needs and the most practicable means of satisfying them' (Dennett 1981: 49). One then works out what the system ought to do given those beliefs and desires and predicts that it will behave in that way. Thus, adopting the intentional stance towards a system involves employing normative principles and attributing a modicum of rationality to the system. Suppose that one adopts the intentional stance towards a system and that doing so enables one to reliably predict its behaviour, something not afforded by any other predictive stance practically available. Then the system in question is an intentional system and has the intentional states so attributed to it. As Dennett puts it, *'What it is* to be a true believer is to be an *inten-*

tional system, a system whose behaviour is reliably and voluminously predicted via the intentional [stance]' (1979: 15). In short then, Dennett ties having intentional states to the predictive effectiveness of attributing such states. A consequence of this, a consequence that Dennett is happy to endorse, is that lower animals and machines such as chess-playing computers (and, perhaps, even thermostats) have intentional states in exactly the same respect in which humans do. For, the adoption of the intentional stance towards such systems enables us to predict their behaviour with considerable accuracy.

Dennett has called his position instrumentalism as the intentional stance is an instrument for the prediction of behaviour and a system has particular intentional states only in so far as the attribution of those states to it would facilitate the accurate and effective prediction of its behaviour. However, he has become wary of the term 'instrumentalism' as it implies that he holds that intentional states are not real or are at best only useful fictions. Certainly, he does not wish to identify intentional states with internal physical states of intentional systems. On the contrary, the intentional states of a system are global states rather than isolable, functionally distinct internal states. Nevertheless, it is an objective fact that the intentional stance works with respect to many systems and intentional states are as real as such abstracta as centres of gravity and lines of latitude. Thus, Dennett has come to prefer the term 'mild realism' when characterizing his position (see Dennett 1991).

Dennett describes folk psychology as a 'rationalistic calculus of interpretation and prediction – an idealizing, abstract, instrumentalist interpretation method that has evolved because it works and works because it has evolved' (1981: 48–9). Thus, he regards his instrumentalist or mild realist theory of intentional states as laying bare the nature of folk psychology. Or, alternatively, as laying bare the nature of intentional states as viewed from the perspective of folk psychology.

For Dennett, the fact that human behaviour can be predicted by means of the adoption of the intentional stance, and, therefore, the fact that we have intentional states, has a lot to do with the nature of our inner workings. For the nature of our inner workings is responsible for the fact that we interact with the external world in such a way as to make our behaviour amenable to prediction from the intentional stance. Dennett distinguishes folk psychology from sub-personal cognitive psychology. The latter is concerned with explaining how we manage to be intentional systems and so, unlike folk psychology, it is concerned with the nature of our inner work-ings. Sub-personal cognitive psychology proceeds by decomposing the mind–brain into distinct functional sub-systems. These sub-systems are seen as manipulating representations and communi-cating with one another in such a way as to generate and sustain the facts concerning our behavioural interactions with the world that folk psychology is concerned with describing and predicting. The representations postulated by the sub-personal cognitive psy-chologist are concrete entities within the brain. Moreover, they have contents attributed to them. However, argues Dennett, they are not to be identified with such personal-level intentional states as beliefs and desires. An important point about such sub-personal represen-tations is that though they are concrete entities, they don't really have content as the brain is merely a syntactic system that mimics a semantic system. Thus, content attribution at the sub-personal level is an entirely instrumentalist business.

Whenever the sub-personal cognitive psychologist postulates a representation- manipulating sub-system within the mind–brain she effectively postulates a homunculus. For something is a representa-tion only if used as such by an intelligent agent. However, this is not a disaster as that sub-system could itself be decomposed into a team of less intelligent homunculi (each executing simpler representation-manipulating tasks) that in turn could be decom-posed into yet less intelligent homunculi and so on. The end result of this decomposition process is the specification of a team of inter-acting homunculi whose tasks are so simple that they could be exe-cuted by a physical device amenable to description and prediction from the physical stance. For Dennett, giving a complete account of how we manage to be intentional systems involves decomposing the mind–brain into such a team of simple physical mechanisms. And the theories of sub-personal cognitive psychology are an impor-tant staging post on the route to such a complete decomposition.[5]

Unlike Davidson, Dennett has directly engaged with Fodor and has produced the following prominent objection to CTM. It is highly unlikely that each of an individual's distinct intentional states will correspond to a distinct state of her brain. This will be the case even if the mind–brain is a computer for it is commonplace for a computer to have representational states that have consider-able predictive value even though they do not directly correspond to any internal state of the computer. In his review of *The Language of Thought* (1978c) Dennett gives the example of a chess-playing computer that is described by a rival programmer as thinking that it should get its queen out early. However, despite the considerable predictive value of this intentional state attribution, nowhere in the machine is there a representation that has the content *get your queen out early*. In response to this objection, Fodor has pointed out that he is not committed to the view that all of our intentional states are explicitly represented within us (that is, that for every intentional state there is a corresponding sentence of LOT tokened in the brain that has the appropriate content). To recall a point made in chapter 3, some of our intentional states are dispositional and it is only our core intentional states that are explicitly represented within us. Moreover, on pain of infinite regress, not all of the rules that a computer applies can be explicitly represented; the most basic rules must be hard-wired into the machine. However, if a representational state of a computer is to have any causal powers then that state must be identical to one of the computer's internal physical states; otherwise, its having causal powers will be a complete mystery. (See Fodor 1978b, 1987, ch. 1.)

So much for my account of Davidson, and Dennett's respective positions. The question arises as to whether Fodor can be defended against the Davidsonian and Dennettian challenge. To do this question justice would necessitate embarking on a substantial project way beyond the confines of this book. I shall confine myself to a few comments that might serve as signposts to a substantial defence of Fodor's position.[6] First, one might doubt that Davidson and Dennett have produced sufficient justification for their view of the role that considerations of rationality play in the attribution of intentional states. I am not alone in finding clear and substantial arguments for Davidson's and Dennett's key claims difficult to discern in their work. Thus, I would question whether either has done enough to defeat the following train of thought. It is an open empirical question to what extent minded creatures are rational. Indeed, there is considerable evidence in the psychological literature to suggest that in certain domains the thought processes of perfectly normal human beings often fall far short of being rational (for a helpful review, see Botterill and Carruthers 1999). Psychologists discuss these questions at great length and find no inherent problem in the idea that in certain domains human individuals often reason in a manner that fails to satisfy good rules of reasoning or even the rules that they explicitly endorse. Moreover, as Fodor points out in his discussion of Dennett (see Fodor 1978b), when we attempt to predict the behaviour of our fellows, we often assume that they fall far short of being rational. The specifics of such assumptions are based upon observing their performance in tasks involving reasoning. For example, watching you play chess I note that there are certain familiar traps that you are prone to fall into (you are a sucker for a knight's fork). Consequently, when playing chess with you, rather than predict that you will make intelligent moves, I fully expect you to fall into the most unsubtle of traps and duly set those traps for you. Davidson and Dennett can concede all of this, for their position only rules out the possibility of systematic, across-the-board irrationality. Thus, they can argue that the cases that psychologists document and folk psychologists exploit are localized to specific subject matters or types of reasoning problem and take place against a general background of rationality. Nevertheless, the above considerations do appear to put pressure on the idea that thinkers are inherently rational or that intentional state attribution is by its very nature governed by principles of rationality or principles concerning what one ought to believe and desire. For they suggest that the question of the extent to which we are rational is an empirical question and that its answer reports a contingent fact that can in turn be explained by reference to lower-level facts. Continuing in this vein, the Fodorian might point out that in so far as the attribution of intentional states rests upon considerations of rationality, this is a reflection of the nature of folk psychology *qua* empirical theory of the workings of human individuals. The idea is that it is a key assumption of folk psychology that human individuals are largely rational, an assumption that is reflected in the nature of the generalizations of folk psychology. But given that folk psychology is an empirical theory, if its core assumptions and generalizations are true then they are only contingently true. And if they are true their truth is open to explanation by appeal to lower-level (and ultimately physical) phenomena in the way that the truth of the generalization that water expands when frozen is open to explanation in lower-level terms. In short, both Davidson and Dennett have badly misconstrued the nature of the practice of attributing intentional states.

Second, Fodor could concede that being rational is constitutive of having intentional states in the respect that it is metaphysically or conceptually impossible for a creature to have intentional states and be systematically irrational. To see why Fodor could make this concession consider the property of being a painkiller. There is a constitutive connection between being a painkiller and easing pain; to be a painkiller just is to be something that would ease pain on being ingested by an individual suffering from pain. Aspirin is a painkiller. Yet, there is an explanation to be given as to how aspirin manages to meet the constitutive conditions for being a painkiller. Such an explanation will appeal to the chemical properties of aspirin and the workings of the central nervous system and is entirely contingent. Similarly, if being rational is constitutive of having intentional states then there is an explanation to be given as to how those creatures that meet such constitutive conditions for having intentional states manage to do so. CTM could then be offered as the relevant explanation that applies to human individuals. Fodor gestures towards such a line of thought in his entry in Guttenplan (1994).

Third, there are reasons for thinking that Davidson's and Dennett's positions have elements or implications that are counterintuitive. We have seen that they both think that human individuals are complex physical systems that can be described in intentional terms. But in virtue of what, one might ask, do human individuals (unlike such complex physical systems as trees and automobiles) satisfy such descriptions? Davidson's answer is that we satisfy such descriptions in virtue of being interpretable by a radical interpreter who attributes intentional states to us (in accord with the constitutive principles of interpretation) on the basis of evidence concerning the physical events impinging upon us, our physical responses to such events and so forth. Dennett's answer is that we satisfy such descriptions in virtue of the fact that our behaviour can be accurately predicted on the basis of them. One implication of this is that there is never a determinate fact of the matter concerning what an individual believes, desires and so on. For there are always going to be rival and incompatible interpretations of a person each of which accords with the constitutive principles of rationality and fits the evidence available to the radical interpreter. For Davidson, all such interpretations are equally legitimate. Similarly, for every predictively effective attribution of intentional states to an individual, there is going to be rival and incompatible attribution that is predictively just as effective. For Dennett, both such attributions are equally legitimate, an implication he is happy to endorse. Moreover, Davidson binds intentional descriptions to the possibility of interpretation and Dennett binds them to predictive utility to such an extent as to imply that we don't really have intentional states. For intentional descriptions cannot be objectively true in the way that biological, chemical and physical descriptions can be true as the truth value of such descriptions has nothing to do with interpretation or predictive utility. I think that Fodor would regard the importation of systematic indeterminacy into the intentional realm and the anti-realist implications of Davidson's and Dennett's positions as constituting a *reductio ad absurdum* of those positions. I would sympathize with such a charge. A less extreme assertion would be this: a commitment to intentional realism and an opposition to the indeterminacy thesis should constitute the default position in the philosophy of mind. That is not to say that we should hold onto this position in the face of any attack upon it. But we have a right to demand more by way of argument for its rejection than would appear to be provided by Davidson or by Dennett.

Fourth, there is a particular problem associated with Dennett's position that I alluded to above. Dennett resists the identification of intentional states with the internal states that cause us to behave as we do. Consequently, he makes it a mystery as to how intentional states could play a role in the causation of behaviour. This is a major limitation of his theory as it is a central assumption of folk psychology that intentional states cause both behaviour and other mental states.

Fifth, Dennett's position has an unfortunate implication. For him, any system whose behaviour can be accurately and effectively predicted from the intentional stance has intentional states in just the respect that we humans have. Thus, machines such as chess-playing computers and simple animals have intentional states. But, one might argue, such an implication constitutes a *reductio ad absurdum* of Dennett's position.

That completes my discussion of the threat to Fodor's position presented by the work of Davidson and Dennett. My comments on behalf of Fodor are by no means conclusive, but I think that I have done enough to suggest that it is not unreasonable to be optimistic about the prospects of constructing a thoroughgoing and convincing defence against the Davidsonian and Dennettian challenge.

Searle

John Searle is another contemporary philosopher of mind of great significance who has developed a philosophical theory of the intentional very much at odds with Fodor's CTM. Searle labels his position 'biological naturalism'. In a nutshell, biological naturalism is the view that mentality is a feature of the brain caused by neurophysiological processes in a respect analogous to that in which the liquidity of a sample of water is a feature of the sample that is caused by the constituent molecules of H_2O and the relations between them. And just as liquidity is a feature of the sample as a whole rather than of its constituent molecules, mentality is a feature of the brain as a whole rather than of its constituent parts. Thus, the project of accounting for our mentality is an empirical project that must concern itself with the neurophysiological processes that take place within the brain.

I am not going to discuss Searle's positive view of the intentional. Rather, I shall focus on a pair of arguments that Searle has produced that are supposed to refute key assumptions of orthodox cognitive science and that, if successful, might be taken to put pressure on Fodor's CTM.

The first of Searle's arguments appears in 'Minds, Brains, and Programs' (1980) and features the famous Chinese room thought experiment. Here Searle's target is a position he calls strong artificial intelligence. According to strong AI an 'appropriately programmed computer really is a mind in the sense that computers given the right programs can literally be said to *understand* and have other cognitive states' (1980: 183). Here is how Searle's attack on strong AI goes.

Searle imagines himself locked in a room. The room contains a batch of sheets of paper with symbols of Chinese printed upon them. These symbols mean nothing to Searle as he can neither speak nor read Chinese. The room also contains a booklet containing instructions written in English informing Searle how to correlate symbols of Chinese with symbols of Chinese. As they are written in English, Searle is able to understand these instructions. Through a slot in the door additional sheets with Chinese symbols printed on them are delivered to Searle. He responds to this input by following the English instructions that he has been given. This involves considering the formal or syntactic properties of the input symbols and correlating them with Chinese symbols printed on the batch of sheets stored in the room, and then copying those symbols onto sheets of paper before delivering them to the outside world via the slot in the door. It turns out that the input symbols are questions written in Chinese and that the output symbols that Searle produces when he follows the English instructions constitute sensible answers to those questions. Thus, Searle's Chinese-symbol-manipulating behaviour mimics that of an individual who understands Chinese despite the fact that Searle has no grasp of Chinese. The crucial point is that Searle does exactly what a computer does for he manipulates symbols by means of the application of symbol-manipulating rules and only has access to the formal or syntactic properties of the symbols that he manipulates. As Searle doesn't understand Chinese despite the fact that his input–output behaviour mimics that of a Chinese speaker, it follows that no computer – regardless of how it is programmed – is capable of understanding Chinese or any other language.[7] Therefore, strong AI collapses.

How are we to respond to Searle's argument? There has been much discussion of Searle's argument and I think that it has become clear that it doesn't present Fodor or the friends of orthodox cognitive science much to worry about. For it is no part of Fodor's CTM or of orthodox cognitive science that engaging in the kind of symbol-manipulating activity executed by Searle in the Chinese room is sufficient for understanding a language. Here, in broad outline, is the kind of response that I think the Fodorian should give to Searle's argument.[8] Searle in the Chinese room does not understand Chinese despite the fact that his symbol-manipulating activity simulates a core element of the behaviour of a Chinese speaker who genuinely understood Chinese. He doesn't understand because his symbol-manipulating activity is too isolated and self-contained. Unlike a genuine Chinese speaker, Searle does not (and is not disposed to) produce Chinese sentences in response to non-symbolic objects that impinge upon him. For example, if Fang was let into the room Searle would not respond by producing the Chinese analogues of 'who let that dog into the room?', 'does it bite?', 'how do I get it out of here?' Moreover, again unlike Chinese speakers, Searle can only respond to sentences of Chinese by producing sentences of Chinese. For example, suppose that he is fed the Chinese equivalent of 'There is a bomb under the chair you are sat upon. To defuse it you need to invert the chair'. He is not disposed to rise from his chair and invert it.

Suppose that we built a robot that had a video camera attached to it so that it was sensitive to objects in the external world. In addition, suppose also that it is capable of moving around the world, grasping objects and the like. Inside the robot is housed a complex computer consisting of computational sub-systems that interact with one another. The computer is fed input from the video camera and so is sensitive to the external world. It also produces output which causes the robot to behave in certain sorts of ways. In short, the computer is hooked up both to the robot's perceptual system and to its motor system. Now suppose that the computer was programmed in such a way that its symbol-manipulating activity played a significant causal role in sustaining a long-running process of interaction with the external world (a process that included navigating that world, picking up objects and suchlike). Finally, suppose that the computational activity was such that the robot, on being presented with written sentences of Chinese, sometimes responded not by producing a sentence of Chinese, but by behaving in a way that was appropriate given the meaning of the input sentence. And that it sometimes produced appropriate sentences in response to non-symbolic objects impinging upon it. In short, the robot's behaviour simulates that of a genuine speaker of Chinese in a far more substantial respect than does Searle in the Chinese room.

The important question is this: does the robot understand Chinese? I think that we should give an affirmative answer to this question. Note that to say that the robot understands Chinese is not to say that any of the computational sub-systems inside it understand the symbols that they manipulate. However, those symbols could still have meaning in virtue of their causal relations to the external world, their causal relations to other symbols or the role that they play in causing the robot to behave as it does. Moreover, it would seem necessary to describe the computational activity that takes place within the robot in order to explain its ability to understand Chinese. If all this is plausible then Searle's argument – construed as an attack on orthodox cognitive science or Fodor's CTM – fails for it suggests how symbol manipulation can play a fundamental role in supporting a cognitive capacity.

In chapter 9 of *The Rediscovery of Mind* (1992) Searle launches an attack on what he identifies as the central assumptions of cognitive science. Given that Fodor endorses these assumptions, if Searle's argument works then Fodor's CTM is thereby undermined. The assumptions that Searle is hostile to can be expressed in the following terms:

> The brain is intrinsically a computer, that is, a system that manipulates syntactically structured symbols by means of the application of symbol-manipulating rules. Thus, the brain's activity has both a physical/neurophysiological description and a higher-level computational description. It is in virtue of its computational nature that the brain's activity sustains cognition. Consequently, an adequate explanation of human cognitive capacities must describe the brain's activity in computational terms; the physical/neurophysiological properties of the brain's activity have little or no role in such explanations.

Searle's central objection to these assumptions is that it is a fundamental mistake to say that the brain is intrinsically a computer; for,
given the nature of computation, nothing is intrinsically a computer.
Here is how he reasons. There is a fundamental distinction between
intrinsic and observer-relative properties. The intrinsic properties of
an object are the properties that it has irrespective of how it is seen,
described or used by minded agents. In other words, an object's
intrinsic properties are its objective features. Familiar examples of
such properties are physical, chemical and biological properties;
in short, the kinds of properties that the physical sciences are concerned with. Searle would also add certain intentional properties to
this list. For example, it is an intrinsic property of me that I believe
that Fang is ferocious; my having this property is an objective
feature of reality that has nothing to do with the way I am described
or interpreted by my fellows. In contrast, the observer-relative properties of an object are the properties that it has in virtue of the way
that it is seen, described or used by minded agents. The property
of being a chair is a familiar example of such a property. An object
is a chair in virtue of the way that it is seen or used by human subjects. Thus, nothing is intrinsically a chair and the intrinsic properties that any particular chair has are not sufficient for its being a
chair. Other examples of observer-relative properties are the semantic properties of public language symbols; for example, 'dog' means
dog in virtue of the beliefs, desires and intentions of the individuals who use that word.

Members of the cognitive science community characterize computation in terms of the manipulation of syntactically structured
symbols and are keen to point out that syntax and computation are
multiply realizable. In their attempts to explain how a physical
system such as the brain could be a computer, and to deal with the
anticipated objection that nothing in the brain looks like a symbol,
they produce an account of syntax that implies that syntax is
observer-relative. For the standard cognitive science account of
syntax has it that a system's internal states are syntactically structured symbols if and only if we can treat, count, use or interpret
them as syntactically structured symbols or assign to them syntactic properties. As Searle puts it, 'syntax is not intrinsic to physics.
The ascription of syntactical properties is always relative to an agent
or observer who treats certain physical phenomena as syntactical'
(1992: 208). Consequently, nothing is intrinsically a computer so it
just couldn't be the case that the brain is intrinsically a computer.
But what we need to appeal to in order to account for cognition are

not observer-relative properties but objective features of the brain that are causally responsible for our intentional states (for example, the physical–neurophysiological properties of the brain). In other words, syntactic and computational properties are of entirely the wrong sort to figure in legitimate accounts of cognition.

Searle accepts that the brain is such that its states can be assigned syntactic properties. But he also points out that the same is true of any complex physical system. His idea is that for any complex physical system there will be some language and associated rules for manipulating the sentences of that language, such that it is possible to map the states of the system onto the symbols of the language (in the manner described in chapter 3) in such a way that the system's internal causal transactions implement applications of the symbol-manipulating rules to the symbols of the language. In short, the brain is not intrinsically a computer and is no more a computer than any complex physical system.

Searle takes particular exception to theorists such as Marr and Chomsky who postulate unconscious computational processes in order to account for, respectively, our visual and linguistic capacities. As these processes are unconscious, the symbols that are manipulated when they occur are not manipulated by us. In this respect, they contrast with the case where I consciously manipulate symbols of propositional logic by applying the rules of that logic. But as something is a symbol only if it is used as such, Marr and Chomsky effectively postulate homunculi in our heads. And postulating homunculi is bad psychology as it threatens circularity or infinite regress.

Searle anticipates the objection that the brain differs from most other physical systems whose internal states can be assigned syntactic properties in that the brain, like an artefactual computer, is an information processor. Searle responds by arguing that the brain does not process information in the respect in which computers do. For we build and program computers with a view to encoding information and solving information-processing problems, something that is clearly not true of brains. Thus, the semantic and syntactic properties of a computer's states are not intrinsic properties but are 'all in the eye of the beholder' (1992: 222). To characterize the brain's activity in information-processing terms is to assign observer-relative properties to it rather than to describe its intrinsic properties and so such a characterization has no legitimate place in a scientific explanation of cognition.

How are we to respond to Searle's argument? Does he succeed in undermining the core assumptions of orthodox cognitive science? As it stands, I find his argument far from convincing as he provides little justification for the crucial claim that syntactic properties are by their nature observer-relative. The response that I would favour has the following broad outlines. Consider a complex physical system such as a pond whose internal states could be mapped onto the symbols of some formal language. The possibility of effecting such a mapping is not a sufficient condition for the pond's being a manipulator of syntactically structured symbols. So long as no intelligent agent actually ascribes syntactic properties to the pond's states and uses the pond to, for example, solve logic problems, the pond's states do not have syntactic properties in any substantial respect. The pond would be like a chair-shaped natural object which, though physically such that it could be used as a chair, never had been so used. Now consider an artefactual computer whose states are explicitly conceived as being syntactically structured symbols by its intelligent users. Searle is right to say that in this case the syntax is observer-relative. But note that human users of artefactual computers not only ascribe syntactic properties to their states. In addition they ascribe semantic properties and most users of computers would find them totally useless unless they made such attributions. As we have seen, Searle would agree that the semantic properties of the states of artefactual computers are as observer-relative as their syntactic properties. We could characterize the distinction between the pond and the artefactual computer in the following terms. The pond – in virtue of its intrinsic physical properties – has states that potentially have certain observer-relative syntactic properties. The distinction between the pond and the artefactual computer is analogous to that between an object that is physically such that it could be used as a chair but isn't so used, and an object that I used as a chair (and was made with that use in mind). The states of the computer actually have observer-relative syntactic properties whilst the states of the pond only potentially have certain observer-relative syntactic properties.

Thus far, I am in agreement with Searle. However, I think that we should be wary of generalizing from such cases as the pond and the artefactual computer. Syntax and semantics are to be distinguished. Nevertheless, there is a close relationship between the two. Syntactic properties are properties of symbols and symbols are, by their very nature, the kinds of things that have semantic properties. Moreover, the syntactic properties of the symbols of a language have a systematic bearing on the meanings of those symbols so that syntactic differences and similarities between distinct symbols make for semantic differences and similarities between those symbols. In assigning a syntax to a system such as a pond or an artefactual computer one is preparing the way for the attribution of semantic properties to its states and is placing strong constraints on any such attribution. For example, one can't legitimately assign the syntax of the language of propositional logic to the physical states of a system and then interpret the state that one maps onto (P & Q) as meaning *Fang is ferocious and Fang likes chasing joggers* and the state that one maps onto (P & R) as meaning *Christmas falls in December*. What this suggests is that the states of a system could not intrinsically have syntactic properties without intrinsically having semantic properties. For if the states did not intrinsically have semantic properties then, a fortiori, their putative syntactic properties would not have any bearing on their intrinsic semantic properties. In short, there could only be intrinsic syntactic properties where there are intrinsic semantic properties.

There is a familiar distinction between original and derived intentionality, a distinction that Searle explicitly endorses. Natural language symbols, road signs, maps and the like mean what they mean in virtue of the way they are used, understood, interpreted and the like, by human individuals. They inherit their meaning from other meaningful items, namely, the intentional states of human individuals. In short, such symbols have derived intentionality. But on pain of infinite regress, not all meaningful items could get their meaning from other meaningful items; some meaningful items must have non-derived or original intentionality. Presumably, human intentional states have original intentionality. This distinction is, of course, Searle's distinction between intrinsic and observer-relative properties applied to the semantic realm.

The states of a pond or an artefactual computer have, at best, derived intentionality. But it would be a mistake to consider such systems and conclude that intentionality is, by its very nature, always derivative. Similarly, it may well be a mistake to conclude that syntactic properties are, by their very nature, non-intrinsic on the basis of an examination of systems such as ponds and artefactual computers. The fact that the states of such systems do not intrinsically have syntactic properties is bound up with the fact that those states do not have original intentionality. This leaves open the possibility that there are systems (for example, human brains) whose states have original intentionality and also intrinsically have syntactic properties. The states of such systems would be structured and the identity of their parts and the relations between them would have a systematic and disciplined bearing on their meaning.

This completes my response to Searle's attack on the idea that the brain is intrinsically a computer. I don't claim to have conclusively established that a system could intrinsically have syntactic properties (and, thus, intrinsically be a computer). But I think I have established that by focusing on systems whose states do not have intrinsic intentionality, he has not done enough to justify his conclusion.

Connectionism

In *The Language of Thought* (1975) Fodor argued that a commitment to CTM underlay virtually all contemporary theories of cognitive processing. Whatever the truth value of that claim in 1975 it certainly wasn't true a decade later. For the mid-1980s witnessed the rise of an alternative to CTM, an alternative that has won many friends within the cognitive science community. The alternative in question is connectionism.[9] Connectionism is a view about the architecture of the mind and the nature of the processes that underlie and support human cognition.[10] It constitutes a rival to CTM in that connectionist systems (typically) do not manipulate syntactically structured symbols nor do they encode information in their memories by means of such symbols. In this section I will give a brief account of the nature of connectionism, indicate the respects in which it constitutes a challenge to CTM, and discuss how Fodor has responded to this challenge.[11]

Connectionist systems are networks of simple units or processors. The following describes a paradigmatic connectionist system. The units of the network are arranged into three layers, namely, an input layer, an intermediate layer and an output layer. At any point in time each unit is in a state of activation, a state that has a numerical value (an inactive unit has zero as its value). Each unit requires a certain amount of stimulation in order to become active; this is its threshold value. Each unit in the input layer is linked by a number of connections to each unit in the intermediate layer and each of those units is similarly linked to each unit in the output layer. These connections are weighted and the weight of a connection has a numerical value. Impulses are transmitted along the connections linking units in the input layer to units in the intermediate layer and along those connections linking the latter units to units in the output layer. The strength of an impulse emitted by a unit (which has a numerical value and is the output of the unit) is a function of the unit's level of activation. The strength (and, hence, numerical value) of the impulse received by a unit is a product of the strength of the initial input fed into the connection and the weight of that connection. For example, if a unit sends an impulse of value 2 down a connection of weight 3, then the impulse received by the receiving unit will be of value 6. The connections fall into two types, namely, excitatory and inhibitory. The level of stimulation a unit receives as input is the sum of the values of the impulses it receives via excitatory connections minus the sum of the values of the impulses it receives via inhibitory connections. If an inactive unit receives input of a value that exceeds its threshold value then it will become active and its state of activity will be a function of the extent to which the stimulation exceeds the threshold value. Units in the input layer are stimulated from outside the system and when they are so stimulated impulses are passed along the connections to the intermediate layer so stimulating activity there. Impulses are then passed to the output layer resulting in patterns of activity at that layer. Consequently, the system transforms patterns of activation at the input layer into patterns of activation at the output layer. The system's input–output behaviour is determined by the nature and weight of the connections along with the threshold values of the units and that behaviour can be altered by adjusting the connection weights.

For the connectionist, the mind–brain is a connectionist system or an ensemble of such systems. But how, one might ask, could this be so? How could a system like the one described in the preceding paragraph support cognition? The crucial point is that the patterns of activation at the input and output layers can have semantic properties; that is, they are representations. To see this, consider the following (fictional) network.

The network is a recognition network. That is, it has the function of identifying individuals on the basis of descriptions of their salient properties. The input layer consists of a number of units each of which serves to express a distinct property that an individual might have. These properties include those of being a dog, being a pigeon, being black, being grey, engaging in snarling behaviour, engaging in squawking behaviour and so on. For example, if the unit that serves to express the first of these properties is highly active, then it represents the individual that the network has to identify as being a dog. Hence, patterns of activation at the input layer constitute descriptions of individuals presented to the system and each distinct pattern encodes a distinct description. The output layer consists of four units, and distinct patterns of activation at that layer encode the names of distinct individuals. For example, the pattern ⟨1,1,0,1⟩ encodes Fang's names and the pattern ⟨0,0,1,1⟩ encodes Squawk's name. The threshold values of the network's constituent units and the weight of its connections are such that, given a reasonably accurate description of an individual that the network has been trained to recognize as input, the system will generate that individual's name as output.[12]

The representations that the system manipulates take the form of patterns of activation involving many distinct units. These representations are not syntactically structured symbols. There is a respect in which the input representations have parts and are such that their meaning depends on the meaning of those parts. However, such representations do not have an internal syntactic structure as they are more akin to lists than they are to sentences. The absence of syntax is very much apparent in many other connectionist systems where complex concepts are expressed by patterns of activation that do not even have components (that is, sub-patterns) that serve to express their constituent concepts.

The recognition system can be said to store a body of information concerning the properties of Fang, Squawk and a whole collection of individuals. However, such information is not stored by means of syntactically structured symbols located in the system's long-term memory (as it would be in the case of a standard commercial computer). Rather, it is encoded by a network of connections that serves to encode everything that the system knows or believes en masse. Consequently, if human recognitional capacities are supported by a system like the connectionist system that I have described, then the CTM story of recognition would be false. Generally, if the mind is a connectionist system, or an ensemble of such systems, then CTM is false. For intentional processes would not involve the manipulation of syntactically structured symbols and our beliefs would not be stored by means of distinct, syntactically structured symbols.

However, a qualification is needed as connectionism and CTM are not mutually exclusive for two reasons. First, it is in principle possible that the mind decomposes into sub-systems some of which are connectionist systems and some of which are orthodox computational systems. For example, recognition could be executed by a system of the former type and logical reasoning by a system of the latter type. Second, it is possible for an orthodox computer to be implemented in a connectionist system. In such a case, the patterns of activation of the connectionist system that encode complex concepts will have components that encode the constituent concepts of those complex concepts. Distinct patterns that encode complex concepts that have a constituent concept in common will, accordingly, have a sub-pattern of activation in common. And, the internal relations between the sub-patterns that encode simple concepts will encode syntactic relations between those simple concepts. Thus, it is in principle possible for the mind to be a computer implemented in a connectionist system. However, it should be noted, most advocates of connectionism do not wish to endorse such an implementationalist position.

Fodor has not ignored the connectionist challenge. In an important and much discussed series of papers he has argued that connectionism cannot account for the systematicity of human cognitive capacities and, for that reason, ought to be rejected.[13] In the remainder of this section I will outline and examine Fodor's argument.

Suppose that two distinct cognitive capacities are such that a human subject has one if and only if she has the other. Then, those capacities are systematically related. Fodor claims that certain of our cognitive capacities are systematically related in this way. For example, as we have already seen, he holds that thought is systematic in the respect in which anybody capable of thinking that a stands in relation R to b (for any objects a and b, and any relation R) is also capable of thinking that b stands in relation R to a, and vice versa. For example, one doesn't find people who are capable of thinking that John loves the girl yet are not capable of thinking that the girl loves John (just as one doesn't find people capable of understanding the sentence 'John loves the girl' yet are not capable of understanding the sentence 'the girl loves John'). Fodor thinks that this is a contingent feature of thought in the respect that there are metaphysically possible creatures whose thought is not systematic in this way. However, it is nomologically necessary that human thought is systematic. In addition, Fodor argues that human inferential capacities are systematic. For example, it is a law of human psychology that individuals who infer P from P & Q & R also infer P from P & Q (and vice versa).

As we saw in chapter 3, Fodor claims that CTM has a straightforward explanation of systematicity and that it has such an explanation constitutes an argument in its favour. By way of brief recapitulation, here is how that explanation goes. First of all consider the systematicity of thought. Thinking that aRb (that is, thinking that a stands in the relation R to b) involves tokening a complex structured symbol of LOT. This symbol contains distinct parts one of which refers to object a, one of which refers to object b, and one of which expresses relation R. These parts are combined in such a way as to express the content *aRb*. Thus, thinking that aRb involves deploying a psychological mechanism that has access to simple symbols of LOT and the capacity to combine them into a complex symbol that has a particular internal structure. Now thinking that bRa is merely a matter of redeploying the resources deployed in thinking that aRb. In particular, it involves combining the very same simple symbols into a complex symbol whose internal structure is analogous to that of the symbols tokened in thinking that aRb. Hence, a classical system[14] that can think aRb is thereby able to think bRa.

Now consider the systematicity of inference. On the classical picture, inference is a causal process where a computational mechanism takes a symbol of LOT as input and produces a symbol of LOT as output. This mechanism is sensitive to the components of the complex symbols it takes as input and the manner in which they are combined and the output that it produces depends upon such properties of the input. In terms of the properties that the computational mechanism responsible for inference is sensitive to, P & Q & R and P & Q are somewhat similar. For they share some of the same simple symbols as parts and have analogous internal structures. Given this similarity, it is to be expected that there is a similarity in the effects that P & Q & R and P & Q cause the inferring mechanism to produce.

In sum, classical systems are such that their representational and inferential capacities are systematic. Therefore, in characterizing the mind as a classical system, the classicist has a ready explanation of the systematicity of human cognition. However, Fodor argues, connectionism doesn't have such a ready explanation of systematicity. This is because connectionist representations that express complex concepts do not generally have parts that serve to express the constituent concepts of the complex concept in question. For example, suppose that a particular connectionist system is capable of expressing the concept JOHN LOVES THE GIRL by means of a pattern of activation over a number of nodes. Unlike a representation in LOT or a natural language, this representation does not have parts that serve to express the constituent concepts JOHN, LOVES and THE GIRL.

Consequently, there is no guarantee that the system will be capable of expressing the complex concept THE GIRL LOVES JOHN. For expressing that concept will not be a matter of redeploying the very resources deployed in expressing the concept JOHN LOVES THE GIRL. Moreover, suppose that the system is capable of expressing both P & Q and P & Q & R. As the representations that serve to express these concepts do not have any constituent parts in common, there is no guarantee that their tokenings will have the same causal ramifications within the system. For example, the fact that tokenings of the pattern of activation over input units that expresses P & Q & R routinely cause tokenings of the pattern of activation over output units that expresses P is no guarantee that tokenings of the pattern that expresses P & Q routinely cause tokenings of the pattern that expresses P. In short, as connectionist systems are not generally systematic, to describe the mind as a connectionist system is to leave it a mystery why human cognition is systematic.

It is important to realize that Fodor is not denying the claim that there can be systematic connectionist systems or the claim that connectionism is consistent with systematicity of human cognition. His point is that it is nomologically necessary that human cognition is systematic and it is this fact that connectionism cannot explain. For, given that connectionist systems are not guaranteed to be systematic, the systematicity of human cognition would be a mere accident were the mind a connectionist system. Hence, to assert that the mind is a connectionist system would be to leave it a complete mystery why it is nomologically necessary (as opposed to a mere accident) that human cognition is systematic. Here is how the point is made in Fodor and McLaughlin (1990: 107):

> No doubt it is possible for Smolensky [a prominent connectionist] to wire a network so that it supports a vector that represents *aRb* if and only if it supports a vector that represents *bRa*. . . . The trouble is that although the architecture permits this, it equally permits Smolensky to wire a network so that it supports a vector that represents *aRb* if and only if it supports a vector that represents *zSq*; or, for that matter, if and only if it supports a vector that represents the last of the Mohicans. The architecture would appear to be absolutely indifferent between these options. . . .
>
> In contrast, as we keep saying, in the classical architecture, if you meet the conditions for being able to represent *aRb, you cannot but meet the conditions for being able to represent bRa*. . . . So then: it is built into the classical picture that you can't think *aRb* unless you are able to think *bRa*, but the connectionist picture is neutral on whether you

can think *aRb* even if you can't think *bRa*. But it is a law of nature that you can't think *aRb* if you can't think *bRa*. So the classical picture explains systematicity and the connectionist picture doesn't. So the classical picture wins.

How convincing is this critique of connectionism? There are at least three lines of defence that the friend of connectionism might seek to pursue. First, it might be argued that Fodor hasn't produced sufficient vindication for his claim that human cognition is systematic. His evidence, such as it is, rests upon a consideration of such simple thoughts as the thought that John loves the girl and the thought that the girl loves John, and such simple inferences as those of inferring P from P & Q & R and P from P & Q. But the fact that our ability to think such simple thoughts and make such simple inferences are systematically related hardly implies that our cognitive abilities with respect to more complex thoughts and inferences are so related. It is true that in Fodor and Pylyshyn (1988) the point is made that the systematicity of language comprehension implies the systematicity of thought as understanding a sentence of a natural language involves tokening a thought that represents its syntactic and semantic properties. But one might object that it is an unjustified idealization to portray our linguistic capacities as being systematic.

Second, how clear is it that classicism explains systematicity? It has been claimed that Fodor, rather than explaining systematicity, does nothing more than issue a promissory note (Matthews 1997). To fulfil this promise would, at the very least, involve specifying the atomic symbols of LOT, the formation rules of LOT and the rules of inference that are applied to the sentences of LOT. Moreover, it would involve describing the psychological mechanisms that apply the formation rules of LOT and those that implement the rules of inference applied to its sentences. A related point is that classical systems do not necessarily have systematic representational powers. For example, a classical system might be capable of tokening the complex, structured symbol aRb yet be unable to recombine the constituents of that symbol so as to token bRa. (Aizawa 1997; Matthews 1997.)

The third line of defence involves questioning the claim that connectionism cannot explain the systematicity of cognition. I think that there is considerable mileage in this line of defence, a version of which can be described in the following terms. It is widely conceded that there can be connectionist systems that are systematic and, as we have seen, Fodor is willing to make this concession. Now consider a connectionist system that is systematic. Surely the systematicity of this system can be explained by appeal to such features of the system as the number of nodes in its input and output layers, the threshold values of the nodes and the nature and weight of the connections linking them, the precise manner in which concepts are encoded by means of patterns of activation over these nodes and suchlike. In short, such an explanation will be a connectionist explanation of the systematicity of a particular connectionist system. Of course, such an explanation will be limited in the number of systems to which it applies and it will be significantly more complicated than the general explanation that Fodor proffers for the systematicity of classical systems. But for all that, it is still an explanation. What this suggests is that if the mind is a connectionist system then its systematicity could be explained in connectionist terms. Does it follow from this that the connectionist can explain systematicity? Unlike the classicist, the connectionist needs to have a detailed theory of the nature and workings of the mind in order to have any hope of constructing an explanation of systematicity. Merely to hypothesize that the mind is a connectionist system is not thereby to explain systematicity. And it is probably fair to say that no connectionist has a sufficiently developed and detailed theory of the mind to be in any position to construct a connectionist explanation of the systematicity of cognition. So there is a respect in which the connectionist cannot explain the systematicity of cognition. Nevertheless, Fodor has given us no reason for thinking that the connectionist cannot in principle explain systematicity. It would be gratuitously premature to reject connectionism solely on the grounds that its advocates cannot currently explain systematicity.

Fodor might respond by saying that the connectionist explanation that I am envisaging would not explain the nomological necessity of systematicity. For it would not explain why the mind had the particular connectionist architecture specified in the explanation rather than one of the myriad connectionist architectures that would not support systematicity. But it is far from clear that the connectionist is required to meet this demand. For the connectionist can say that it is a law of psychology that the mind has the particular architecture that she describes and that this law cannot be explained in psychological terms. After all, Fodor's account of the structure of science implies that many special science laws can only be explained by appeal to lower-level phenomena and laws. In the case in question, perhaps what is needed is an evolutionary account of why the mind has the particular architecture that it has and Fodor has given us no reason for believing that such an account could not be forthcoming. Moreover, have we any reasons to believe that Fodor can explain why the mind is a classical system rather than a system of some non-classical form?

In this context it should be pointed out that there are salient features of the mind that are much more amenable to explanation from the connectionist perspective than they are from the classical perspective. For example, humans have content-addressable memories. That is, we are able to recall information from memory on the basis of descriptions of the content of the target memory item. (If someone asks you the name of the ferocious dog that Cain is so obsessed with you are effortlessly able to reply 'Fang'.) Connectionist systems, such as the object recognition system described above, are inherently well suited to supporting content-addressable memories. However, the same cannot be said of classical systems. Orthodox commercial computers store information in specific memory locations and to retrieve the item stored in any such location the computer must be informed of the specific address of the required item. This is not to say that a classical system could not have a content-addressable memory. In principle, such a system could store items of information in locations that were systematically related to the content of that information. Thus, the system could be programmed to compute the location of any given item of information from a description of its content so enabling it to retrieve that item without taking recourse to an exhaustive search of its memory. However, the key point is that classical systems do not by their very nature have content-addressable memories. This suggests the following argument against Fodor: CTM, unlike connectionism, makes it a mystery why it is nomologically necessary that we have content-addressable memories.

In light of the above considerations, it would be somewhat premature to reject connectionism on the basis of Fodor's systematicity argument. However, it does not follow from this that CTM collapses in the face of the connectionist challenge. Despite its popularity, it has yet to be conclusively established that connectionism has the resources to account for any of our cognitive capacities. Reflecting this, CTM is still widely held within the cognitive science community. The fact of the matter is that given our current state of knowledge it is not possible to adjudicate the dispute between CTM and connectionism. This is, as they say, a matter for further empirical research.

Conclusion

In this chapter I have discussed four of the most important and prominent challenges to CTM. Although these challenges are to be taken very seriously indeed, and although there are no knock-down objections to them, I hope to have shown that there are grounds for thinking that they do not fatally wound Fodor.

5

Explaining Mental Content

Introduction

We have seen that CTM is the centrepiece of Fodor's attempt to construct a physicalist vindication of folk psychology. However, as it stands, CTM has a major limitation: it fails to account for the semantic or intentional properties of our intentional states. Why, for example, does my belief that Fang is ferocious (or the sentence of LOT involved in my tokening that belief) have that content as opposed to some other content or no content at all? Therefore, to complete his project, Fodor must supplement his CTM with a theory that accounts for the intentional properties of our intentional states in physicalist terms. Fodor has constructed such a theory and that theory, along with Fodor's criticisms of competing theories, is the subject of this chapter.[1]

Naturalistic Theories of Content

Few philosophers question the reality of the properties that populate the theories of such non-intentional special sciences as chemistry, biology, geology and the like, or doubt that such properties ultimately reduce to or supervene upon physical properties. Consequently, it is generally recognized that the physicalist will have succeeded in accounting for the intentional properties of our intentional states if she can account for those properties by appeal to properties recognized by respectable non-intentional special sciences. The project of so accounting for the intentional properties of our intentional states is generally called the naturalization project. The aim of those who engage in the naturalization project is to construct a viable naturalistic theory of content; that is, a theory that accounts for the contents of our intentional states by appeal to properties recognized by respectable non-intentional natural scientific disciplines (be they physics or higher-level special sciences).

In the nineteenth century the Austrian philosopher and psychologist Franz Brentano argued that intentionality was the mark of the mental and that the physical was incapable of generating intentionality thus implying that mental phenomena resided outside the physical realm. Brentano's claim that the intentional resists naturalization has been echoed in the work of such influential twentieth-century philosophers as Quine (1960) and Wittgenstein (1953), not to mention more recent luminaries such as Hilary Putnam (1992) and John McDowell (1994). This dominant theme has served to create a climate where physicalist friends of intentional psychology have felt an urgent need to establish both that and how the contents of our intentional states are ultimately determined by their physical properties. This is reflected in the following quotes from Fodor.

> The worry about representation is above all that the semantic (and/or the intentional) will prove permanently recalcitrant to integration in the natural order; for example, that the semantic/intentional properties of things will fail to supervene upon their physical properties. What is required to relieve the worry is therefore, at a minimum, the framing of *naturalistic* conditions for representation. (1984a: 32)

> If the semantic and the intentional are real properties of things, it must be in virtue of their identity (or maybe their supervenience on?) properties that are themselves neither intentional *nor* semantic. If aboutness is real, it must be really something else.
>
> And, indeed, the deepest motivation for intentional irrealism derives from a certain intuition; that there is no place for intentional categories in a physicalistic view of the world; that the intentional can't be *naturalized*. (1987: 97)

What form should a naturalistic theory of content take? One answer is that it should specify necessary and sufficient conditions for the instantiation of intentional properties; conditions that, of course, appeal only to non-intentional properties recognized by respectable scientific disciplines. Such necessary and sufficient conditions would lay bare the nature or essence of intentional content. One way they could do this is by specifying an identity relationship akin to that that holds between the property of being water and the property of being H_2O. Since Kripke (1980) the standard view of such identity relations is that they are metaphysically necessary (that is, true in all possible worlds) though not knowable a priori. Alternatively, they might be the product of a process of conceptual analysis reporting a definition or some other truth of meaning (akin to x is a bachelor if and only if x is an unmarried man).

We have seen that Fodor has developed an account of the structure of science according to which the special sciences appeal to properties and laws that do not generally identify or reduce to those of lower-level sciences. Inter-theoretic bridge laws are thin on the ground; the law that x is water if and only if x is composed of H_2O molecules being the exception rather than the norm. (See Fodor 1974.) Moreover, he is also sceptical about the prospects of conceptual analysis; the track record of philosophers and linguists who have attempted to analyse any particular concept or define the words that express that concept is so poor as to suggest that their project is hopelessly misguided. (See Fodor 1975, ch. 3, 1998a, chs 3 and 4.) Consequently, it is no surprise that Fodor's engagement in the naturalization project does not constitute a search for necessary and sufficient conditions for content. Rather than attempt to reduce content to something non-intentional, he seeks to specify lower-level non-intentional properties that are capable of exhaustively generating the kinds of contents that our intentional states have. These lower-level determinants of content are to be expressed by means of a sufficient condition. Thus, Fodor's theory of content takes the form of the provision of a sufficient condition for content. But, one might ask, is this sufficient condition supposed to apply to our intentional states and thus account for their contents? Or, on the other hand, is it supposed merely to establish that and how content could be generated by lower-level non-intentional properties regardless of whether or not it is satisfied by our intentional states? If the latter is the case, then, at least on the face of it, it is no objection to Fodor that the sufficient condition that he presents is not satisfied by our intentional states. In *Psychosemantics* (1987) Fodor explicitly states that his theory of content is intended to specify a sufficient condition that is satisfied by our intentional states. For example, he writes:

I want a *naturalized* theory of meaning; a theory that articulates, in nonsemantic and nonintentional terms, sufficient conditions for one bit of the world to *be about* (to express, represent, be true of) another bit. I don't care . . . whether this theory holds for *all* symbols or for all things that represent . . . I'm prepared, that is, that only mental states (hence, according to [CTM], only mental representations) should turn out to have semantic properties *in the first instance*; hence that a naturalized semantics should apply, strictu dictu, to mental representations only.

But it had better apply to them. (1987: 98–9)

However, by the time of the later work 'A Theory of Content, II' (1990c) Fodor has relaxed his ambitions so that he would be satisfied with any sufficient condition, even a condition that our intentional states did not satisfy. For example, he writes 'It's enough if I could make good the claim that "X" would mean such and such if so and so were to be the case. It's not incumbent on me to argue that since "X" does mean such and such, so and so is the case' (1990c: 96).

I think that Fodor's initial ambition was the right one to have and thus that an important element of evaluating his theory involves addressing the question of whether or not it is satisfied by our intentional states. This is for two reasons. First, how are we to determine if a proposed condition is sufficient for content independently of a consideration of whether it is satisfied by our intentional states? Second, given that Fodor's project is to vindicate folk psychology, it is important that he establishes that and how the internal states driving our behaviour really have the contents that folk psychologists routinely ascribe to them. The uncovering of a sufficient condition for content isn't going to do this unless it is satisfied by our intentional states. If Fodor's theory does not apply to our intentional states then either some other theory does, or those states do not literally have the contents that we take them to have. Clearly, Fodor has to be committed to the idea that if his theory does not apply to us then some alternative theory must do. Yet, as we shall see, he thinks that the major competitors to his theory have disastrous consequences for they imply either that our intentional states do not have determinate contents or that no two individuals or time slices of the same individual ever share an intentional state. In short, Fodor holds that the alternatives to his theory would inadvertently serve to undermine the viability of folk psychology were they true.

So Fodor had better hope that his theory actually applies to our intentional states as he implicitly commits himself to the claim that a failure so to apply would fatally undermine folk psychology.

Fodor's Theory of Content

Fodor's approach to the naturalization problem is dictated by his commitment to CTM. According to CTM, the contents of our intentional states are inherited from sentences of LOT. And the content of any given sentence of LOT is determined by the meaning of its component symbols and the syntactic structure of the sentence. Consequently, the task of naturalizing content reduces to that of accounting for the meanings of the simple symbols or words of LOT.

Fodor recognizes that different types of symbol have their content determined in different ways so that no one single theory will apply to all of the symbols of LOT. He proposes a functional–causal role theory for the logical symbols of LOT. And, echoing Kripke (1980) and Putnam (1975b), he proposes a causal chain story for proper names. Neither of these stories are told in any detail, reflecting his view that the hardest and most important part of the naturalization project is that of dealing with those symbols of LOT that are neither proper names nor logical symbols; that is, symbols that are the analogues of such English words as 'horse', 'red', 'proton', 'virtuous' and the like. For Fodor, the content of such a symbol is a matter of the property that it expresses.

Fodor's theory is inspired by a very crude theory according to which the meaning of a symbol is determined by the property that it causally covaries with. Thus, for example, according to the causal covariation theory, the LOT symbol HORSE means *horse* because tokenings of that symbol are caused by, and only by, horses.[2] The causal covariation approach is also known as informational semantics as, in the technical sense of the term, the information that a symbol carries is a matter of the property with which it causally covaries. The theory that Fodor offers constitutes a sophisticated development of this crude informational theory, placing him in a long tradition of tying meaning to aetiology (a tradition whose prominent members include B. F. Skinner 1957, Stampe 1977 and Fred Dretske 1981).

According to the informational theory, the meaning of the simple symbols of LOT is determined by their causal relations to the properties that they express and has nothing to do with the relations that they bear to other symbols. Hence, in principle, a creature could have a symbol in its LOT that meant *horse* without having any other symbols in that language. In other words, it could have the concept HORSE and be capable of thinking about horses without having any other concepts or be capable of having any other thoughts. This feature of the informational theory makes it an atomistic theory. According to non-atomistic theories, the meaning of a symbol depends upon its relations to other symbols so that a creature could not have a particular concept unless it had a battery of related concepts. For example, a non-atomist might argue that to grasp the concept HORSE it is necessary that one also grasps the concept ANIMAL and be disposed to infer from the thought x IS A HORSE the thought x IS AN ANIMAL.

Fodor is a staunch atomist as he believes that non-atomistic theories of content have implications that undermine the viability of folk psychology and intentional psychology in general. This goes a long way towards explaining the appeal that the informational theory holds for him. Quite apart from its atomistic credentials, there are other reasons for taking the informational theory seriously. First, by appealing to causal relations the theory appeals to something that is naturalistically kosher. And, one might suspect, the naturalist has few other viable options. Second, a cursory look at natural language lends support to the theory. For example, most competent adult speakers of English are disposed to utter 'horse' in response to horses and we are reluctant to attribute a grasp of the meaning of that word to children or foreigners who give evidence that they are not so disposed or who are disposed to utter 'horse' in response to non-horses. Third, there are cases of meaning or representation in the natural world with respect to which the informational theory clearly applies. For example, the height of the mercury column in a mercury thermometer represents the ambient temperature because the height of the column causally covaries with the temperature. If this were not the case how could the height of the column represent the temperature?

However, despite its appealing characteristics, the informational theory faces a major problem: that of finding a place for error or misrepresentation. We all misrepresent the world from time to time as in the case where I see a cow on a dark night and mistakenly conclude that it is a horse. In such a case a cow on a dark night causes a tokening of HORSE. The informational theory seems to rule out the possibility of this kind of error or misrepresentation. For it implies that as cows on a dark night as well as horses cause tokenings of HORSE that symbol must mean not *horse* but *horse or cow-on-a-dark-night*. In other words, the theory implies that HORSE has a disjunctive content. In the light of such a problem, the advocate of the informational theory needs to modify the theory in such a way as to avoid being forced to make a mistaken attribution of a disjunctive content in such cases. In Fodor's terminology, what is needed is a solution to the disjunction problem.

To make matter worse, as Fodor emphasizes in 'A Theory of Content, II' (1990c), there is another familiar kind of case where the cause of an LOT symbol does not fall within its extension, namely, representation in thought. For example, thoughts about hay sometimes cause thoughts about horses; and, thus, sometimes cause a tokening of HORSE. When this happens we do not have a case of error or misrepresentation; when a thought about hay causes me to think about horses it is not a case where I misrepresent a thought about hay as a horse. Such cases seem to force the advocate of the informational theory to attribute to horse a disjunctive content that includes not only *cow-on-a-dark-night* as a disjunct but also *thought-about-hay*.

If we are to hold onto the idea that mind–world causal relations lie at the heart of mental meaning, we need to uncover some non-intentional property that the causal connection between horses and HORSE has that that between cows on a dark night and HORSE (and that between thoughts about hay and HORSE) does not; a property that explains why the former rather than the latter plays a role in determining the meaning of HORSE. The discovery of such a property would facilitate the modification of the informational theory in such a way as to solve the disjunction problem.

Fodor considers, and finds wanting, several attempts to solve the disjunction problem in the above-described way. First, there is Dretske's (1981) idea that the content-determining causal connections are those that hold in the period when a symbol is being learned. According to Dretske, the content of a symbol depends upon what property its tokenings covary with in the learning period. Misrepresentation occurs when, outside the learning period (once the content of the symbol for the subject has been fixed), a tokening of the symbol is caused by something that doesn't have the property that the symbol covaried with in the learning period. In 'Semantics Wisconsin Style' (1984a) and Chapter 4 of *Psychosemantics* (1987) Fodor presents the following compelling objections to Dretske's line of thought. First, there is no principled, nonarbitrary way of saying when the learning period ends and mis-representation becomes a possibility. Second, the theory can apply only to symbols that are learned and hence not to the symbols of LOT assuming that that language is innate. Third, it is not true of learned symbols that they covary with the property that they express during the learning period. Consider the English word 'horse'. At best, utterances of this word by me were caused by, and only by, horses during the period when I was learning this word. But had I been confronted by a cow on a dark night I would have responded by uttering 'horse'. The truth of this counterfactual entails that 'horse' didn't covary with horses in the learning period for the relevant notions of causal connection and causal covariance are counterfactual supporting.

A second approach to the disjunction problem involves appealing to optimal circumstances. It's true that cows sometimes cause me to token HORSE, but usually when this happens conditions are not ideal with respect to determining the nature of the object before me. This is the case when I am confronted by a cow on a dark night; had conditions been ideal (which would involve its not being dark) I would not have misidentified the cow as a horse. This leads quite naturally to the thought that it is the causal connections that hold in ideal or optimal conditions that determine meaning, where these conditions are to be described in psychophysical terms, that is, in terms of lighting conditions, spatial relationship to the distal stimuli and suchlike. Given this, in cases of misrepresentation a symbol is caused by something that would not have caused it had conditions been ideal.

Fodor argues that the main problem with this attempt to solve the disjunction problem is that it does not apply to belief or thought in general and therefore not to the symbols of LOT. This is due to the role that beliefs play in belief fixation. Many of the causal relationships between properties instantiated in the extra-mental world and the symbols of LOT that express them are mediated by beliefs. For example, beliefs about what horses look and sound like and the kind of environment that they typically inhabit mediate the horse–HORSE connection in me. A consequence of this is that being in the psychophysically described optimal circumstances with respect to a horse is no guarantee that that horse will cause me to token HORSE. For, I could have beliefs which interfere with this process; for example, I could believe that I am in an environment populated by cows in pantomime horse costumes as a result of which the horse causes me to token COW. (See Fodor 1987, ch. 4.)

A third attempt to solve the disjunction problem involves appealing to teleological considerations. The basic idea is that a symbol expresses the property that it covaries with in those circumstances where the mechanism that produces it is performing its proper function. 'Proper function' here is to be understood in evolutionary terms so that it is the proper function of mechanism M to produce tokens of symbol S in response to instances of property P if and only if M was selected for in virtue of producing tokens of S in response to instances of P.[3]

Fodor's primary objection to the teleological theory is that it is afflicted with a problem of indeterminacy and that, as a consequence, it fails to solve the disjunction problem. This can be seen by considering the famous case of the frog and the fly. Frogs have an in-head mechanism M that, in response to certain distal stimuli, produces a state S that in turn causes the frog to snap. Flies, when they impinge upon a frog's visual system, typically set off such a causal chain and as a result end up being swallowed and ingested. This is clearly a good thing to happen to a frog and it is in virtue of such effects that M has been selected for. Now what is the function of M? One possible answer is that it is to detect flies. If M is a fly detector then, according to the teleological theory, S has the content *fly*. Another possible answer is that, due to the fact that all the flies in the frog's environment are little ambient black things (LABT for short) and all the LABTs are flies, M is an LABT detector; for M was selected for in virtue of producing tokenings of S in response to LABTs. If that is the function of M then, on the teleological theory, S has the content *LABT* rather than *fly*. Fodor's point is that there is nothing that the advocate of the teleological theory can appeal to in order to justify the preference of one of these stories to the other. In particular, counterfactuals cannot be appealed to, for the basic idea driving the theory is that it is the mechanism's actual history that determines its function. Therefore, the teleological theory entails that S has no determinate content; there is, for example, no fact of the matter as to whether S has the content *fly* or *LABT*. (See Fodor 1990b.)

So how does Fodor attempt to modify the informational theory in such a way as to deal with the disjunction problem? The appeals to a learning period, to optimal circumstances and to proper function constitute attempts to characterize in non-intentional terms circumstances in which tokenings of a symbol of LOT are caused by, and only by, instances of the property that it expresses. Fodor doubts that there could be any such circumstances and so he adopts a different tactic. Reflecting on the natural language case where he mistakes a cow for a horse and consequently utters 'horse', Fodor notes the following:

> misidentifying a cow as a horse wouldn't have led me to say 'horse' *except that there was independently a semantic relation between 'horse' tokenings and horses*. But for the fact that the word 'horse' expresses the property *of being a horse* (i.e. but for the fact that one calls horses 'horses') it would not have been *that* word that taking a cow to be a horse would have caused me to utter. Whereas, by contrast, since 'horse' does mean *horse*, the fact that horses cause me to say 'horse' does not depend on there being a semantic – or, indeed, any connection between 'horse' tokenings and cows. (1987: 107–8)

Fodor describes a natural language case merely for expository purposes; given that tokenings of the LOT symbol HORSE underlie utterances of the English word 'horse' the same point can be made of the former symbol. Reflecting on cases such as the above, Fodor concludes that the key difference between the causal connection between a symbol and the property that it expresses, on the one hand, and that between the symbol and properties that it does not express, on the other, is that the latter depends on the former but not vice versa. For example, horses cause tokenings of HORSE as do cows on a dark night. Cows on a dark night wouldn't cause tokenings of HORSE were it not the case that horses did, but not vice versa. In other words, break the causal connection between horses and tokenings of HORSE and you thereby break that between cows on a dark night and tokenings of HORSE; but breaking the latter connection will not thereby break the former connection. Expressed in Fodor's now famous terminology, the connection between cows on a dark night and tokenings of HORSE asymmetrically depends on that between horses and tokenings of HORSE. This leads Fodor to propose the following sufficient condition, a condition that constitutes the heart of his naturalistic theory of content:

Simple, non-logical symbol S expresses the property P if:

(i) it's a law that Ps cause tokenings of S; and
(ii) for any property P* not equivalent to P, if it's a law that P*s cause tokenings of S then that law asymmetrically depends upon the law that Ps cause tokenings of S.

The theory appeals to causal laws as Fodor regards the relevant causal connections as counterfactual supporting and holds that 'counterfactual supporting generalizations are (either identical to or) backed by causal laws' (1990c: 93).

To say that a law asymmetrically depends upon another is to commit oneself to the truth of certain counterfactuals; specifically, it is to say that if, contrary to fact, the latter law did not hold then neither would the former, but not vice versa (that is, the latter would hold even if, contrary to fact, the former did not). If, following Lewis (1973) and Stalnaker (1984), we understand counterfactuals in possible world terms, then to say that law Y asymmetrically depends upon law X is to say that: (i) in the nearest possible world where the law X does not hold neither does the law Y; and (ii) in the nearest possible world where the law that Y does not hold it is nevertheless a law that X.[4]

How convincing is Fodor's theory of content? The remainder of this chapter will be devoted to addressing this question.

Atomism and Conceptual Role Semantics

Fodor's theory of content is atomistic as it implies that the meaning of the primitive non-logical symbols of LOT are not determined by their relations to other symbols of that language. Expressed in terms of concepts (recall that for Fodor concepts are LOT symbols), his position is that the content of our simple concepts is not determined by their relationships to any of the other concepts in our conceptual scheme. Consequently, it is in principle possible for an individual to have DOG thoughts without being capable of having CAT thoughts, ANIMAL thoughts or thoughts involving any other concept. Fodor regards the atomistic credentials of his theory as a great virtue despite the fact that most philosophers of mind and cognitive scientists take atomism to be an untenable doctrine. In this section I will explain why Fodor is so committed to atomism and examine his objections to the most widely held non-atomistic theory of content (namely, conceptual role semantics).

According to the non-atomist, any meaningful item – be it a symbol or a concept – belongs to a system of meaningful items and inherits its content from at least some of the distinctive relations that it bears to these other items. One version of such a view might have it that, for example, for a person to grasp the concept DOG she must also grasp such concepts as ANIMAL, BARKS, BITES POSTMAN and so on, and that these concepts must stand in the appropriate evidential and inferential relations to one another. That is, she must take X BARKS as evidence for the conclusion that X IS A DOG, be disposed to infer from X IS A DOG that X IS AN ANIMAL and so on. Fodor labels the evidential and inferential relations that a concept bears to other concepts its epistemic liaisons. Thus, according to the non-atomist, the content of our concepts is determined by the epistemic liaisons that they bear to other concepts in our conceptual scheme.

Non-atomism has considerable intuitive appeal. This can be seen by considering how we go about determining whether an individual grasps a particular concept or understands the meaning of a given word. Suppose we want to determine whether or not a child grasps the concept AARDVARK or knows the meaning of the word 'aardvark'. Typically, we would ask such questions as 'what is an aardvark?' and if the child's answers suggested that she did not believe aardvarks to be animals, to have grey leathery skins, to eat termites and so on, then we would conclude that she did not grasp the concept AARDVARK or that she did not know what 'aardvark' means. In short, non-atomism would seem to underlie the methods that we use in settling questions as to whether an individual grasps a particular concept or knows the meaning of a particular word.

The intuitive pull of non-atomism is emphasized by a consideration of the much discussed case of Mrs T (Stich 1983: 54–6). Mrs T was a governess employed by the Stich family who, as a young woman, had had a keen interest in politics and had been shocked by the assassination of President McKinley. In old age she began to suffer from progressive memory loss and got to the stage where she would assert that 'McKinley was assassinated' whilst remaining neutral on the question of whether he was dead or alive. Indeed, she seemed to have forgotten what the difference between being dead and being alive amounts to. Stich raises the question of whether, despite her pronouncements, Mrs T really believed that McKinley had been assassinated. He reports that 'For just about everyone to whom I have posed this question, the overwhelmingly clear intuitive answer is no. One simply cannot believe that McKinley was assassinated if one has no idea what assassination is, nor any grasp of the difference between life and death' (1983: 56). In other words, this case suggests that in order to grasp the concept ASSASSINATION one also has to grasp the concept DEAD and, *inter alia*, be disposed to infer X IS DEAD from X WAS ASSASSINATED.

Such non-atomistic intuitions might suggest the need to develop a theory of content that, unlike Fodor's theory, finds a place for the evidential and inferential relations that hold between concepts. Clearly, it would be no good to argue that, for example, DOG means *dog* in virtue of the evidential and inferential relations that it bears to such concepts as ANIMAL, BARKS, CHASES POSTMEN and so on. Such a claim would fail to count as a legitimate naturalist theory of content by dint of its circularity: it attempts to account for the content of the target concept by appealing both to other concepts and to the intentional process of drawing an inference. However, there is a straightforward way of holding onto the central insight of the claim whilst avoiding the problem of circularity. As drawing an inference is a causal process (a process where a belief causes another belief) appeals to evidential and inferential relations can be replaced with appeals to causal processes. But how are we to avoid presupposing the contents of other concepts in order to account for the content of the target concept? By attempting to account for the contents of the members of our conceptual scheme en masse in a manner akin to the way in which theoretical terms are defined in terms of one another (see Lewis 1970). In broad outline, the resulting theory would account for the contents of the simple symbols of LOT (and, therefore, of our concepts) in terms of the causal relations that they bear to one another and, perhaps, to sensory inputs and motor outputs. Such a theory constitutes a functionalist attempt to construct a naturalist theory of content and is standardly known as conceptual role semantics (CRS for short).[5] CRS is widely held within the philosophical community. Wilfred Sellars (1963) is often cited as an early advocate of CRS and prominent contemporary champions of the theory include Block (1986), Field (1977), Loar (1981) and Lycan (1984).

Does CRS constitute a viable alternative to Fodor's atomistic theory? Fodor has two main objections to CRS. First, it has implications that undermine the viability of intentional psychology (be it folk psychology or any scientific refinement of folk psychology). Thus, it is a theory that is of no use to Fodor given that his aim is to vindicate folk psychology. In practice, Fodor writes as if this consequence of CRS constitutes a *reductio ad absurdum* of the theory. Second, CRS is inconsistent with a central feature of thought, namely, its compositionality. Let us consider these objections in some detail.

Holism is non-atomism taken to its logical extreme; according to the holist, the content of a symbol or concept is determined by the entirety of its relations to the other items in the language or conceptual scheme to which it belongs. Thus, symbols or concepts that belong to distinct languages or conceptual schemes cannot be equivalent in meaning. Fodor thinks that the advocate of CRS (and of non-atomism in general) is effectively committed to holism as there is no principled way of distinguishing between those causal connections that determine the meaning of a symbol or concept and those that don't. That is to say, if one holds that some of the relations that a symbol or concept bears to other symbols or concepts determine its content then one cannot avoid the holistic conclusion that all of its relations to other symbols or concepts determine its content. A traditional way of endorsing non-atomism whilst avoiding holism would involve appealing to the analytic–synthetic distinction. Roughly speaking, an analytic sentence is one that is true in virtue of its meaning (the sentence 'all bachelors are unmarried men' is an obvious candidate for an analytic sentence). A synthetic sentence, on the other hand, is one whose truth value partly depends upon extra-linguistic fact as in the case of 'all bachelors over the age of 30 are lonely'. The basic idea is that it is those causal connections between symbols that correspond to analytic truths that play a meaning-determining role. For example, suppose that I believe both that dogs are animals and that they bite postmen. Consequently, tokenings of DOG will tend to cause tokenings of both ANIMAL and BITES POSTMEN in my head. But only the former causal connection plays a role in determining the content of DOG as it is analytic that 'dogs are animals' and (if true) only synthetically true that 'dogs bite postmen'.

In the context of naturalizing content, this proposal faces an obvious problem. The analytic–synthetic distinction is a semantic distinction so that to say that the DOG–ANIMAL connection plays a role in determining the content of DOG (whilst the DOG–BITES POSTMEN connection does not) because it is analytic that 'dogs are animals' (but not that 'dogs bite postmen') is to run the risk of circularity. One cannot legitimately account for the meaning of a symbol by making a tacit appeal to its meaning. What is needed, then, is some principled way of distinguishing the analytic sentences in which 'dog' figures from the synthetic ones in non-semantic terms. It is far from obvious how this is to be done.

Fodor's main objection to the proposal involves an endorsement of Quine's (1953) attack on the analytic–synthetic distinction:

> I take it very seriously that there is no principled distinction between matters of meaning and matters of fact. Quine was right; you can't have an analytic/synthetic distinction. In the present context, this

means that you can't have a principled distinction between the kinds of causal relations among mental states that determine content and the kind of causal relations that don't. The immediate consequence is that you can't have functionalism [i.e. CRS] without holism; if *any* of the function of a mental state bears on its content, then *all* of its function bears on its content. (Fodor 1990a, p. x)

This rejection of the analytic–synthetic distinction is of a piece with Fodor's hostility to the view that our concepts can be defined or that concepts are definitions, a hostility that I discussed in chapter 3. And it places on any advocate of CRS who wishes to resist holism the unenviable burden of undermining Quine's hugely influential arguments.[6]

But why, one might ask, is the de facto holism of CRS a problem? Fodor's answer runs as follows. Holism implies that, barring cosmic accident, no two individuals or time slices of the same individual ever share a concept and, thus, ever share an intentional state. To see why, consider an example. It is highly unusual for two distinct individuals, or time slices of the same individual, to be entirely alike with respect to their beliefs about dogs. There is always going to be some belief about dogs that the one has that the other does not share. Suppose that I believe that dogs are dangerous, a belief that you do not share. Then, in my head there will exist a causal connection between DOG and DANGEROUS, a connection that does not exist in your head. Consequently, the symbol DOG has a divergent causal role in our respective heads and thus, according to holism, a divergent content. Notice that the same will be true of DANGEROUS; it is part of the causal role of that symbol in my head – but not part of its causal role in your head – that it is causally connected to DOG. Clearly, the same will be true of any symbol causally connected to DANGEROUS in either of our respective heads, and, in turn, of any symbol causally connected to such a symbol. In short, a holistic CRS implies that what initially looks like a minor difference in beliefs involving a shared concept ramifies throughout the conceptual schemes of the respective individuals in such a way that they do not share a single concept or, therefore, a single intentional state. Notice, this also implies that whenever an individual abandons a belief or acquires a new belief then the contents of all her other beliefs change.

Fodor goes on to argue that if no two individuals, or time slices of the same individual, ever share an intentional state then the laws or generalizations of intentional psychology (folk or scientific) will at most only subsume one individual (or time slice of one individual). And if this is the case, then there are effectively no intentional laws or generalizations thus making intentional psychology explanatorily and predictively toothless. In short then, Fodor thinks that holism undermines the viability of intentional psychology; for him, CRS constitutes a form of suicide semantics. Hence, it is no surprise that he regards the atomism of informational theories as being a great virtue. (See Fodor 1990b, introduction, 1987, ch. 3; Fodor and LePore 1992, chs 1 and 6.)

It might be objected that the inability of individuals to share concepts and intentional states does not in itself undermine the value of intentional laws or generalizations. This is because intentional laws can quantify over contents in such a way that distinct individuals can be subsumed by the same law despite the fact that they fail to share a single intentional state. For example, consider the familiar law that if a person wants it to be the case that P, and believes that the best way to bring it about that P is by doing Q, then, *ceteris paribus*, she will do Q. Clearly, this law could subsume the psychological life of individuals who have quite distinct beliefs and desires. However, the existence of such abstract laws will hardly serve to save intentional psychology. As Fodor convincingly puts it:

> laws that quantify into opaque contexts, e.g.: $(x)(y)(if\ x\ believes\ that\ y$ *is dangerous then ceteris paribus x tries to avoid y)*, look to be in deep trouble if holism is true, since such laws purport to generalize over organisms *in virtue of the shared intentional contents of their mental states.* Similarly for laws that constrain the mental states of given organisms across time, including, notably, the laws that govern belief fixation in reasoning, learning and perception (about 96.4% of serious psychology, at a rough estimate). Suppose, for example, that it's a law that, *ceteris paribus*, the more of the xs an individual comes to believe are F, the more the organism comes to believe that $(x)Fx$. Such a law would presuppose that an organism can hold the same (quantified) belief for different reasons at different times. But it's hard to square this with an intentional holism that implies that changing any one of one's beliefs changes the content of all the rest. (1990b: 82 n. 2)

Apart from appealing to the analytic–synthetic distinction, various attempts have been made to establish that CRS does not have the disastrous consequences that Fodor describes. One move, which Fodor takes to be implicit in much of the cognitive science literature (Fodor and LePore 1994: 17), involves an appeal to content similarity and can be expressed in the following terms. Perhaps holism rules out the possibility of distinct individuals (or distinct time slices of the same individual) sharing a concept or having intentional states with identical contents. But it doesn't rule out the possibility of their having similar concepts or having intentional states with similar contents. For example, it is consistent with holism that the concept that I express with the word 'dog' is similar to that that you express with 'dog'. Likewise, the belief that you express with the sentence 'dogs are fond of biting postmen' may well have a similar content to that that I express with the same sentence. All that is required for the laws of intentional psychology to have general application is for them to invoke the notion of content similarity and for it to be the case that distinct individuals often have intentional states with similar contents.

As Fodor and LePore point out (1994: 18), it is incumbent on the advocate of such a proposal to provide a substantial account of what it is for the intentional states of distinct individuals to be similar in content, and it is far from clear how this is to be done. They recognize that there is an everyday sense in which two individuals can have similar beliefs. For example, we might say that two people have similar beliefs when one believes P, Q, R and S whilst the other believes P, Q and R. Alternatively, we sometimes say that two people have similar beliefs when they differ in the strength of their commitment to the truth of a particular proposition; for example, when one believes P very strongly whilst the other believes P less strongly. However, such familiar notions of belief similarity are of no use to the holist as for two individuals to have similar beliefs in either of these respects they must have some beliefs that are identical in terms of their content.

Another attempt to cash out the notion of content similarity that Fodor and LePore examine is this: 'two beliefs are similar if they participate in mostly the same inferences' (1994: 20). They argue, convincingly, that this move won't work for two reasons. First, it is difficult to see how two beliefs could participate in 'mostly the same' inferences if there were not certain inferences in which they both participated. But inferences are individuated in terms of their premises and conclusions: for you to have made the same inference as me, you must have reached the same conclusion from the same premises. Hence, for your belief to participate in 'mostly the same inferences' as my belief, we must have some beliefs that have identical contents, a possibility that the holist rules out. Second, we need a principled answer to the question of which inferences a given concept enters into determine its content, an answer that we just don't have. We need an answer to this question as it is clearly the case that many of the inferences that we make play no role in determining the content of our concepts. For example, I believe that ripe tomatoes are red and so am disposed to infer from X IS RED to X IS THE COLOUR OF A RIPE TOMATO. Shakespeare, never having come across a tomato, was not remotely disposed to make this inference yet that didn't prevent him from having the concept RED.

In sum, then, the holist owes us a substantial account of content similarity, an account that shows how two individuals can have concepts or intentional states that have similar contents without their having concepts or intentional states that have identical contents. Fodor and LePore are sceptical that such an account has been produced: 'It's not, of course, incoherent to imagine a notion of "similar belief" which . . . is compatible both with meaning holism and with their being robust intentional generalizations. The trouble is . . . that nobody seems to have any idea what this useful sense of "similar belief" might be' (1994: 19).

A second attempt to establish that CRS does not undermine the viability of intentional psychology is due to Peter Carruthers (1996, ch. 4). Carruthers argues that Fodor fails to establish that CRS leads to holism. This is because the beliefs that a subject has, though they influence the actual effects of tokenings of the symbols of her LOT, do not influence their causal role in the manner envisaged by Fodor. Consider the following example. Suppose I believe that dogs are ferocious, a belief that you do not share. Then, in me, tokenings of DOG will cause tokenings of DANGEROUS, something that is not true of you. According to Fodor, here is a case where a symbol of LOT diverges in its causal role in our respective internal economies. Carruthers, however, disagrees, for in the counterfactual situation where you believed that dogs are dangerous, tokenings of DOG in you would also cause tokenings of DANGEROUS. In short, when comparing the causal role of a given symbol in the heads of distinct individuals, one must consider not so much the actual effects of tokenings of that symbol, but, rather, the effects that those tokenings would have in counterfactual circumstances where the individuals in question agree in their beliefs.

My objection to Carruthers's argument is that it runs the risk of implying that, for example, my LOT symbol DOG has the same causal role as your CAT and thus, assuming CRS, that my DOG and your CAT have the same content. In virtue of what I believe about dogs, tokenings of DOG in my head tend to cause tokenings of

BARKS, BITES POSTMEN, LOVES TO SWIM and so on, effects that, I take it, tokenings of CAT in your head do not tend to cause. But suppose that I changed my beliefs about dogs (or, more accurately, adjusted the sentences of LOT in my belief box that contain the symbol DOG) so that I came to believe that dogs have all the characteristics that you actually believe cats to have. Making this change would involve modifying the sentences in my belief box so that for every sentence in your belief box of the form CATS ARE F there would be a sentence in my belief box of the form DOGS ARE F, and vice versa. In principle, there is nothing to stop me from changing my beliefs in this way. If I changed my beliefs in this way, then my tokenings of DOG would cause just the same effects in me that your tokenings of CAT actually cause in you. If we individuate causal roles in the manner recommended by Carruthers, the upshot would appear to be that my DOG and your CAT have just the same causal role in our respective internal economies. Such examples will abound so that Carruthers only rescues CRS from the clutches of holism at the cost of conflating divergent concepts held by distinct individuals.

Another suggestion as to how the advocate of CRS can avoid holism is provided by Botterill and Carruthers (1999, ch. 7). They argue that it is only those causal connections that a symbol of LOT enters into that are lawful, or that are necessary for the laws of psychology to hold, that play a role in determining its content. So, for example, as it is not a law of psychology that thinking about slugs causes cringing, then the fact that thinking about slugs causes me to cringe does not imply that tokenings of SLUG in my head have a content that diverges from that of tokenings of SLUG in the head of a slug enthusiast. The main problem with this line of thought is that it runs the risk of implying that creatures belonging to species that have different psychologies cannot share concepts. To see this consider an example. Suppose a species of creature inhabits an environment where it is preyed upon by snakes and has evolved in such a way that whenever it thinks that there is a snake in the vicinity it comes to think that it is in grave danger. In short, it is a law of this creature's psychology that tokenings of SNAKE cause tokenings of DANGER. Another species of creature that inhabits the same environment, rather than being preyed upon by snakes, itself preys upon snakes. Thus, tokenings of SNAKE in this creature cause not DANGER but FOOD. The Botterill and Carruthers position would appear to have the upshot that SNAKE in the respective heads of these distinct species of creature cannot have the same content; or at the very least, they make it a mystery as to how they could share the concept

SNAKE. But it strikes me that nothing that I have said about these creatures suggests that they do not share the concept SNAKE.

So much for Fodor's first objection to CRS. His second objection appeals to the idea that content is compositional (Fodor and LePore 1992, ch. 6). According to Fodor, content is compositional in the respect that the content of a complex concept is exhaustively determined by the content of its constituent concepts and the manner in which they are combined. Assuming CTM, the idea is that the content of a complex LOT symbol is determined by the content of its constituent symbols and its syntactic structure (in other words, LOT has a combinatorial semantics). Thus, if one knows the meaning of each of the constituent concepts (that is, LOT words) of THE DOG BIT THE POSTMAN and appreciates its syntactic structure, then one knows all that is necessary to work out the meaning of that complex concept or symbol. For Fodor, the chief evidence that content is compositional is the productivity and systematicity of thought; if content wasn't compositional, then how could thought be productive and systematic? Thus, rejecting Fodor's premiss is to relinquish thereby one's ability to account for two salient features of thought.[7]

Fodor argues that the compositionality of content causes a major problem for CRS. Given that content is compositional, for content to be determined by causal role, causal roles must themselves compose. That is, it must be the case that the causal role of a complex concept is exhaustively determined by the casual role of its component concepts (and the manner in which they are combined). But, argues Fodor, causal roles do not compose owing to the role that beliefs play in determining the causal role of complex concepts. To see this consider Fodor and LePore's examination of the complex concept BROWN COW. They accept that there is a causal connection between BROWN COW and ANIMAL and between BROWN COW and NOT GREEN COW in virtue of, respectively, the existence of causal connections between COW and ANIMAL and between BROWN and NOT GREEN. However, suppose that you believe that brown cows are dangerous whilst not believing that either brown things or cows are generally dangerous. Then in your head there will be a causal connection between BROWN COW and DANGEROUS despite the fact that there is no connection between either BROWN and DANGEROUS or COW and DANGEROUS. In short, in virtue of your beliefs about brown cows, BROWN COW will have a causal role over and above that of its constituent concepts. Put in general terms, casual roles do not compose. But as causal roles do not compose whereas content does, then the content of a concept cannot be a matter of its causal role.

As we saw in chapter 3, in his recent work Fodor has invested a great deal of energy into undermining a view of concepts widely held in the cognitive science community. This is the view that concepts are prototypes. Fodor is opposed to the prototype theory as he sees it as being at odds with his atomism and as constituting a version of CRS. To see why, consider the example of DOG once more. If the concept DOG is a prototype then it is constitutive of grasping that concept both that one represents dogs as tending to have certain features and that one is disposed to make such inferences as X IS A DOG therefore X IS LIKELY TO BARK, X BARKS therefore X IS LIKELY TO BE A DOG and so on. That is, part of what it is to have the concept DOG is to have a battery of other concepts and to be disposed to make certain inferences involving those concepts. Notice, though, that Fodor can consistently hold that there is such a thing as a prototypical dog and that, as a matter of empirical fact, many of those individuals who grasp the concept DOG have a mental representation of the prototypical dog, a representation that mediates the causal connection between dogs and tokenings of DOG within them.

Fodor's critique of the prototype theory echoes his second objection to CRS as he argues that concepts cannot be prototypes as, generally speaking, prototypes do not compose; that is, the prototypes of complex concepts are generally not determined by the prototypes of their constituents.[8]

In this section we have seen that Fodor has some substantial objections to CRS and to any non-atomistic theory of content. Thus, he has some powerful reasons for endorsing atomism and seeking to construct an atomistic theory of content. But how are we to square all this with the fact that many of us appear to have non-atomistic intuitions of the kind described at the beginning of this section? What, for example, is the atomist to say about Mrs T?

In this context, it is very important to appreciate that Fodor can consistently accept that many of the mind–world causal connections that determine the content of our concepts (LOT symbols) are mediated by theories or bodies of beliefs. Similarly, he can concede that, as a matter of fact, to acquire certain concepts we must form a body of beliefs as to the nature of the property expressed by the target concept. For example, suppose that in order to acquire the concept AARDVARK a human individual has to form a body of beliefs or a theory as to the salient characteristics of aardvarks otherwise she would not be remotely disposed to respond to aardvarks by tokening AARDVARK. It is just that the precise nature of this body of beliefs is irrelevant to the content of AARDVARK; in principle two individuals could have radically different theories about aardvarks but still share the concept AARDVARK, as their respective theories both served to mediate a causal connection between aardvarks and tokenings of AARDVARK. Once this is appreciated, it becomes clear that the atomist is in a good position to deal with our prima facie non-atomistic intuitions and practices. First, it is consistent with atomism that one finds it implausible that a person could acquire any given concept without having a prior grasp of a whole battery of other concepts. For, if they don't have a prior grasp of a whole battery of concepts, how could they form a body of beliefs that could serve to mediate a causal connection between the property expressed by the target concept and tokenings of that concept? Second, it is consistent with the truth of atomism that a good way of determining whether a person grasps a particular concept involves determining whether she has true beliefs about the property expressed by the concept. For example, suppose that an individual asserts that she believes that 'aardvarks are grey, leathery, termite-eating mammals'. Then she has provided evidence that her beliefs are such as to mediate a causal connection between aardvarks and her tokenings of AARDVARK. If, on the other hand, she appears not even to believe that aardvarks are mammals then, assuming that she grasps the concept MAMMAL, we have evidence that her beliefs are not such as to mediate an aardvark–AARDVARK connection. For, if a person who grasps the concept MAMMAL doesn't believe that aardvarks are mammals, then she is hardly likely to respond to an encounter with an aardvark by tokening AARDVARK.

The previous point ties in with Fodor's analysis of the case of Mrs T. Fodor accepts Stich's claim that Mrs T does not believe that President McKinley was assassinated despite her repeated utterance of the sentence 'McKinley was assassinated'. But this is not because there is any constitutive relation between grasping the concept ASSASSINATION and having such beliefs as that when a person has been assassinated, she is thereby dead (a belief that Mrs T does not hold). Rather, it is because the required causal connection between assassinations and tokenings of ASSASSINATION has broken down: 'In no useful way were her tokenings of ASSASSINATION . . . causally connected with assassinations. Remember, Mrs. T was prepared to apply "assassinated" to people whom she didn't even think were dead. What better evidence could we have that, for

Mrs. T, ASSASSINATION and assassinations had come unstuck?'
(Fodor 1987: 93).

A final point on the prima facie intuitive implausibility of
atomism is that there are cases where the non-atomist – and particularly the advocate of CRS – is committed to the claim that two
individuals fail to share a concept, which clashes with common
sense. Hence, it is far from obvious that non-atomism has any clear-
cut advantages over atomism in terms of its intuitive plausibility.
In *Psychosemantics* Fodor presents an example of such a case. The
ancient Greeks had a theory about stars very much at odds with
that widely held today. For they 'believed that stars are little holes
in the sky which the heavenly fires show through' (1987: 88). Consequently, the relation that the ancient Greeks' concept STAR bore to
their other concepts is very much at odds with that that our concept
STAR bears to the other concepts that we hold. For example, I am
not remotely disposed to infer the belief that x is a hole in the sky
from the belief that x is a star. Given this divergence of inferential
role, the non-atomist is committed to the idea that the ancient
Greeks did not share our concept STAR. But this is clearly at odds
with common-sense intuition. For, common sense has it that the
ancient Greeks shared our concept STAR but differed from us in that
they had a whole collection of beliefs about stars that we do not
hold and which we take to be false. If this were not the case, then
we would have no hope of understanding or characterizing the
beliefs that the ancient Greeks expressed by using the word that is
standardly translated as 'star'. Indeed, that translation would be
illegitimate.

Some Potential Problems for Fodor's Theory

In this section I will consider some frequently raised objections that
would appear to cause problems for Fodor's theory of content. In
addressing these problems, Fodor has displayed a considerable
degree of ingenuity and has introduced some additions and modi-
fications to his position.

The first objection runs as follows. Fodor has a very austere conception of the nature of meaning: for him, the meaning of a symbol
or concept is solely a matter of the property that it expresses. Thus,
symbols or concepts that express the same property or, alternatively,
have the same reference are semantically equivalent. For example,
as the properties of being water and being H_2O are identical, the

concepts WATER and H$_2$O express the same property, have the same reference and enter into the same mind–world causal laws. Therefore, it is an implication of Fodor's theory that these two concepts have the same content. But, so the objection continues, this is a problem as Frege (1952) has given us compelling reasons for thinking that WATER and H$_2$O do not have the same content despite the fact that they express the same property or have the same reference. For example, the sentence 'water is H$_2$O' is informative whereas the sentence 'water is water' is not. How could this be the case if 'water' and 'H$_2$O' (and thus WATER and H$_2$O) were semantically equivalent? Similarly, one can rationally believe that water is wet whilst doubting that H$_2$O is wet. According to Frege, there is a second component to meaning, namely, sense or the mode of presentation of reference. The charge against Fodor is that his theory ignores sense and for that reason is at best incomplete (in naturalizing only one component of the content of our concepts) and at worst flat false (in implying that, for example, WATER and H$_2$O are equivalent in content).[9]

Fodor responds to this objection by taking the bull by the horns and denying that there is such a thing as sense. Thus, WATER and H$_2$O are equivalent in terms of content. However, they are different concepts as the latter, unlike the former, is a complex concept that includes as its components the concepts HYDROGEN, 2, and OXYGEN. This idea is incorporated into Fodor's attempt to deal with the sense-motivating facts described in the previous paragraph. In effect, he wheels in syntax to do the job that sense is widely invoked to do. This is how his idea goes. Intentional states are individuated not just in terms of their content and the relation involved, but also in terms of the syntax of the sentence of LOT involved. Thus, for you and I to share a belief we must both have a sentence of LOT in our respective belief boxes that agrees in its semantic and syntactic properties. So, for example, if the sentence in your belief box is WATER IS WET and the one in mine is H$_2$O IS WET then our respective beliefs do not belong to the same type despite the fact that they have the same content. Consequently, an individual can rationally believe that water is wet whilst doubting that H$_2$O is wet, for to do that is not the same as to believe that water is wet and simultaneously doubt that water is wet. And the sentence 'water is H$_2$O' is informative in a way in which 'water is water' is not, for an individual who has the concept WATER can acquire a new belief on being presented with the former sentence but not on being presented with the latter. (See Fodor 1989c, 1990b, 1994a, ch. 1.)

This is clearly a controversial line of thought. I will restrict my critical comments to the following point. Fodor risks running together two levels that he stresses are distinct, namely the intentional level and the computational or syntactic level. He holds that special science laws are underpinned by lower-level mechanisms. For example, suppose that it is a law of some special science that Xs cause Ys. Then, whenever an X is tokened, that token will be identical to (or constituted by) a lower-level phenomenon that (in virtue of the laws holding at that lower level) sets off a causal chain that eventuates in the tokening of a distinct lower-level phenomenon that is identical to (or constitutes) a tokening of Y. For Fodor, the laws of intentional psychology are computationally or syntactically implemented. Hence, whenever an intentional state causes another intentional state, there is a lower-level syntactic description of that process.

Fodor appeals to the idea that the relationship between the intentional and the syntactic is that syntactic processes implement intentional laws in order to deal with the accusation that CTM implies that content has no legitimate role to play in psychological explanation. According to this accusation, as computers are sensitive only to the syntactic properties of the symbols that they manipulate, CTM implies that the content of our intentional states has no bearing on their causal ramifications. But if content is causally inert in this way, then it has no legitimate role to play in psychological explanation.[10] Fodor's response is that CTM has no such implications as the intentional and the syntactic reside at different levels in the hierarchy of the special sciences. (See Fodor 1987, appendix, and his reply to Devitt in Fodor 1991c.) My point is that such a defence of intentional psychology would appear to be inconsistent with the idea that intentional psychology must individuate intentional states partly in terms of their syntax. For that idea entails that intentional psychology must appeal to syntactic properties in framing its laws and explanations and that, therefore, the intentional and the syntactic reside at the same level. It is clear that intentional psychology needs to appeal to properties of intentional states other than their referential content (be it sense or syntax). This is because, as Fodor stresses in 'Methodological Solipsism Considered as a Research Strategy in Psychology' (1980), the causal powers of intentional states are not wholly determined by their referential content. For example, given that Jocasta is Oedipus' mother, the belief that Oedipus has married Jocasta and the belief that he has married his mother have the same referential content. Yet it is the latter belief that causes him to gouge out his eyes and that we must appeal to in order to explain his behaviour.

A second objection to Fodor's theory of content has to do with deferential concepts. Like most people I am not very good at recognizing elms; I am just as likely to token ELM when confronted by a beech as I am when confronted by an elm. But for all that, I grasp the concept ELM; it is just that I defer to experts when it comes to the question whether a given object falls within the extension of ELM. The objection that this suggests is that Fodor's theory implies that most people do not grasp the concept ELM as there is not the required causal connection between elms and their tokenings of the LOT symbol ELM; at best, in most people's heads ELM has a wider extension that includes both elms and beeches. The same can be said of many of my concepts including GOLD, DIAMOND and PROTEIN, not to mention such arcane concepts as NEURON and ELECTRON.

In *The Elm and the Expert* (1994a) Fodor develops a line of thought with respect to deferential concepts (concepts with respect to whose application we defer to experts) that furnishes a reply to the above objection. Contrary to appearances, there is a causal connection between elms and my tokenings of ELM and I can distinguish elms from beeches. In the normal course of things, when I am confronted by a tree I do not care to which species it belongs. In those cases where I do care I utilize an expert (in this case a botanist) so that I token ELM if and only if the tree in question is an elm. The situation is not relevantly different from that where we employ instruments of observation or laboratory equipment in order to determine whether or not we are being confronted by an instance of a particular property. In other words, just as there is a causal connection between acids and tokenings of ACID, there is a causal connection between elms and tokenings of ELM; in the former case the connection is mediated by an instrument of observation (for example, a piece of litmus paper) and in the latter case it is mediated by an expert. As Fodor puts it: 'From the point of view of informational semantics, the situation is *absolutely normal*: that my *elm* and *acid* thoughts have the content that they do depends on their being mechanisms that reliably correlate them with instantiations of elmhood and acidhood respectively' (1994a: 35).

This is certainly an ingenious response but I have my worries. First, it makes it too easy to grasp a concept. There are many concepts whose existence I am in some sense aware of but which I cannot be said to fully grasp. For example, I have heard talk of muons but I know little about them apart from the fact that they are of interest to physicists. However, I am more than willing to defer to experts when it comes to the question determining whether or not the property of being a muon has been instantiated in my immediate environment. Fodor would thus seem to be committed to the highly questionable claim that I grasp the concept MUON. Second, for reasons that become apparent later, if the causal connection between elms and tokenings of ELM is expert-mediated then it is not a law that elms cause tokenings of ELM. For being impinged upon by an elm will not be sufficient for bringing about a tokening of ELM and in those cases where an elm fails to cause a tokening of ELM (due to the absence of an expert) no *ceteris paribus* condition of psychology will have been violated.

A third objection to Fodor's theory of content is that the theory implies that many of our concepts, rather than expressing properties instantiated in the external world, express properties of proximal stimuli. For example, whenever I see a cow and subsequently token COW, the cow in question causes a certain pattern of retinal stimulation. Call this particular type of pattern of retinal stimulation R. Then there is as reliable a causal connection between instances of R and tokenings of COW as there is between cows and tokenings of COW. Moreover, the cow–cow would appear to depend asymmetrically upon the R–cow connection. Given that the latter connection mediates the former in the nearby possible world where Rs do not cause tokenings of COW, neither do cows. Yet in the nearby possible world where cows don't cause tokenings of COW (perhaps because the laws of optics are such that cows do not affect the retina in the way that they do in the actual world) Rs still do. Therefore, Fodor's theory implies that COW has the content *R* rather than *cow*.

Fodor's reply is that there is no such typical pattern of retinal stimulation that mediates the cow–cow connection. Sometimes (for example, when one believes one is in cow-infested waters) glimpsing a cow out of the corner of one's eye is enough to cause a tokening of COW and in such a case the pattern of retinal stimulation involved is going to be very different from that produced in a head-on confrontation with a cow. 'Given the vast number of ways that cows may impinge upon sensory mechanisms, a perceptual system which made COW tokenings intimately dependent upon specific proximal projections wouldn't work as a cow spotter' (Fodor 1990c: 109). This is a fair point but it does not serve to save Fodor's theory from the spirit of the objection. No matter how varied the sensory stimulations that can cause tokenings of COW, it seems likely that all such tokenings are immediately preceded by instances of the same type of neural state, a neural state causally upstream of the sensory stimulation. So why doesn't COW refer to a certain type of neural state? Fodor modifies his theory somewhat in attempting to deal with this kind of case. For a symbol S to express property P, it is not enough that it is a law that instances of P cause tokenings of S and that the required dependency relations hold. In addition, S must be robust; that is, it must be the case that tokenings of S are sometimes caused without the instantiation of P. But in the case under discussion, this condition is not satisfied as COW is only tokened when it has been preceded by the neural state in question.

Fodor seems to be suggesting that robustness is necessary for content. If this is so then his modification won't work as there is a counter-example; that is, a case of a perfectly meaningful symbol that is not robust, a symbol that is never tokened in the absence of the property that it expresses. An input transducer is a mechanism that takes physical, non-symbolic events as input and generates a symbolic output which is subsequently processed by some cognitive processor. The retina is an example of an input transducer. Input transducers are constructed in such a way as to be sensitive to certain intrinsic physical properties of their input. For example, the retina is sensitive to such properties of light waves as their intensity, wavelength and so on. Consequently, each of the distinct symbols that the retina is capable of producing as output will causally covary with a specific type of physical input. The crucial point is that the symbols produced by the retina represent or express the very properties that they are invariably caused by as the job of the retina is to generate representations of the intensity, wavelength and so on of the light waves that stimulate it. In other words, the retina will produce an output symbol S that expresse property P only if it is stimulated by an instance of P. In short, the symbols produced by the retina are not robust.

A fourth objection arises from Putnam's (1975b) Twin Earth scenario. Twin Earth is a planet that is a duplicate of Earth apart from the fact that the stuff that its residents call 'water' (and which fills their rivers and lakes, comes out of their taps, etc.), though just like water in terms of its superficial properties, has a quite different chemical composition (summarized as XYZ). In virtue of this fact, XYZ falls outside the extension of our concept WATER as that concept only applies to H_2O. The objection is that Fodor's theory implies that both XYZ and H_2O fall within the extension of WATER. Here's why. XYZ has just the same superficial properties as water; its visual appearance, taste, smell and feel is indistinguishable from that of water. Consequently a perceptual encounter with a sample of XYZ would have just the same effect on me as a perceptual encounter with a sample of water. Therefore, if it is a law that water causes tokenings of WATER then it is equally a law that XYZ causes tokenings of WATER. As the superficial properties of XYZ are determined by its chemical constitution, these laws symmetrically depend on one another. Breaking the XYZ–WATER connection would involve altering the functioning of the human perceptual apparatus or changing such laws as the laws of optics. And doing this would have the effect of breaking the water–WATER connection.

In 'A Theory of Content, II' (1990c) Fodor offers two independent replies to this objection. The first runs as follows. There is nothing in Putnam's story that rules out the possibility of our coming to be able to distinguish between water and XYZ. As the two substances are chemically different, it must be nomologically possible to develop a reliable test for telling them apart, a test that, perhaps, involves the use of technical laboratory equipment. Fodor argues that the possible world where we have such a reliable test is relevant to the question of the dependency relations between the various causal connections in which WATER figures. WATER is a kind concept; that is, we operate with the intention of applying WATER only to samples of stuff that have the same chemical constitution as the local samples of colourless, odourless, tasteless liquid. In virtue of this intention, in the nearest possible world where we can distinguish water from XYZ, we will apply WATER to water but not to XYZ.[11] Thus, breaking the XYZ–WATER connection does not bring down the water–WATER connection. But not vice versa.

I am not entirely convinced by this reply. In the possible world that Fodor refers to, in a direct perceptual encounter with a sample of XYZ we would be affected in just the same way as we would by a sample of water. Thus, to break the XYZ–WATER connection we would have to refrain from applying the concept WATER to colourless, odourless, tasteless liquids on the basis of a direct perceptual encounter. That is, we would have to refrain from applying WATER on the basis of the methods that we standardly and routinely employ in the actual world. My worry is that this makes that possible world irrelevant, for in it the water–WATER connection is not mediated in anything like the same way that it is in the actual world. What Fodor needs is a possible world where the water–WATER connection is just as it is in the actual world (that is, mediated in just the same way) and where there is no XYZ–WATER connection.

Fodor's second way of dealing with the problem posed by XYZ involves a modification to his theory. There is no XYZ around here; the property of being XYZ is uninstantiated on Earth. To fall within the extension of WATER, XYZ would have to feature in the local environment or in the actual history of tokenings of WATER. Thus Fodor amends his theory by saying that for a symbol 'X' to express the property X it has to be the case that 'Some "X"s are actually caused by X's' (1990c: 121). A potential objection to this suggestion is that it undermines Fodor's ability to account for the content of concepts that express uninstantiated properties, concepts such as UNICORN and GHOST.[12] Fodor cheerfully admits this but suggests that such concepts might well not be primitive and thus can be handled in the same way as SQUARE CIRCLE. But Fodor needs to tell us what the constituent concepts of GHOST and UNICORN are without committing himself to the thesis that such concepts can be defined (recall that Fodor thinks that few, if any, of our concepts can be defined).

A fifth objection is that Fodor's theory fails to account for an important element of meaning, namely, its normativity. The idea lying behind this objection is that normativity is an essential component of meaning in the respect that if a symbol has a particular meaning then there will be infinitely many facts concerning how it ought to be used in various possible circumstances over and above any facts concerning how it would be used in those circumstances. And how a symbol ought to be used is partly constitutive of its meaning so that to attribute a particular meaning to a symbol is to imply a whole battery of normative facts. Similarly, when an individual misapplies a concept (for example, when she thinks that the anteater before her is an aardvark) she has violated a norm governing the application of that concept; she has done something she ought not have done. Moreover, there are norms of theoretical and practical reasoning. For example, there are rules or standards of inductive reasoning that I violate when I make a sweeping generalization about the Finnish national character on the basis of meeting one or two Finns. In jumping to my conclusion from the premises from which I began, I have done something that I ought not have done.

The objection is that Fodor fails to account for such meaning-constitutive normative facts as facts about causal connections and dependency relations holding between them are not capable of generating normative facts.[13]

One response to this objection is to say that there is no problem of normativity over and above the problem of misrepresentation.

That to say that to use a symbol in a particular way is to use it in a way it ought not be used, is to say no more than that such a use would constitute a case of misrepresentation. Thus, advocates of the normativity objection need to give us some compelling reasons for thinking that Fodor's theory fails to explain why, for example, a horse-caused tokening of cow misrepresents its cause as a cow. In 'A Theory of Content, II' Fodor expresses sympathy with this line of thought (see Fodor 1990c, n. 35).

A second response that I favour denies that crucial premiss that normativity is an essential component of meaning. That is not to deny that there are normative facts but these facts are a product of such intentional states as our intentions, expectations and the responses that we and our fellows make to certain uses of symbols, applications of concepts and inferential moves. Consider the English word 'cow'. I intend to use this word in a way that is consistent with its meaning in the wider community and to fail to do so is to fail to live up to this intention. Similarly, my fellows expect me to use this word in a way that is consistent with its public meaning and are prone to criticize me if I fail to meet this expectation (after all, such usage hardly makes for communication and mutual understanding). Moreover, if I discovered that I had violated my intentions with respect to the use of 'cow', I would be disposed to engage in self-criticism and regret. My thought is that such facts about our intentions, expectations and responses (facts that Fodor can account for in naturalistic terms) determine the normativity of public language symbols. Something similar can be said with respect to the application of concepts and the inferential processes that we execute. We desire to hold beliefs that are true, to purge our belief systems of false beliefs and to make inferential leaps that have a high probability of taking us from true beliefs to true beliefs. Moreover, we criticize the ignorant and indifferent, those who hold false beliefs and those who make inferential leaps that do not preserve truth. Consequently, when I misapply a concept or reason badly, I have acted in a way that runs counter to much of what I hold dear or in a way that violates some of my most fundamental intentions and desires. Moreover, I have done precisely the sort of thing that evokes the criticism and condemnation of my fellows. My point is that it is such facts about our desires and intentions along with our critical responses that are responsible for the normative facts that surround our application of concepts and theoretical and practical reasoning.

If I am right, then normativity is not an essential component of meaning and can be accounted for in non-circular terms by an appeal to our intentional states and responses. Of course none of this is conclusive; my comments could do with much by way of extension and elaboration, something that cannot be done in this context. However, I think I have done enough to suggest that the normativity objection to Fodor's theory is hardly conclusive.

Some More Telling Objections

There are reasons for doubting that Fodor's theory actually applies to our intentional states. For, in the case of many of the simple non-logical symbols of LOT, the required laws do not hold. To see this, consider the case of my LOT symbol AARDVARK. For this symbol to satisfy Fodor's sufficient condition for meaning *aardvark* it would have to be the case that it was a law that aardvarks cause me to token AARDVARK. Suppose that I am confronted by an aardvark in broad daylight. This creature will have many, many distinct properties. For example, it will be an animal, a mammal, a quadruped, leathery, grey and so on. The human object recognition system works in such a way that I will not explicitly represent all of the properties that the aardvark has. On the contrary, I will represent the aardvark as having only a small subset of the properties that it actually has despite the fact that I have symbols in my LOT that express many of the properties that, so to speak, I turn a blind eye to. It is a good thing that this is the case for two reasons. First, it would take up lots of space to represent explicitly all of the properties that the aardvark has that I am capable of representing. Second, some of the aardvark's properties will require a lot of processing if their possession by it is to be detected. For example, it will take a lot more processing to work out that it is an aardvark than it will to work out that it is an animal. To do the former would be to waste valuable cognitive resources if I wasn't interested in the question to what particular species the animal before me belonged. To generalize the point, if when we exercised our recognition capacities we were to represent explicitly anything more than a small subset of the properties of the object before us, we would run the risk of cognitive breakdown in every perceptual encounter. The mechanisms that underpin our recognition capacities must be highly selective when it comes to detecting and representing properties of the objects with which we interact. They are designed in such a way as to focus on those properties of objects that are relevant to us given our plans, projects, purposes and interests. In other words, the object recognition process is cognitively penetrable.

Consequently, there is no guarantee that I will represent the aardvark as an aardvark (that is, by tokening AARDVARK). I might merely represent it as being a grey, leathery mammal in virtue of the fact that, on this particular occasion, I am not interested in the question of the species to which the creature before me belongs. Generalized, the point is that it is often the case that an aardvark impinges on an individual without causing her to token AARDVARK. Does it follow from this that it is not a law that aardvarks cause tokenings of AARDVARK? The laws that Fodor has in mind are *ceteris paribus* laws and it is consistent with its being a law that *ceteris paribus* Xs cause Ys that sometimes an X occurs without causing a Y. In such cases, the operative idealizations of the special science that frames the law in question will have broken down so that all else is not equal. However, in the case where, because of my interests at the time, the aardvark does not cause me to token AARDVARK, it does not appear to be the case that the operative idealizations of psychology have broken down. For my failing to token AARDVARK is a product of the design and proper functioning of the psychological mechanisms involved in object recognition. Moreover, my failure to token AARDVARK can be explained in psychological terms; for example, by appeal to the design of the object recognition system and the fact that I am not particularly interested in the arcane question to what species the creature before me belongs. In short, it isn't a *ceteris paribus* law that aardvarks cause tokenings of AARDVARK as it is perfectly possible for a person to perceive an aardvark and not token AARDVARK in response without there being any breakdown in the operative idealizations of psychology. Thus, Fodor's theory doesn't explain why AARDVARK means aardvark. A parallel argument can be applied to many other simple, non-logical symbols of LOT with the consequence that Fodor's theory of content does not generally apply to human intentional states.[14]

Not all mind–world causal transactions are cognitively penetrable in the way that object recognition is. For example, many of the processes that take place in the early stages of visual perception are in no way influenced by our intentional states. As such processes involve the production and manipulation of representations or symbols there are, presumably, laws relating external stimuli to the tokening of such symbols. This raises the possibility that Fodor's theory applies to such symbols and, thus, that it accounts for the content of our visual states. However, there is reason to believe that in the case of such visual states, the asymmetric dependence condition of Fodor's theory is not satisfied.

One of the tasks of the visual system is to determine the colour of objects impinging on the individual. When an individual tokens a retinal image, implicit in that image is information concerning the colour of the object(s) impinging upon her visual system. This information is extracted and made explicit by the processes of early vision. In order to extract this information, the visual system must make all sorts of assumptions concerning how various colours affect the visual system or show up in the retinal image. These assumptions are hard-wired into the visual system and are such that, for example, red objects usually cause a tokening of RED whenever they impinge upon a human individual's visual system. Thus, it is a law that red objects cause tokenings of RED. However, these assumptions only apply within a narrow range of lighting conditions. Call those conditions C. Consequently, in certain alternative lighting conditions (call them C*) it is orange objects that cause tokenings of RED. Thus, it is a law that orange objects cause tokenings of RED (in C*) just as much as it is a law that red objects cause tokenings of RED (in C). In this case, it is difficult to see how the orange–RED connection could be broken without breaking the red–RED connection; it would appear that these connections stand and fall together. Given the nature of the human visual system and the laws of optics that hold in our world, orange objects cannot but cause tokenings of RED (in C*) if red objects cause tokenings of RED (in C). To break the former connection without breaking the latter would involve effecting substantial changes in the workings of the visual system or substantial changes in the laws of optics. Thus, the possible world where there is a red–RED connection but no orange–RED connection is at some distance from the actual world. It is far from clear that this possible world is nearer to the actual world than that where the orange–RED connection is broken by effecting changes that also bring down the red–RED connection. In short, it would appear that the orange–RED connection symmetrically depends (rather than asymmetrically depends) on the red–RED connection. Parallel arguments will apply to all symbols generated by cognitively impenetrable processes. Thus, Fodor's theory does not apply to such symbols.

It might be objected on Fodor's behalf that the argument of this section at best only establishes that Fodor's theory does not apply to human representational states. But, so the objection continues, Fodor's aim is only to specify a sufficient condition for content and such a condition need not be satisfied by any of our states. Hence, my objection is beside the point. In response I would say that, for the reasons that I outlined earlier in the chapter, it is a major limitation of Fodor's theory if it does not apply to human representational states. Moreover, I think there is a case that suggests that Fodor's theory doesn't even present a plausible sufficient condition for meaning.

Visual experiences, though they are to be distinguished from such intentional states as beliefs, are like beliefs in having content; our visual experiences serve to represent such salient properties of distal objects as their shape, size, colour, spatial relation to us and so on. The question arises why our visual experiences have the contents that they do. Our visual experiences play an important role in determining how we act when we attempt to navigate the external world and manipulate the objects that populate that world. It is my contention that the informational theory is particularly implausible when applied to visual experiences as it finds no place for the behavioural ramifications of visual experiences in determining their content. Hence, I prefer a theory according to which the content of such experiences is largely a product of the manner in which they influence our behaviour when we attempt to interact with the external world. (For further details see Cain 2000.)

Consider the following case. I and I* are two creatures belonging to different species. There is a type of visual experience (call it V) that I is capable of tokening and which satisfies Fodor's sufficient condition for meaning *square*. Similarly, there is a type of visual experience that I* is capable of tokening (call it V*) that satisfies Fodor's sufficient condition for meaning *square*. However, V and V* have quite different causal powers with respect to the behaviour of the creatures that token them. Whenever I tokens V and, taking that experience at face value, attempts to interact with the object that caused it, he behaves in a way that would be an appropriate way to behave towards a square-shaped object. In short, tokenings of V play an important role in causing I to behave in a square-wise manner towards the distal objects that cause such tokenings. Whenever I* tokens V* and, taking that experience at face value, attempts to interact with the object that caused it, he behaves in a way that would be an appropriate way to behave towards a circular-shaped object. In other words, tokenings of V* play an important role in causing I* to behave in a circle-wise manner towards the distal objects that cause such tokenings. This is the case despite the fact that square-wise behaviour belongs to I*'s behavioural repertoire. Consequently, if a square-shaped object caused I* to token V* (as such objects are prone to do) then I* would subsequently behave towards that object in a maladaptive way. For example, if he tried to pick the object up he would be prone to drop it and if he tried to circumnavigate the object he would be prone to crash into it. In short, he would behave in such a way as to suggest to an onlooker that he misperceived the shape of the object before him. My contention is that, in virtue of this difference between the causal powers of V and V*, those experiences have quite different contents. V has the content *square* whereas V* has the content *circle*.[15] If I am correct in saying this then Fodor's sufficient condition is not sufficient after all. For, V* meets his condition for meaning *square* yet has no such content. How could V* mean *square* given that its tokenings cause I* to behave in a way that would be inappropriate with respect to a square-shaped object?

Conclusion

CTM alone is not sufficient to account for all of the salient properties of our intentional states. For CTM does not explain why our intentional states have the contents that they have or reveal how physical properties could generate semantic or intentional properties. Consequently, in order to construct a thoroughgoing physicalist vindication of folk psychology, Fodor needs to supplement CTM with a naturalistic theory of content. Fodor has risen to this challenge and has constructed a theory that takes the form of the specification of a sufficient condition for a simple, non-logical symbol of LOT to express a property. That condition appeals to mind–world causal laws and relations of asymmetric dependence holding between such laws. Fodor's theory is resolutely atomistic and I have attempted to defend his commitment to atomism. Moreover, I have argued that Fodor's theory can be defended against many objections that have been levelled against it. However, in the later stages of the chapter I have argued that there are reasons for doubting that Fodor's theory applies to the intentional states of human individuals and that the sufficient condition for content that he presents is in fact sufficient.

6

Individualism and Narrow Content

Introduction

A major debate in recent philosophy of mind has focused on a question concerning how psychology (be it folk or scientific psychology) classifies or individuates intentional states. The question is that of whether psychology individuates mental states in terms of properties that supervene on our intrinsic physical properties. The individualist argues for an affirmative answer to this question. The advocate of the opposing view – generally known as externalism – argues that the nature of the world external to the subject and her relations to that world plays an important non-causal role in determining what psychological properties she instantiates.

Fodor has been one of the most significant contributors to this debate. He has always accepted that folk psychology is externalist in nature, yet for many years he argued that scientific psychology is individualistic and that it must employ a notion of narrow content (that is, a kind of content that is exhaustively determined by our intrinsic physical properties). Thus, despite the fact that he regarded scientific psychology as a closely related refinement and extension of folk psychology, he held that there existed a major difference between the two. More recently, he has abandoned the view that scientific psychology is individualistic and that it must employ a notion of narrow content. In this chapter I will examine Fodor's arguments for individualism, his account of the nature of narrow content and the reasons for his change of heart.[1]

The Nature of the Issue

To get clear on the nature of the issue under discussion consider the following example. In my pocket I have a one pound coin, an object that is engaged in an ongoing process of causal interaction with the world external to it. This coin has certain intrinsic physical properties, for example, it has a particular molecular structure. Its possession of these properties is a matter of how it is in and of itself and is entirely independent of the nature of the external world and its relations to that world.[2] Such intrinsic properties are to be contrasted with certain other physical properties that my coin has; for example, the properties of being located ten kilometres from Trafalgar Square and of being heavier than the pebble resting on my desk. These properties are relational properties; my coin has them in virtue of the nature of certain objects external to it and its relations to those objects. Now consider the property of being a one pound coin. This is not a physical property of my coin – a fortiori, not one of its intrinsic physical properties – as it is not recognized by the science of physics. Nevertheless, it is an important property salient in economics and everyday commerce. Is my coin a one pound coin solely in virtue of its intrinsic physical properties or, alternatively, partly in virtue of the nature of the external world and its relations to it? In other words, does the property of being a one pound coin belong to a family of properties that supervene upon the intrinsic physical properties of the objects that instantiate them?[3] If such a supervenience relationship does hold then anything that is a physical duplicate of my coin (and therefore has just the same intrinsic physical properties) will also be a one pound coin. It is clearly possible for my coin to have a physical duplicate that is not itself a one pound coin. For example, imagine a member of an isolated Amazonian tribe who manufactured an object physically just like my coin for the purpose of ornamentation, an object that is neither used to facilitate the exchange of goods and services nor was made with the intention of so being used. Surely this object would not be a one pound coin. Therefore, such economic properties as being a one pound coin do not supervene upon the intrinsic physical properties of objects that instantiate them. If something is a one pound coin then it is so partly in virtue of the nature of the external world and its relations to that world. More specifically, in virtue of being embedded in a complex network of social and economic practices, being used with certain aims in mind and having a particular casual origin (that is, the kind of origin that counterfeit coins do not have).

Are the properties in terms of which psychology individuates our intentional states like that of being a one pound coin in the respect that they fail to supervene on our intrinsic physical properties? If so, then the relationship between the mind and the external world is more than a mere causal relationship; the nature of the external world and our relations to it will enter into the very nature of our intentional states as viewed from the perspective of psychology. The individualist answers this question in the negative. As Tyler Burge characterizes it, individualism is the doctrine that 'the mental natures of all a person's or animal's mental states (and events) are such that there is no necessary or deep individuative relation between the individual's being in states of those kinds and the nature of the individual's physical or social environments' (1986: 3–4). Strictly speaking, the individualist need not endorse the claim that a subject's psychological properties supervene upon her intrinsic physical properties. For like Descartes, who is often held up as a paradigmatic individualist, she can endorse substance dualism and conceive of the mind as being a non-physical entity the nature of whose states are independent of the external world. However, few contemporary philosophers find substance dualism tenable and so, as a matter of fact, the supervenience claim is central to the position of the contemporary individualist.

Individualism and Folk Psychology

Individualism implies that individuals who are physical duplicates will be psychologically alike no matter how much their respective home environments diverge. Consequently, a popular externalist tactic is to construct a twin scenario, that is, a thought experiment involving a pair of physical duplicates who inhabit divergent environments, and then to argue that the protagonists of this scenario differ with respect to their intentional states. There are two famous twin scenarios that are widely taken to establish that folk psychology individuates non-individualistically. The first twin scenario is inspired by Putnam's (1975b) attempt to establish that 'meanings ain't in the head'. In a distant galaxy there is a planet called Twin Earth that is very much like our own planet. On Twin Earth there is a community of individuals who speak a language very much like English, a community that has a member – call him Oscar2 –

who is a physical duplicate of Oscar, a fellow who lives here on Earth. Members of both these linguistic communities apply the word 'water' to the local colourless, odourless liquid that falls as rain, fills their rivers and streams, quenches their thirst and so on, and intend to apply that word only to stuff that has the same physical microstructure as the local 'water'. One significant difference between Earth and Twin Earth is that the stuff they call 'water' on Twin Earth – the colourless, odourless liquid that fills their rivers and lakes, falls as rain, quenches their thirst and so on – has a physical microstructure that differs from that of the stuff that we call 'water'. For it is XYZ rather than H_2O. In virtue of this difference the English word 'water' has a different extension from that of the Twin English word 'water'; H_2O, and only H_2O, falls within the extension of the former whereas XYZ, and only XYZ, falls within the extension of the latter. Similarly, English sentences containing the word 'water' have different truth conditions from their Twin English counterparts. For example, the English sentence 'water is wet' is true if and only if H_2O is wet whereas the corresponding Twin English sentence is true if and only if XYZ is wet. Due to this difference of extension and truth conditions, the word 'water' has one meaning on Earth and quite another on Twin Earth. And an upshot of this is that the twins, being fully fledged members of their respective linguistic communities, mean different things by the word 'water' (or understand that word differently) despite their physical identity. This leads Putnam to conclude that the meaning of a natural kind word on an individual's lips is partly determined by the nature of the external world that she inhabits.

Putnam was primarily concerned with linguistic meaning but his argument can easily be extended to generate the conclusion that folk psychology individuates thoughts involving natural kind concepts non-individualistically. Here is how such an extension might run. We use language to express our thoughts. For example, Oscar uses the sentence 'water is wet' to express one of his beliefs. Reflecting the linguistic case, due to the nature of his home environment, this belief is about H_2O and is true if and only if H_2O is wet. Similarly, the belief that Oscar2 expresses with the sentence 'water is wet' is about XYZ and is true if and only if XYZ is wet. Due to this difference in extension and truth conditions, Oscar's 'water' thoughts differ in content from those of his twin. And as folk psychology individuates intentional states partly in terms of their content, from the perspective of folk psychology, the twins diverge in their intentional states.

The second argument for the claim that folk psychology is non-individualistic was developed by Tyler Burge (1979) and has the advantage of being nowhere near as outlandish as the Putnam-inspired argument. It is also more general as it applies not just to intentional states involving natural kind concepts. Burge proceeds by describing an individual who has beliefs involving a concept that he only partly understands. He then describes a counterfactual situation in which the individual is physically just as he is in the actual world but in which his social environment is somewhat different. Burge argues that the actual thoughts involving the concept that the individual doesn't fully understand diverge in content from the corresponding counterfactual thoughts and thus that, from the point of view of folk psychology, the actual individual has thoughts that differ in content from those of his counterfactual self.

More specifically, here is one of the cases that Burge presents and takes to be conclusive. An individual has a collection of arthritis beliefs; that is, beliefs 'attributed with content clauses containing "arthritis" in oblique occurrence' (1979: 77). Many of these beliefs are true, for example, that he has had arthritis for years, that stiffening joints is a symptom of arthritis, that certain sorts of aches are characteristic of arthritis and so on. He also has the false belief that he has arthritis in his thigh as he doesn't know that arthritis is, by definition, an inflammation of the joints and that you can't develop it in your thigh.

Burge describes a counterfactual situation in which the individual is physically just as he is in the actual situation. In this counterfactual situation linguistic practices are such that the word 'arthritis' is typically applied, and defined to apply, to rheumatoid conditions both of the joints and outside the joints. In other words, in the counterfactual situation the word 'arthritis' does not mean *arthritis*. Burge argues that due to this fact about linguistic practices in his home environment, the individual in the counterfactual situation 'lacks some – probably all – of the attitudes commonly attributed with content clauses containing "arthritis" in oblique occurrence' (1979: 78). He concludes that:

> The upshot of these reflections is that the patient's mental contents differ while his entire physical and non-intentional mental histories, considered in isolation from their social context, remain the same. . . . The differences seem to stem from differences 'outside' the patient considered as an isolated physical organism, causal mechanism or seat of consciousness. The difference in his mental contents is attrib-

utable to differences in his social environment . . . such differences are ordinarily taken to spell differences in mental states and events. (1979: 79)

In short then, we have a case of physical identity, yet, from the point of view of folk psychology, mental divergence. Hence, folk psychology individuates mental states non-individualistically.[4]

Putnam's and Burge's arguments are widely taken[5] as being decisive, but from the fact that folk psychology is non-individualistic, it doesn't follow that scientific psychology is non-individualistic. There might be a mismatch between their respective taxonomies due to a divergence in their theoretical assumptions or their explanatory ambitions. Indeed, Fodor takes the Putnam and Burge arguments to be decisive, but for many years held that scientific psychology is individualistic and that, in so far as it individuates mental states in terms of their content, must appeal to a kind of content – namely narrow content – that is locally supervenient. We can now turn to Fodor's arguments for the claim that scientific psychology is individualistic.

Individualism and the Computational Theory of Mind

Fodor has presented arguments for the conclusion that scientific psychology individuates intentional states individualistically that might be labelled 'arguments from the computational theory of mind'. According to such arguments, scientific psychology is committed to CTM and – given the nature of computation – this commitment entails that it is individualistic.

The first such argument is presented in 'Methodological Solipsism Considered as a Research Strategy in Cognitive Psychology' (1980). Methodological solipsism is an approach in psychology that considers the individual in isolation from her environment, attempting to describe her internal mental life in such a way that makes no assumptions about the nature of the external world. In ignoring the individual's environment and making no assumptions about its nature, such a psychology must describe and individuate intentional states in terms of properties that supervene on the individual's intrinsic properties. Assuming the truth of physicalism, a methodologically solipsistic psychology would therefore individuate intentional states in terms of properties that supervene upon the intrinsic physical properties of the subjects that fell within its domain of enquiry.

Fodor argues that contemporary cognitive psychology is methodologically solipsistic and thus, in virtue of its physicalist predilections, individuates in such a way as to respect the local supervenience of the mental on the physical. His reasoning runs thus. Cognitive psychology is committed to CTM. Now computers only have access to the formal or syntactic properties of the symbols that they manipulate, being blind to their semantic properties (which are determined by features of the world external to the computer). Consequently, cognitive psychology is committed to the idea that intentional processes only have access to the formal or syntactic properties of the representations that they manipulate; in other words, it endorses the formality condition. This endorsement of the formality condition entails that the concern of cognitive psychology is to 'study mental processes *qua* formal operations on symbols' (1980: 232) and thus, that it will ignore the semantic properties of mental representations and states individuating such representations and states in terms of their formal or syntactic properties. In the case of physically realized computers, such properties supervene on their intrinsic physical properties so that physically identical computers will be formally or syntactically identical. In short, cognitive psychology, in studying and attempting to characterize the computational processes executed by the mind–brain, will consider the individual in isolation from the environment and will individuate mental representations and states formally or syntactically and, therefore, individualistically.

It is important to realize that Fodor is not denying that mental representations and states have semantic or intentional properties, nor that there are intentional laws that are implemented by the computational mechanisms that cognitive psychologists seek to describe. Indeed, he recognizes the legitimacy of a rich tradition in scientific psychology that is concerned with the intentional properties of our mental states, a tradition that he labels 'naturalistic psychology'. However, he thinks that cognitive psychology is not concerned with intentional properties and he doubts that naturalistic psychology will bear fruit until the completion of the rest of science.

As should be clear from chapters 2 and 3, I think that this account of the nature of cognitive psychology is mistaken. The aim of cognitive psychology is to account for such intentionally characterized cognitive capacities as our ability to find out about the nature of the external world by means of perception, categorize objects, recognize faces, recall past events, solve problems, understand the utterances of our fellows and so on. Assuming CTM, part of the task of accounting for such capacities involves describing the computational mechanisms that underlie their exercise in syntactic terms. But such mechanisms are able to support cognition only because they solve appropriate information-processing problems. Moreover, as we saw in connection with Marr's theory of vision, that they are able to solve such problems depends upon contingent features of the external world. Consequently, a putative explanation of a cognitive capacity that merely characterized the computational processing (*qua* formal symbol manipulation) that underlay that capacity would not constitute a full explanation of the capacity in question. A complete explanation must characterize the information generated by the computational mechanisms (and thus attribute contents to the symbols so manipulated) plus those contingent features of the world that enable the information to be generated in the way that it is. Therefore, cognitive psychology can hardly be methodologically solipsistic in the manner described by Fodor. It must be stressed that none of this implies that cognitive psychology individuates intentional states non-individualistically. For it is consistent with all that I have said that the contents that cognitive psychology attributes to our intentional states are narrow.

A somewhat different argument for the conclusion that a scientific psychology committed to CTM is thereby individualistic is described by Fodor in *The Elm and the Expert* (1994a).[6] The argument runs as follows. Higher-level laws are implemented by lower-level mechanisms. For a higher-level law of the form 'Fs cause Gs' to be implemented by the lower-level mechanism that MFs cause MGs (where MF and MG are micro-properties that realize, respectively, F and G) it must be the case that the instantiation of the property F is sufficient for the instantiation of MF and that the instantiation of the property MG is sufficient for the instantiation of G. A scientific psychology committed to CTM holds that intentional laws are implemented by computational mechanisms. Given the general nature of the implementation relation, this implies both that there are computationally sufficient conditions for the instantiation of intentional properties and that there are intentionally sufficient conditions for the instantiation of computational properties. But this requirement isn't satisfied where the intentional properties in question are broad (that is, are such as not to supervene upon our intrinsic physical properties). For example, having a token of the LOT symbol WATER

IS WET in one's belief box is not sufficient for believing that water is wet, as is established by Putnam's Twin Earth scenario. This case shows that instantiating a computational property is not sufficient for instantiating a broad intentional property. Moreover, there are cases that show that instantiating a broad intentional property is not sufficient for instantiating a computational property. A representation of the form 'a is F' will have the same truth conditions (and hence, the same broad content) as a representation of the form 'b is F' whenever a and b are numerically identical (as are the Morning Star and the Evening Star, and Jocasta and Oedipus' mother, to pick two familiar examples). Consequently, in such cases – cases that Fodor labels 'Frege cases' – believing that a is F is not sufficient for tokening the LOT symbol 'a is F' as the broad content of the belief in question could equally be expressed by the LOT symbol 'b is F'. This is not merely a case where a higher-level property is multiply realizable. For, as Fodor stresses in 'Methodological Solipsism' (1980), the psychological ramifications of an intentional state – and, therefore, the laws that it enters into – depend crucially on how the referent of the state is represented. For example, if Oedipus represents Jocasta as MOTHER then his belief that he has married that woman will have quite different mental effects than if he had represented her as JOCASTA.

The upshot of the above considerations, the argument concludes, is that computational mechanisms can implement intentional laws only if those laws are narrow; that is, only if those laws appeal to intentional properties that are locally supervenient. Consequently, a scientific psychology that is both intentional and committed to CTM must employ a notion of narrow content.

I will discuss this argument below in the context of a consideration of Fodor's abandonment of individualism. For now, I will restrict myself to raising the following doubts. With respect to the point that the instantiation of computational properties is not sufficient for the instantiation of broad intentional properties, one might wonder whether Fodor is overestimating the demands made by the implementation relation. Perhaps all that is required is that there be context- or environment-relative computationally sufficient conditions. Consider a community of creatures who are embedded in a particular environment that is such that instantiating a particular computational property in that environment is sufficient for instantiating a particular broad intentional property. For example, we are embedded in an environment such that tokening WATER in our belief box whilst embedded in that environment is sufficient for having a water belief. Why wouldn't it be the case that the broad intentional laws governing the mental lives of these creatures were implemented by computational mechanisms whose ability to implement the intentional laws in question depended upon the details of their environmental embedding?

What about the claim that the instantiation of broad intentional properties is not sufficient for the instantiation of computational properties and that tokens of one and the same broad intentional state can have quite different causal ramifications? The point might be made that Fodor is unfairly assuming that the advocate of broad intentional psychology is compelled to individuate intentional contents solely in terms of truth conditions. But can't she argue that although truth conditions are an important component of the content of our intentional states, they are not the only component? In short, can't she appeal to something like Fregean senses to distinguish between broad thoughts involving co-referential concepts?

The Argument from Causal Powers

Arguments for and against individualism fall into one of two distinct categories. On the one hand, there are arguments that rely heavily on quite specific claims about the theoretical commitments, practices and explanatory ambitions of contemporary scientific psychology.[7] On the other hand, there are those of a metaphysical or a priori nature. Such arguments appeal to considerations concerning the nature of causation, laws and scientific explanation in general. Perhaps it is not clear to which of these categories the above-described Fodorian arguments belong. However, there can be no doubt that Fodor's most prominent argument for individualism belongs to the metaphysical or a priori category. This argument first appeared in *Psychosemantics* (1987) and is supplemented by the paper 'A Modal Argument for Narrow Content' (1991a). It can be labelled the argument from causal powers and can be described in the following terms.

A primary aim of science is to construct causal explanations. Constructing a causal explanation involves subsuming events under a causal law. For example, explaining why an event e_2 occurred involves specifying a prior event e_1 and a law to the effect that events of type E_1 (that is, the type to which e_1 belongs) cause events of type E_2 (that is, the type to which e_2 belongs). Such causal laws 'subsume the things they apply to in virtue of the causal properties of the things that they apply to' (1987: 34).[8] Fodor argues that this fact has consequences for the way that sciences individuate the phenomena that fall within their domain of enquiry: sciences must individuate phenomena in terms of their causal powers. Thus, a science will allot distinct token phenomena to the same type if and only if they are relevantly similar in their causal powers. Similarly, a property will be taxonomic in a science only if it affects the causal powers of whatever has it. It follows from this that scientific psychology must individuate in terms of causal powers. This entails that scientific psychology must individuate intentional states individualistically as the intentional states of physical duplicates will be equivalent in their causal powers; such properties that distinguish between physical twins do not affect the causal powers of their intentional states and so have no place in a scientific taxonomy.

As it stands, this argument is hardly conclusive. On the one hand, one might question the premiss that science must always individuate in terms of causal powers. On the other, one might argue that the intentional states of physical twins do not always agree in their causal powers. Fodor invests a good deal of energy into defeating the second of these potential lines of objection, and it is here that the power and interest of reflections lie. Before examining that line of thought, some comments on the plausibility of the claim that science individuates in terms of causal powers are in order.

Fodor's claim that sciences individuate in terms of causal powers has not won universal acceptance.[9] Nevertheless, Fodor's claim has considerable intuitive plausibility and it is not difficult to appreciate why he takes it to be self-evidently true. A major aim of science is to uncover causal laws and produce illuminating causal explanations. And, one might wonder, how could a putative science that failed to individuate the phenomena falling within its domain of enquiry in terms of their causal powers capture the causal laws operating within that domain or produce illuminating causal explanations? For one thing, as it would classify phenomena in a manner that cross-cut their causal powers, any given type would include members whose behaviour was governed by a battery of distinct causal laws. It would have great difficulty expressing any of these causal laws, as it would not recognize the properties that featured in them and thus would not have the appropriate vocabulary. Moreover, although the putative science could produce true singular causal statements, such statements would fail to specify the property of the cause in virtue of which it brought about the effect. For example, suppose that the statement 'the event that took place in

Cain's kitchen at 3.00 p.m. caused the water to boil' is true. This statement does not constitute an illuminating explanation of the water's boiling; it leaves it a mystery why that event caused the effect that it happened to cause. A much better explanation would describe the cause as a heating of a sample of water to 100° Celsius. For, given that it is a law that heating a sample of water to 100° Celsius will cause it to boil, it is in virtue of being such an event that the cause causes the boiling. (Davidson 1967.) In short, the putative science runs the risk of being unable to produce illuminating causal explanations.

Suppose that we concede the point that sciences generally individuate in terms of causal powers. What reasons does Fodor give us for concluding that the causal powers of our intentional states are locally supervenient so that the intentional states of twins will agree in their causal powers no matter how much their local environments diverge? Fodor is not claiming that objects that are physical duplicates always agree in their causal powers. For example, he points out that the property of being a planet affects the causal powers of whatever instantiates it: 'whether you are a planet affects your trajectory, and your trajectory determines what you can bump into; so whether you're a planet affects your causal powers' (1987: 43). In order to be a planet one has to be an unsupported body orbiting a star. Consequently, as Fodor concedes, a planet could have a physical duplicate that was not a planet (suppose the duplicate was a stationary chunk of matter resting on the surface of a much larger chunk of matter that was a planet). But a point to notice about a planet and its non-planet twin is that the former is subject to proximal forces (for example, gravitational pull) that the latter is not, a difference that makes their divergence in causal powers intelligible and explicable. In the case of Putnamian twins, the difference between their respective home environments is not such that their outer surfaces are subject to physically divergent impingements. As we shall see, this point is closely related to one of Fodor's main reasons for denying that twins could have mental states that diverged in their causal powers.

The Putnamian twins might appear to constitute a problem for Fodor for the following reason. Suppose that a thirsty Oscar forms a desire for a glass of water. This causes him to engage in behaviour that eventuates in his acquiring some H_2O. The corresponding desire of Oscar2 causes him to behave in a manner that results in his getting XYZ rather than H_2O. Fodor responds to such putative counter-examples to his position by making an important point about the nature of causal powers. Something can have a particular causal power without ever exercising that power. For example, an aspirin tablet could have the power to ease pain even though it was never ingested and thus never eased a single pain. All that is required is that it be the case that were the aspirin ingested, or had it been ingested by an individual in pain, then it would have eased their pain. Consequently, when determining whether or not something has a particular causal power, it is necessary to consider not merely the effects that it has actually caused, but the effects that it would have caused in certain counterfactual circumstances. It follows from this that 'identity of causal powers has to be assessed *across* contexts not *within* contexts' (1987: 35). Thus, when determining whether the mental states of Oscar and Oscar2 have the same causal powers, it is necessary to consider not just the effects that their respective states actually caused, but the effects that they would have caused in certain counterfactual circumstances. When we take into account the relevant counterfactuals we see that we do not have a case of a divergence in causal powers: were Oscar2 located on Earth (that is, in Oscar's context) his desire would have landed him with H_2O and were Oscar located on Twin Earth (that is, in Oscar2's context) his desire would have landed him with XYZ.

The above reply is decisive, but the Putnamian twins present Fodor with a far more substantial problem. Intentional states routinely cause both intentional states and behaviour. Such effects have intentional properties. The intentional and behavioural effects of Oscar's water thoughts differ in their intentional properties from the corresponding effects of Oscar2's twater thoughts (that is, his twin-water thoughts, his thoughts about XYZ). For example, Oscar's desire for water causes him to form an intention to get a glass of water and to engage in water-seeking behaviour, whereas Oscar2's desire for twater causes him to form an intention to get a glass of twater and to engage in twater-seeking behaviour. What this suggests is that Oscar's water thoughts diverge in their causal powers from Oscar2's twater thoughts, as the former have the power to cause water thoughts and behaviour, a power that the latter do not have. Similarly, Oscar2's twater thoughts have a power that Oscar's water thoughts do not have, namely, the power to cause twater thoughts and behaviour.

Application of the cross-context test does nothing to unseat this conclusion, for were Oscar transported to Twin Earth his water thoughts would remain water thoughts and the behaviour that they caused would still be water behaviour. The corresponding point holds true of Oscar2. As scientific psychology is concerned with explaining behaviour and the tokening of intentional states, it seems reasonable to conclude that this difference in causal powers is one that scientific psychology should care about, and thus that it should assign Oscar's water thoughts to a different psychological type from Oscar2's twater thoughts.

Fodor will have none of this and puts a lot of effort into defeating this putative counter-example to his individualist thesis. Essentially, he has two arguments for the conclusion that the intentional states of the Putnamian twins agree in their causal powers. The first appears in *Psychosemantics* (1987) and the second in 'A Modal Argument for Narrow Content' (1991a). I will discuss these arguments in turn.

Fodor introduces a pair of properties that clearly don't count in any scientific taxonomy. The properties in question are that of being an H-particle and that of being a T-particle. A physical particle is an H-particle at time t if and only if Fodor's dime is heads up at t. Similarly, a physical particle is a T-particle if and only if Fodor's dime is tails up at t. If Fodor flips his dime from being heads up to being tails up, then every particle in the universe will change from being an H-particle to being a T-particle. Do H-particles and T-particles differ in their causal powers? There is certainly a difference between these two types of particles as H-particles enter into H-particle interactions, something that T-particles do not. However, Fodor thinks, this difference does not make for a difference in causal powers for the following reason. For the causal powers of a particle to depend upon the orientation of Fodor's dime, there would have to be a causal mechanism or a fundamental law of nature to mediate that dependency. But there aren't any such mechanisms or laws; the orientation of Fodor's dime is not capable of affecting every physical particle in the universe. In short, to claim that the property of being an H-particle or that of being a T-property affects causal powers is to postulate 'crazy causal mechanisms' or 'impossible laws'.

To hold that the intentional states of the Putnamian twins differed in their causal powers would involve postulating crazy causal mechanisms or impossible causal laws. If the intentional states of the twins differed in their causal powers, then the causal powers of such states would depend upon the character of the environment in which the individual who had them resided. For there to be such a dependency relationship there would have to be some mediating mechanism that enabled the character of an individual's environment to affect the causal powers of his intentional states without affecting his physiology.

> But there is no such mechanism; you *can't* affect the causal powers of a person's mental states without affecting his physiology. That's not a conceptual claim or a metaphysical claim, of course. It's a contingent fact about how God made the world. God made the world such that the mechanisms by which environmental variables affect organic behaviours run via their effects on the organism's nervous system, or so, at least, all the physiologists I know assure me. (1987: 40)

As it stands I don't think that this argument is entirely convincing. It is far from clear that to claim that the mental states of the Putnamian twins diverge in their causal powers is thereby to commit oneself to the existence of the kind of causal mechanisms and laws that Fodor finds 'crazy and impossible'. To have a particular causal power, an object must have the ability to produce events of a type that count as exercises of the power in question. And this requires that there are possible worlds close to the actual world where the object causes such an event. For example, to be a painkiller, a tablet need not actually ease anyone's pain. But it must cause an easing of pain in the nearby possible worlds where it is ingested by an individual who is in pain. For the externalist, there are causal powers that are such that their exercise involves causing an event that has certain relational properties. The nature of these powers is such that to possess them an object's environment must be, so to speak, amenable. Consider the power to engage in water behaviour. This power is such that an individual who was not embedded in a watery world would not be capable of executing water behaviour, that is, the type of behaviour that constitutes an exercise of this power. For there is no nearby possible world where any of her behaviour has the relational property of being water behaviour.

If such externalist causal powers are genuine causal powers, then there are two distinct ways in which the nature of an object's environment can affect its causal powers. The first way is causal. For example, an iron bar might become magnetic in virtue of its proximity to a magnet. This is a case where facts about the iron bar's environment and it relations to that environment cause it to acquire the power of being magnetic. The second way is constitutive rather than causal. The nature of an externalist causal power is such that to have that power one must be embedded in an appropriate environment. If an object is not so embedded, then none of its actual effects, or the effects that it produces in nearby possible worlds, will have the relational properties necessary to count as an exercise of the power in question. This enables us to make perfect sense of how two objects that were identical in respect of their intrinsic physical properties could diverge in their externalist causal powers in virtue of differences between their respective home environments or their relations to that environment.

What the above implies is that the kind of dependency relationship between the environment and the causal powers of intentional states that the externalist envisages in claiming that Oscar and Oscar2 have intentional states with divergent causal powers is a constitutive rather than a causal relationship. Being non-causal, the existence of such a dependency relationship does not require mediation by the kinds of causal mechanisms and laws that Fodor describes as 'crazy and impossible'. In short, Fodor saddles his opponent with a commitment that she does not make.

It might be argued that there is something illegitimate about externalist causal powers; either that they are not genuine causal powers or that they shouldn't be recognized by a bona fide science. However, Fodor has produced no such argument. Of course, many of the causal powers that science cares about are locally supervenient, magnetism and solubility being salient examples. But nothing about science in general can be read off from this fact. As Fodor points out, sciences employ non-equivalent taxonomic schemes and often cross-classify phenomena, as the causal powers that matter for individuation will differ from one science to the next. So why isn't it possible that some higher-level sciences, especially those concerned with intentional phenomena, legitimately recognize externalist causal powers?

A related point is that it is not an inevitable part of the externalist's position that changes in an individual's environment will bring about changes in the causal powers of her mental states (Davies 1986). Indeed, the standard view of the Putnamian twins is that were Oscar to be transported to Twin Earth, the content of his water thoughts and behaviour would remain unaffected. However, it has to be conceded that it is also widely held that if Oscar remained on Twin Earth for a considerable period of time (a period during which he interacted with an awful lot of XYZ) then his water thoughts would eventually become twater thoughts. And it is not inconceivable that at a point in time after this change he could be a physical duplicate of one of his previous selves whose thoughts were water – rather than twater – thoughts.

Once again, this possibility does not land the externalist with a commitment to any 'crazy causal mechanisms or impossible laws'. I take it that the intuition driving Fodor is that causation is local. That is, for a physically constituted event to cause a physically constituted event that is at a considerable distance from it, the cause must set off a chain of physically constituted events each member of which is contiguous to its immediate cause and to its immediate effect. This intuition is certainly plausible and widely held, but it has no relevance to the case under discussion. Suppose that we accept that a change in an individual's environment can cause a change in the causal powers of her mental states without having any effect on her intrinsic physical properties. The point to note is that the effect of this causal process is not constituted by a physical movement of the individual's body or by a physical change within her body. Consequently, it is no great miracle that it took place without a prior physical change within her body; it wasn't the kind of event that required such a cause. If a particular causal power involves an ability to produce an event of a relationally individuated type, then it is perfectly intelligible how an object's possession of this causal power could be affected by a change in its relational properties without any change in its intrinsic physical properties.[10]

How are we to square all this with the commitments of Fodor's physiologist friends? As we have seen, the externalist need not endorse the possibility that an environmental event can cause a subject to execute behaviour involving a bodily movement without causing a prior event in her nervous system. Indeed, it is consistent with externalism that the physiologist is committed to the claim that the causal powers of our internal states are locally supervenient. Physiology is concerned with our internal states *qua* physiological states and not *qua* psychological states even though the former often constitute the latter. If this were not the case then physiology and psychology could hardly be distinct sciences. Physiology is not particularly concerned with the intentional properties of our internal states and behaviour (be those intentional properties broad or narrow). For example, it will not recognize the difference between an arm-raising done with the intention of hailing a taxicab and a physically identical movement done in order to stretch an aching limb. Similarly, it will not recognize the difference in causal powers between Oscar's water thoughts and his twater thoughts. But nothing about the causal powers of our internal states *qua* psychological states follows from this and a psychologist who drew a distinction between the intentional states of the twins would not be casting any aspersions on the individuative practices of her physiologist colleagues.

What is the externalist to say about H-particles and T-particles? Do they differ in their causal powers? The externalist has two options. The first is to bite the bullet and concede that H-particles differ in their causal powers from T-particles. To make this concession is not necessarily to imply that the property of being an H-particle and that of being a T-particle should figure in the taxonomy of any science. For they could affect causal powers but not in a way that is relevant to any science. However, there is a problem with this line of thought. If the properties are not relevant to any science then presumably there are no laws governing the behaviour of H-particles *qua* H-particles (or T-particles *qua* T-particles). In other words, the properties do not feature in any causal laws. But if they do not feature in any causal laws then how could they affect the causal powers of whatever has them?

The second option is to claim that H-particles and T-particles do not differ in their causal powers or, alternatively, that the properties do not affect causal powers. This necessitates finding some difference between the properties of being an H-particle and being a T-particle, on the one hand, and those of being a water thought and being a twater thought, on the other, that explains why the latter, but not the former, affect causal powers. There are grounds for optimism that such a difference can be found. Perhaps, ironically, Fodor's second argument for his thesis that the mental states of the Putnamian twins agree in the causal powers provides a valuable suggestion.

Fodor's second argument for his thesis that the intentional states of the Putnamian twins agree in their causal powers appears in 'A Modal Argument for Narrow Content' (1991a). Here he argues that the difference between the twins and their respective thoughts fails to meet a necessary condition for being a difference in causal powers. This is because there is a conceptual connection between, on the one hand, the difference between the twins and their thoughts and, on the other, the differences between the effects that they produce.

Fodor begins by describing a schema that the case of the Putnamian twins fits, a schema that he labels 'schema S'. Schema S is as follows. C1 and C2 are a pair of causes and E1 and E2 are their respective effects:

C1 differs from C2 in that C1 has cause property CP1 whereas C2 has cause property CP2.

E1 differs from E2 in that E1 has effect property EP1 and E2 has effect property EP2.

The difference between C1 and C2 is responsible for the difference between E1 and E2 in the sense that, if C1 had had CP2 rather than CP1, then E1 would have had EP2 rather than EP1; and if C2 had had CP1 rather than CP2, E2 would have had EP1 rather than EP2. (1991a: 9)

The twin case fits schema S in the following way. C1 is Oscar and C2 is Oscar2. CP1 is the property of being connected to water and CP2 is the property of being connected to twater. E1 and E2 are thoughts of, respectively, Oscar and Oscar2. EP1 is the property of being a water thought and EP2 is the property of being a twater thought. In other words, the difference between being connected to water and being connected to twater is responsible for the difference between having water thoughts and having twater thoughts. For Fodor's opponent, in virtue of the nature of his environmental embedding, Oscar has the power to think water thoughts, a power that his twin does not have.

Fodor argues that not every instance of schema S is a bona fide case of a divergence in causal powers. That is, not every instance of S is a case 'where the difference between having CP1 and having CP2 is a difference in causal powers in virtue of its responsibility for the difference between E1 and E2'. This raises the question whether the Putnamian twin case is a bona fide case of a difference in causal powers. In order to answer this question Fodor formulates a condition that he thinks that any instance of S must satisfy in order to be a bona fide case of a difference in causal powers.[11] He then argues that the twin case fails to satisfy this question and therefore does not count as a genuine counter-example to his individualist thesis.

The necessary condition that Fodor formulates (and labels 'condition C') is essentially this:

The difference between having CP1 and having CP2 is a difference in causal powers in virtue of its responsibility for the difference between having effects that have EP1 and having effects that have EP2 only when this difference between the effects is nonconceptually related to the difference between the causes.

Hence, if there is a conceptual relationship between having CP1 (rather than CP2) and having effects that have EP1 (rather than EP2) so that to have EP1 (rather than EP2) *just is* to be caused by something with CP1 (rather than CP2) then the necessary condition is not satisfied.

Fodor's justification for condition C is twofold. First, it is consistent with his intuitions in that the instances of S which he thinks are bona fide pass the test and those that he thinks are not fail the test. Thus we find him saying: 'My evidence for the acceptability of this condition will be largely that it sorts examples that I have just run through in an intuitively satisfactory way' (1991a: 12). For example, the following is an instance of schema S that Fodor takes to be non-bona fide that fails to satisfy condition C. The difference between Fodor's dime's being heads up and being tails up is responsible for the difference between every particle in the universe being an H-particle and every particle in the universe being a T-particle. This case fails to satisfy condition C 'because the connection between all the world's particles becoming H-particles at time t and my coin's being heads up at t is conceptual. To be an H-particle at t *just is* to be a particle at a time when my coin is heads up' (1991a: 19). And here is an instance of S that Fodor takes to be bona fide that does satisfy C. The difference between being a planet and not being one is responsible for the difference between having a Keplerian orbit and not having such an orbit. This case satisfies C 'because it is true and contingent that, if you have molecularly identical chunks of rock, one which is a planet and the other which is not, then ceteris paribus, the one which is a planet will have a Keplerian orbit, and ceteris paribus, the one which is not a planet will not' (1991a: 19).

The second justification for C is that it coheres with Humean considerations about the nature of causation. It is an important point of Hume's (1975) theory of causation that causal connections are contingent in the respect that if A causes B, then, in principle, A could have happened without being followed by B. Fodor thinks that this Humean idea implies that if a property affects a thing's causal powers then it is contingent that it does so. As he puts it, '[the] condition is motivated both by our intuitions about the examples and by the Humean consideration that causal powers are, after all, powers to enter into nonconceptual relations' (1991a: 24).

Fodor argues that the case of the Putnamian twins fails to satisfy condition C as there is a conceptual connection between the difference between Oscar and Oscar2 and the difference between the broad contents of their thoughts. He writes, 'it is conceptually necessary that if you are connected to water in the right way then you have water thoughts (rather than twater thoughts)' (1991a: 20), and that 'to have a water thought *just is* to have a thought that is connected to water in the right way' (1991a: 21). Therefore, he concludes, the Putnamian twin case doesn't constitute a counter-example to his individualism as Oscar and Oscar2 do not differ in their causal powers.

What are we to make of this argument? Again, I don't think that it is entirely convincing. I dare say that 'it is conceptually necessary that if you are connected to water in the right way then you have water thoughts (rather than twater thoughts)' and that 'to have a water thought *just is* to have a thought that is connected to water in the right way'. But this is because 'right way' is elliptical for 'in the way that makes your thoughts water thoughts'. In other words, the following sentence may well be conceptually necessary: if you are connected to water in the way that makes your thoughts water thoughts, then you have water thoughts (rather than twater thoughts). Nevertheless, there may still be a property that Oscar has (that his twin doesn't) that is responsible for his water thoughts being water thoughts and that isn't conceptually connected to that property of his water thoughts. Call the specific relation that Oscar bears to water that is responsible for his water thoughts being water thoughts R. Is it conceptually necessary that if one bears R to water then one will have water thoughts? Or alternatively, is it a conceptual truth that to have a water thought *just is* to have a thought that stands in relation R to water? It seems more plausible to say that the truths and necessities involved are metaphysical rather than conceptual.

A second objection has to do with the legitimacy of Fodor's invoking the notion of a conceptual connection. As we saw in chapter 5, a crucial premiss in Fodor's attack on conceptual role semantics (CRS) is his rejection of the analytic–synthetic distinction; if there was such a distinction then CRS would not inevitably lead to holism. But how can someone who rejects the analytic–synthetic distinction help himself to the notion of a conceptual connection? If 'there is no principled distinction between matters of meaning and matters of fact' (Fodor and LePore 1992, p. x) then how can there be a principled distinction between conceptual and non-conceptual connections? And if there is no such distinction, then how can Fodor appeal to the notion of a conceptual connection to defend his individualism?

It might be objected that regardless of whether Fodor can legitimately appeal to the notion of a conceptual connection, he has raised an important point. The idea that I have in mind is that scientific psychology must produce explanations, specify connections and appeal to generalizations that are contingently rather than conceptually true. Consequently, the property of being a water thought and that of being water behaviour cannot legitimately figure in the taxonomy of scientific psychology. For explanations that appeal to these properties will be conceptually rather than contingently true.

I think that there is a way of answering the above line of thought, and doing so in such a way as to reconcile the Humean intuitions that underlie it with an externalist position. There may well be a conceptual connection between water thoughts and water behaviour (in the sense that water behaviour *just is* behaviour that is caused by water thoughts) and it may well be conceptually true that my water thoughts cause water behaviour rather than twater behaviour. But that notwithstanding, the specific causal explanations that an externalist psychology would produce are contingent as would be the generalizations governing the behaviour of our water thoughts. To see this, consider the following. Suppose I switch on an empty kettle. Why did I do that? Because I wanted to boil some water and believed that the kettle was full of water. Surely that is a legitimate causal explanation. The connection between my specific thoughts and the behaviour that they caused is contingent as is the explanation of my behaviour. If you want to know why I am a nephew you can generate from your armchair the following explanation: because I have a parent with siblings. But the explanation as to why I switched on the empty kettle is nothing like that. My behaviour could have had just about any cause, and which cause it had (and, thus, how it is to be explained) is a matter for empirical investigation. Moreover, there is nothing necessary about the specific generalizations that govern my water thoughts. For we can conceive of creatures that are capable of having water thoughts whose water thoughts have quite different causal ramifications than those very thoughts do in us.[12] Therefore, one can assert that a scientific psychology can appeal to a specific water thought in order to explain specific mental and behavioural episodes, and can employ generalizations in which reference to such thoughts figure, without abandoning any Humean intuitions. Hence, although an appeal to Humean considerations may well undermine the scientific legitimacy of the property of being an H-particle, they give no grounds for the conclusion that scientific psychology should not recognize the property of being a water thought.[13]

Narrow Content

Assuming that folk psychology individuates at least some of our intentional states non-individualistically, the philosopher who thinks that scientific psychology is (or should be) individualistic has two options. The first option is to deny that intentional properties have any legitimate role in scientific psychological explanation. Stich (1978a, 1983) has famously taken this option by arguing that scientific psychology should be syntactic and should individuate intentional states in terms of their syntax rather than their semantics. However, this doesn't appear to be a very attractive option for two reasons. First, as we saw in chapter 3, the aim of scientific psychology is to account for our intentionally characterized capacities and it is far from clear how a purely syntactic psychology could account for such capacities. Second, as Fodor points out, there are psychological generalizations that a syntactic psychology cannot capture. These are generalizations involving content-equivalent thoughts that are syntactically different from one person to the next. Suppose that it is a true generalization that thirst causes an intention to drink water. I use the LOT symbol WATER to express the property of being water whereas you – who believe that water is Fang's favourite drink – tend to use the LOT symbol FANG'S FAVOURITE DRINK. Consequently, when my thirst causes me to form an intention to drink water, the syntactic process that takes place in my head will be quite different from that that takes place in your head when thirst causes you to intend to drink water. What these two processes have in common resides at the semantic level so that a syntactic psychology would miss an important generalization. (Fodor 1994a: 50–1.)

The second individualist option is to argue that scientific psychology should employ a notion of narrow content and individuate intentional states in terms of their narrow – as opposed to their broad – contents. But what exactly is narrow content? By definition, narrow content is a kind of content that is locally supervenient. Thus, it is shared by the thoughts of physical duplicates (for example, the Putnamian twins) and the narrow content of a thought is to be distinguished from its truth conditions. The problem facing the champion of narrow content is to give us a substantial and coherent account of what narrow content is. It is important that such an account tells us how individuals who are not physical duplicates can share a narrow thought. One popular tactic is to identify the narrow content of a thought with the causal role that it has in the individual's head. (See e.g. Loar 1981; Block 1986.) This view holds no appeal for Fodor as it inherits all of the problems that bedevil CRS in general. For example, on this account it is far from clear how distinct individuals who are not physical duplicates could share a narrow thought.

Fodor has developed his own distinctive account of the nature of narrow content.[14] According to him, narrow content is a function (in the mathematical sense) that has possible contexts as its arguments and broad contents (which Fodor equates with truth conditions) as its values. In other words, the narrow content of a thought is a function that maps contexts onto truth conditions. Therefore, to have a thought with a particular narrow content involves having a thought that instantiates the appropriate function from contexts to truth conditions. It might be helpful to consider a particular example. Oscar has a belief that he expresses with the words 'water is wet'. The context in which Oscar is embedded is an Earthly one and in that context his belief is true if and only if water (that is H_2O) is wet. But had Oscar's context been Twin Earth, then his belief would have had quite different truth conditions (it would have been true if and only if XYZ is wet). And in other possible contexts in which Oscar could have been embedded, his belief would have had quite different truth conditions. Thus, specifying the narrow content of Oscar's belief involves specifying the various truth conditions that it would have in various possible contexts. Notice that the belief that Oscar2 expresses with the words 'water is wet' instantiates the very same function from contexts to truth conditions. For example, although Oscar2's belief is true if and only if XYZ is wet, were he embedded in an Earthly context it would be true if and only if H_2O is wet. Similarly, although Oscar's belief is true if and only if H_2O is wet, were he embedded in a Twin-Earthly context, it would be true if and only if XYZ were wet. This account of the nature of narrow content implies (as it should do) that physical duplicates have thoughts with just the same narrow contents; unlike the CRS theory, it does not make it unintelligible how non-twins could share a narrow thought. (Fodor 1987, ch. 2.)

There are several features of Fodor's account of narrow content that are worth stressing. First, narrow content is distinct from syntax. A symbol of LOT of a given syntactic type could have a particular narrow content in one individual's head and a different narrow content in the head of another individual. And one and the same narrow content could be expressed by syntactically divergent LOT symbols in the heads of distinct individuals. Second, narrow content is to be distinguished from Fregean sense. For Frege, the reference of a symbol is determined by its sense; therefore, same sense, same reference. The same is not true of narrow content: Oscar's tokenings of WATER refer to H_2O whereas Oscar2's tokenings of the same symbol refer to XYZ. However, narrow content does determine reference relative to context: therefore, sameness of narrow content plus sameness of context equals sameness of reference. Third, Fodor accepts that, strictly speaking, narrow contents are inexpressible. Any attempt to use a sentence to express the narrow content of a thought will fail, as that sentence will be 'anchored' to a specific context, and thus will have some particular broad content. However, Fodor thinks, this does not rule out the possibility of specifying the narrow content of an individual's thought. This is because the psychologist can 'sneak up' on the narrow content of a thought by mentioning the sentence that has the broad content that the thought in question would have (or its narrow content would determine) if it were embedded in the psychologist's context. For example, I can specify the narrow content of the belief that Oscar2 expresses with the sentence 'water is wet' for, as used by me, that sentence has the same broad content that Oscar2's thought would have if he were embedded in my context. I can do this by saying that Oscar2 has a belief with the narrow content that determines the broad content *water is wet* in my context.

In chapter 5 we considered Fodor's attempt to construct a naturalistic theory of content. The aim of that theory is to account for the broad contents of our thoughts. On the face of it, a theory that appeals to mind–world causal connections is ill suited to account for any kind of content that is 'in the head'. This raises the question of whether Fodor is required to supplement his theory of content with another theory that naturalizes the narrow contents of our thoughts. The answer to this question is no. This is because of the close relationship between narrow content and broad content. As the narrow content of a thought is a matter of what broad contents it would have in the various possible contexts in which it could be tokened, once Fodor has naturalized broad content he has effectively naturalized narrow content. For example – and very crudely – my LOT symbol WATER has the narrow content that it has in virtue of the fact that my internal mechanisms are such that it would have the informational content *water* were I embedded in an Earthly context, the informational content *twater*, were I embedded on Twin Earth, and so on.

There are several problems associated with Fodor's account of the nature of narrow content. First, it is somewhat vague and unclear in the respect that Fodor gives us little indication of how contexts are to be individuated or what is involved in being embedded in a particular context. Second, there are going to be practical problems associated with determining and specifying the narrow contents of the thoughts of our fellows, especially those who are not our physical twins and are not embedded in our context. The addition and multiplication functions overlap in that they both map the arguments {2,2} onto the value {4}. If distinct narrow contents can overlap in the same way, then in order to determine the narrow content of a thought it will be necessary to do more than determine what broad content it would have were it embedded in one's own context, and Fodor's way of sneaking up on the narrow content of a thought isn't going to work. To see this consider an analogy. Suppose a machine computes a particular mathematical function. In order to determine which function it computes it wouldn't be enough to determine that for the arguments {2,2} it produced the value {4}, for knowing that wouldn't tell you whether it had computed the addition function or the multiplication function. Similarly, to say that the machine computes the value {4} for the arguments {2,2} isn't to specify any one particular function. For just the same reasons, to determine that Oscar2 has a thought that would have the same broad content that the sentence 'water is wet' has on my lips were he embedded in my context is not thereby to determine which function that thought instantiates. What will have been determined is consistent with Oscar2's having a thought with any of many distinct narrow contents and the description of the thought embedded in the previous sentence will not specify any particular narrow content. Consequently, a narrow psychology would have to do a lot more than Fodor would have us believe in order to determine and specify the narrow contents of the thoughts of the individuals that fell within the domain of its enquiry.

The practical difficulties of engaging in narrow psychology are obscured by the concentration on twins in the literature. If I have a physical twin then I can safely conclude that the narrow contents of his thoughts will be the same as those of my own thoughts. So, perhaps, I can find some way of specifying his narrow thoughts by mentioning my own broad thoughts. But how am I to proceed with respect to an individual who is neither my twin nor embedded in my context? It is far from obvious how I am to work out just what broad contents his thoughts would have were he embedded in my context.

Third, Fodor's account runs the risk of being too coarse-grained with respect to thoughts involving names. I believe that Fang is ferocious. I also believe that Vinnie is ferocious. These beliefs have different broad contents but it would appear that they have the same narrow content as they instantiate the same function from contexts to broad contents. Fang might have been named 'Vinnie': there is a possible world or context where Fang has that name. Similarly, there is a possible world where I am physically just as I am now but where my VINNIE thoughts are about Fang, a context where they are anchored to that dog. In other words, in the context where they are anchored to Vinnie, my VINNIE thoughts are about Vinnie, and in the context where they are anchored to Fang they are about Fang. Exactly the same is true of my FANG thoughts; although they are about Fang, were they anchored to Vinnie (as they could have been with me being physically just as I am now) they would have been about Vinnie. In other words, my belief that Fang is ferocious and my belief that Vinnie is ferocious have identical narrow contents on Fodor's account of the nature of narrow content. The fact that these beliefs differ in broad content is a product of their being embedded in different contexts rather than their having divergent narrow contents. This is a problem for Fodor's account of narrow content, as I do not think that scientific psychology either does or should assign these thoughts to the same psychological type. For they tend to have quite different causal ramifications; my belief that Fang is ferocious will tend to cause me to hide or flee when confronted by Fang, an effect that my belief that Vinnie is ferocious will not. These reflections lead to a related point concerning the role of representations that represent specific individuals in the exercise of our recognitional capacities.

The aim of scientific psychology is to account for our cognitive capacities. One such capacity is the familiar capacity to recognize individuals of our acquaintance. This capacity is manifested whenever an individual, confronted by someone she is acquainted with, forms a true belief to the effect that that person is before her. Such a capacity would appear to be broad in that its exercise involves tokening a belief that is both true and represents a particular person as being present. A standard way of accounting for such capacities involves appealing to representations that represent the observable properties (for example, the appearance) of specific individuals; that represent those individuals as having particular observable properties. The fact that these representations are about specific individuals and that they correctly represent those individuals as having certain properties is central to their ability to underpin and facilitate recognition. For example, consider the representation in my head that represents Fang as having a particular appearance. This representation plays an important role in enabling me to recognize Fang as Fang whenever I am confronted by that beast. If it represented the appearance of some other dog then I would end up mistakenly believing that that dog was before me when confronted by Fang. And if it misrepresented Fang then I would have a tendency to mistake other dogs for Fang or Fang for other dogs. Consequently, a psychological explanation of how I recognize Fang must appeal to representations that are characterized as correctly representing Fang as having a particular appearance. A narrow psychology that had no concern for such broad properties of representations as their reference and truth value would be unable to account for our familiar recognitional capacities. To merely specify the narrow content of my representations of Fang would make it a mystery how those representations enabled me to recognize Fang.

Recalling Fodor's argument from causal powers, the reflections of the preceding paragraph would appear to provide a plausible counter-example to Fodor's claim that the psychological states of physical twins will always agree in their causal powers. Suppose that I have a twin who inhabits a distant locality and has neither met nor heard about Fang. I have a capacity to recognize Fang, a capacity whose nature involves being disposed to believe that Fang is present whenever I am confronted by that dog. My twin has no such capacity. Call the representation that in me correctly represents Fang's appearance R. The representation corresponding to R in the head of my twin will represent the appearance of some other dog (namely, Fang2). Were my twin to meet Fang, he would mistakenly believe Fang to be Fang2 and what would explain his mistake would be Fang's similarity to some other dog that he knew. R in my head has a psychologically salient causal power: it enables me to recognize Fang. R in my twin's head has no such causal power as it does not carry any information about Fang's appearance. But what it does have is the power to enable him to recognize some other dog, namely, Fang2.

Fodor's Rejection of Narrow Content

In *The Elm and the Expert* (1994a) Fodor abandoned his commitment to individualism by announcing that scientific psychology need not be narrow. In this section I shall examine Fodor's reasons for this change of heart. Fodor didn't abandon individualism because he became less persuaded by the argument from causal powers or because he came to doubt the coherence of the notion of narrow content. Rather, he came to think that broad psychology is perfectly acceptable in terms of its predictive and explanatory power, a fact that makes narrow content superfluous. To appreciate the fine details of Fodor's reasoning it is necessary to get clear on an argument for individualism that – though closely related to the considerations discussed above – I have not as yet explicitly described.

Suppose that Oscar returns home from the pub after having several beers. He doesn't want a hangover and believes that an effective way of avoiding a hangover is to drink plenty of water. Consequently, he forms a desire to drink water, a desire that causes him to turn on a nearby tap and take a drink. Oscar2 also turns on a nearby tap and takes a drink but in his case the behaviour is caused by a collection of twater beliefs and desires. From the point of view of broad psychology, Oscar's behaviour and the mental causes of that behaviour are quite different from the corresponding behaviour and mental states of his twin. Therefore, broad psychology would regard the twins' mental life as being subsumed by different psychological generalizations and, accordingly, would offer divergent explanations of their drinking behaviour. However, this violates a powerful intuition that for the purposes of psychological explanation, Oscar's reasons for turning on the tap and drinking are just the same as Oscar2's reasons and, thus, that the respective causal transactions leading from mental states to behaviour are subsumed by one and the same generalization. In short, broad psychology misses important generalizations that subsume individuals inhabiting different environments. In other words, in virtue of being environment-specific, broad psychological generalizations are unacceptably parochial.[15]

In addition to twin cases, so the argument continues, there is another kind of case that undermines the explanatory and predictive value of the generalizations of broad psychology. These are the Frege cases. In Frege cases two individuals share a broad thought yet diverge with respect to the manner in which they represent the referent of their thought. That is to say, they employ different modes of presentation. Assuming CTM, this difference comes down to one of tokening distinct sentences of LOT that have the same broad contents in virtue of containing co-referential expressions. For example, suppose that you and I are standing at a bus stop attempting to get to Belsize Park. We both see a bus approaching, a vehicle that causes me to token the LOT sentence THE BUS TO BELSIZE PARK IS APPROACHING in my belief box. When you finally make out the number displayed on the bus, you token the LOT sentence THE 168 IS APPROACHING in your belief box. Given an identity relationship holding between the 168 and the bus that goes to Belsize Park, our respective LOT sentences contain co-referential expressions and have just the same broad content. Thus, we share a broad thought.

Frege cases cause problems for broad psychology as they act as counter-examples to broad generalizations thus undermining the predictive and explanatory value of those generalizations. Consider the prima facie plausible broad generalization that people try to avoid marrying their mother. Jocasta was Oedipus' mother but Oedipus was unaware of this fact. Oedipus enthusiastically tried to marry Jocasta (and succeeded) and thus constitutes a counter-example to this broad generalization. Therefore, one could not employ this generalization to explain or predict the behaviour of Oedipus or of anyone else who did not know the identity of their mother. Of course, most people know who their mother is, but it is commonplace for an individual to be ignorant of an important identity relationship. For any generalization proffered by the broad psychologist, there are bound to be such cases of ignorance that result in violations of the generalization in question.[16]

Twin and Frege cases pose no problems for narrow psychology. On the one hand, a narrow psychology is capable of capturing generalizations that subsume inhabitants of divergent environments, as it does not individuate thoughts in an environment-sensitive manner. On the other hand, narrow psychology draws a distinction between thinking that Fa and thinking that Fb when a = b and so can frame generalizations that are sensitive to how the individual represents the referents of her thoughts.

In *The Elm and the Expert* (1994a) Fodor argues that there are contingent mechanisms that prevent the proliferation of the kind of twin and Frege cases that would undermine broad psychology.

Given the existence of such mechanisms, the generalizations of broad psychology can be of considerable explanatory and predictive value, the above considerations notwithstanding. Therefore, there is no need for scientific psychology to 'go narrow'; in other words, narrow content is superfluous. But what are the mechanisms that prevent the proliferation of problematic twin and Frege cases?

First, consider twin cases. XYZ is nomologically impossible in that the laws of chemistry prevent anything that is not H_2O from being like water in the respects that XYZ is supposed to be like water. Therefore, the laws of chemistry rule out the occurrence of the kind of twin case that Putnam describes. This, thinks Fodor, has a bearing upon the relevance of the argument from casual powers. For a broad psychology that would draw a distinction between the mental states of Putnamian twins, were there any, will not fail to individuate in terms of causal powers if such twins are nomologically impossible.

Fodor accepts that not all twin cases are nomologically impossible. For example, he accepts the nomological possibility of what he refers to as 'the familiar story about jade and jadeite' (1994a: 30). This case can be described as follows. There are two types of jade that are chemically distinct, namely jadeite and nephrite. Suppose that Oscar lives in an environment where all the jade is jadeite. Members of his community intend to apply the concept JADE only to stuff of the same kind as the local green semi-precious stone. Thus, only jadeite falls within the extension of Oscar's JADE. Were Oscar to apply the concept JADE to a green stone that was composed of nephrite then he would have made a mistake. Oscar2 lives in an environment where there is no jadeite and where all the local green semi-precious stones are composed of nephrite. The intention of the members of Oscar2's community is to apply JADE only to stuff of the same kind as the local semi-precious green stones. Consequently, only nephrite falls within the extension of Oscar2's concept JADE. Hence, Oscar's JADE thoughts differ in broad content from the corresponding thoughts of his twin.

Fodor thinks that the advocate of broad psychology should not be worried by such cases. For, 'though such cases occur, *it is reasonable to treat them as accidents and to regard the missed generalizations as spurious*' (1994a: 30). '*Failures to capture accidental generalizations don't impugn theories*' (1994a: 32) and so scientific psychology is not required to capture accidental generalizations subsuming the twins in such cases. Why, one might ask, should we accept that such twin cases as the jadeite–nephrite case are accidental? I think that the sort of considerations that Fodor has in mind and the power of those considerations can be seen by considering a case that he does not discuss, namely, the arthritis case invented by Burge and described above.

Oscar, recall, has a mistaken belief about arthritis: he believes it is possible to get arthritis outside one's joints, something that is by definition impossible. Oscar2 lives in a community where the word 'arthritis' has a wider application; that word is applied to rheumatoid conditions both inside and outside the joints. In virtue of the differences between the linguistic practices that operate in their respective home environments, Oscar's arthritis thoughts differ in broad content from the corresponding thoughts of Oscar2. Unlike most of his fellows, Oscar behaves like an individual who has a concept that means *tharthritis* rather than *arthritis*. For he applies ARTHRITIS to rheumatoid conditions both inside and outside the joints and the causal role of that concept in his head mirrors the typical causal role of the concept that means *tharthritis* in the head of those who fully grasp that concept. That Oscar behaves in such a way is entirely accidental, as his behaviour is a product of elementary and atypical misunderstanding on his part. Were he to become aware of and rectify his mistake, his subsequent use of the concept ARTHRITIS would be brought into line with that of his fellows and he would no longer behave like a member of a community where ARTHRITIS meant *tharthritis*. And he would no longer be a participant of a twin case. Given all this, Fodor would argue, it is reasonable to conclude that this twin case is an accident as is any generalization that subsumes Oscar and Oscar2. Therefore, it is not incumbent on scientific psychology to capture that generalization.

I sympathize with this Fodorian treatment of the Burge case. However, I am not convinced that it is equally convincing when applied to the jade case. For neither of the participants in that case is in the grip of a misunderstanding or a mistake that is atypical in their respective communities and the application and use that they make of the symbol JADE is entirely in line with that which is standard amongst their fellows.

A third twin case discussed by Fodor has to do with such deferential concepts as ELM and BEECH. I am typical in that I cannot distinguish between elms and beeches and I know little about elms and beeches apart from the fact that they are distinct species of deciduous tree. Consequently, my use of ELM mirrors my use of BEECH; I apply both indiscriminately to elms and beeches and any inference

I am disposed to make from x IS AN ELM I am equally disposed to make from x IS A BEECH. Nevertheless, ELM and BEECH differ in their broad content. Therefore, there are generalizations concerning the behaviour of these concepts that cannot be captured by a broad psychology. As Fodor puts it: 'here, as with twins, broad content individuation misses generalizations that narrow content individuation can express; broad individuation just can't think why what it takes to be thoughts with quite different contents should nevertheless eventuate in what appear to be identical behaviours' (1994a: 34). Fodor argues that the problem for broad psychology evaporates once one realizes an important fact about such deferential concepts as ELM and BEECH. Contrary to appearances, I can tell elms from beeches; I do so by employing an expert. When I care whether or not the tree before me is an elm I consult an expert so ensuring that I will token ELM in response to the tree if and only if it is an elm. I don't normally employ this method as the issue of the elmicity or otherwise of the local trees is not a matter of any great importance to me. A consequence of the fact that I can discriminate between elms and beeches by employing an expert is that, contrary to first appearances, my usage of the concepts ELM and BEECH does not match up. Therefore, there are no generalizations that narrow psychology is needed to capture. This completes Fodor's treatment of the twin cases.

What mechanisms prevent the proliferation of such Frege cases that would serve to undermine broad psychology? Fodor begins by noting that psychology is a special science so that its laws are *ceteris paribus* laws. *Ceteris paribus* laws, unlike strict laws, have exceptions. Thus, broad psychology is only in trouble if cases like that of Oedipus are regular and systematic. However, Fodor argues, they are not, as our perceptual and cognitive systems work in such a way that we are generally aware of those identity relationships upon which the success of our behaviour depends. That we are aware of such identity relations is a prerequisite for the success of our rational behaviour. To see this consider an example. Suppose I want to go to Belsize Park and I (mistakenly) believe that the 24 bus goes there. If I act rationally on the basis of this belief I will board a 24 and thus fail to satisfy my desire. If I am not aware that it is the 168 that goes to Belsize Park (that is, that there is an identity relationship between the bus that goes to Belsize Park and the 168) then, barring an accident, any rational behaviour that I engage in will not result in the satisfaction of my desires. But as rational human behaviour is generally successful in satisfying our desires then it must generally be the case that we are aware of the relevant identity relations. Indeed, the advocate of narrow psychology must accept this; otherwise she cannot make any sense of the widespread success of rational behaviour. The upshot of all this is that cases like that of Oedipus are far from the norm. Rather than undermining broad psychological laws, they count as exceptions consistent with the *ceteris paribus* status of such generalizations. As Fodor summarizes his position: 'That Frege cases don't proliferate is, in fact, a reasonable assumption. "Intentional systems" invariably incorporate mechanisms which insure that they generally know the facts upon which the success of their behaviour depends. That, I suppose, is what perception and cognition are *for*. They operate to insure (inter alia) that stories like *Oedipus* don't constitute the norm' (1994a: 48).

Thus, Fodor concludes, due to the existence of mechanisms that prevent the systematic proliferation of twin and Frege cases, a broad psychology is capable of framing generalizations of considerable explanatory and predictive power. Therefore, as a matter of empirical fact, a scientific psychology has no need to employ a notion of narrow content.

Conclusion

One of the most prominent debates in recent philosophy of mind has concerned the question of whether or not scientific psychology should individuate intentional states individualistically (that is, in terms of properties that supervene upon our intrinsic physical properties). Fodor has made one of the most important contributions to this debate and I have been concerned with describing and evaluating that contribution in this chapter. For many years Fodor was an individualist and produced several distinct arguments for this commitment. According to some of these arguments, scientific psychology is individualistic in virtue of its commitment to CTM. His most prominent pro-individualist argument is that scientific psychology must individuate in terms of causal powers, and as the intentional states of physical twins agree in their causal powers, it follows that it must individuate those states individualistically. Consequently, scientific psychology must employ a notion of narrow content and individuate intentional states in terms of their narrow content. In the mid-1990s Fodor abandoned his commitment to individualism. However, this is not as dramatic a turnabout as might first appear. For Fodor didn't exactly come to reject his earlier arguments or conclude that there is no such thing as narrow content. Rather, he came to the conclusion that, as a matter of empirical fact, scientific psychology can get away with being broad as employing a notion of narrow content would bring few explanatory and predictive benefits.

7

The Modularity Thesis

Introduction

In *The Modularity of Mind*, published in 1983, Fodor advances a thesis concerning the architecture of the mind, a thesis that I shall label the modularity thesis. *The Modularity of Mind* is the most empirical and least philosophical of Fodor's major works: Fodor explicitly characterizes it as a work of psychology and it contains extensive discussion of research in cognitive psychology and psycholinguistics. Accordingly, the work has had more influence and has received more extensive discussion in the psychological than in the philosophical community.[1] Nevertheless, the work is unashamedly speculative in a way that echoes *The Language of Thought* (1975), and in later work he argues that the modularity thesis has significant philosophical implications. The purpose of this chapter is to discuss Fodor's modularity thesis. I shall give a detailed account of the nature of the thesis and of Fodor's arguments for it, discuss its plausibility and examine its philosophical implications.

The Nature of Fodor's Modularity Thesis

Broadly speaking, a modularity thesis is a thesis to the effect that the mind is not a single, homogeneous, general-purpose processing system; rather, it comprises several task-specific sub-systems that operate in relative independence of one another. There are two dimensions along which distinct modularity theses may differ. First, they may differ with respect to the account of the nature of mental modules that they incorporate. For example, champions of competing modularity theses might offer divergent definitions or analyses of the concept of a mental module. Alternatively, they might hold what they regard to be empirical accounts of the nature of mental modules that differ considerably. Second, they may differ with respect to their account of the number and identity of the mental modules in the human mind. For example, the advocate of one thesis might hold that there is a distinct face recognition module whilst a rival regards face recognition as being executed by the very module responsible for object recognition in general.

Consequently, giving an account of Fodor's modularity thesis involves describing both his general conception of the nature of mental modules and his answer to the question of the number and identity of the modules that belong to the human mind. In broad approximation, Fodor thinks of modules as being task-specific, informationally encapsulated sub-systems of the mind that, as a matter of contingent empirical fact, tend to share a particular collection of further properties. And he thinks that there are at least six modules: one for each of the five senses as traditionally conceived along with a language module responsible for linguistic processing. This could do with much by way of elaboration, a task to which I now turn.

Fodor distinguishes between three functionally distinct types of mental mechanism or sub-system; namely, transducers, input and output systems and central systems. The central system is primarily concerned with belief fixation and is the domain of beliefs, desires and the like. Thus, reasoning, problem-solving, constructing scientific explanations and engaging in philosophical reflection are familiar processes that it is the job of the central system to execute. Transducers lie at the interface between the mind and the world. There are two basic types of transducer. On the one hand, input transducers take physical, non-symbolic input and produce symbols as output. The retina is an input transducer that in response to being stimulated by light produces symbolic output that represents the intensity and wavelength of the light falling upon it. Output transducers, on the other hand, take symbolic input and transform it into non-symbolic output. An example of such an output might be a neural firing that subsequently caused a muscle contraction and a bodily movement. Without transducers the mind would be isolated from the world; it would neither be able to obtain information concerning the nature of the external world nor act on the world in such a way as to satisfy its desires. Transducers perform their operations automatically and not by means of computation. For example, when it is stimulated by light, the retina does not execute a complex process of manipulating symbols by means of the application of symbol-manipulating rules in order to determine what output to produce.

Input and output systems lie between the transducers and the central system. Input systems take the symbolic output of input transducers as their input and produce representations of the external world as output. They do this by means of computation. That is, they infer how the external world must be given the deliverances of the transducers that feed them their input. The representations of the external world that input systems generate are fed to the central system and typically result in the tokening of a belief about the nature of the external world. Hence, the general function of input systems is to 'so represent the world as to make it accessible to thought' (1983: 40). For Fodor, there is a distinct input system corresponding to each of the five senses as traditionally conceived. In addition, he contends, there is a language system that constitutes a distinct input system. This system functions so as to generate, from auditory and visual information associated with verbal utterances and written words and sentences, representations of the semantic and syntactic properties of linguistic items.

Output systems take their input (which takes the form of symbols) from the central system and deliver their output to output transducers. Such systems are involved in motor coordination and control. For example, suppose that I decide to utter the sentence 'Fang is ferocious'. An output system sensitive to my decision will execute a computational process that results in various output transducers being fed instructions which cause them to initiate such neural firings, muscle contractions and the like that will result in a vocalization of the sentence 'Fang is ferocious'. In short, the function of output systems is to instruct our bodies to move in such a way that we succeed in performing the actions that we intend or decide to perform.

The central plank of Fodor's modularity thesis is the claim that input systems are modules.[2] But what, in Fodor's eyes, is a module? In keeping with his general hostility to definitions and conceptual analyses, Fodor is unwilling to provide a definition or an analysis of the concept of a module. Instead, he argues that there is a battery of nine properties that input systems generally share and that any psychological system that had all or most of these properties would thereby be a module. These properties are only contingently related and there is no necessity in the fact that input systems have all or most of these properties. However, Fodor places particular emphasis on the property of informational encapsulation. Consequently, it is not a gross distortion to say that for Fodor a module is a task-specific, informationally encapsulated psychological sub-system. Thus, if human input systems turned out to lack most of the properties that Fodor enumerates in discussing the nature of modularity, they would still be Fodorian modules if they were task-specific, informationally encapsulated sub-systems of the mind. The nine properties that Fodor enumerates are as follows.

1. *'Input systems are domain specific'* (1983: 47). That is, they are concerned with a distinctive and quite specific subject matter. In other words, they perform a highly specialized task. Bound up with their specialization, Fodor suggests, is the fact that modules are often sensitive to only a narrow range of quite specific input or stimulation. For example, modules concerned with language perception are only sensitive to, or stimulated by, sounds that are taken to be utterances.

2. *'The operation of input systems is mandatory'* (1983: 52). There are some cognitive processes that we are capable of executing that are under our control in the respect that we can decide whether or not to execute them. For example, I can decide whether or not to think about philosophy and my thinking about philosophy requires a prior decision to do so. We do not have this control over the processes that modules execute; they do what they do automatically and regardless of our choices and decisions. In short, their operations are akin to reflexes. For example, if you hear a sentence of a language that you know then you cannot help but hear it as a sentence; you do not have the power to 'switch off' the processes that result in your hearing it as a sentence as opposed to a pure sound.

3. *'There is only limited central access to the mental representations that input systems compute'* (1983: 55). In the course of generating output from input, computational systems typically generate a whole series of intermediary representations. Modules deliver their output to the central system but not the intermediary representations from which that output was computationally generated. In effect, modules inform other systems of their solution to the information-processing problems that they solve but conceal the

manner in which they produce such solutions. For example, on Marr's theory of vision the output of the visual module is presented to more central processes in order to facilitate such tasks as object recognition. But such processes do not have access to the primal sketch or the $2\frac{1}{2}$-D sketch.

4. *'Input systems are fast'* (1983: 61). Although it is difficult to measure accurately the speed of the processes executed by input systems, it is clear that compared to such central processes as solving a philosophical problem, they are very fast indeed. For example, it takes milliseconds to identify a heard sentence or determine the shape of a distal object impinging on one's visual system. Fodor suggests that this speed may well be related to the mandatory nature of the processes executed by input systems: as these processes are performed automatically one doesn't waste time reflecting on whether and how to execute them.

5. *'Input systems are informationally encapsulated'* (1983: 64). A computational sub-system is informationally encapsulated if there is information stored in the system of which it is a part to which it does not have access (even if that information would help it to perform its target task successfully). Fodor holds that input systems have their own task-specific body of information that they utilize in performing their operations. For example, an individual's language system will have information concerning the lexical items and the grammatical rules of the language that she speaks. Any given input system will have access only to its own specialized body of information; it will have no access either to the specialist information employed by the other input systems or to information stored in the central system and utilized in general reasoning and problem-solving. Consequently, the course of the processing executed by an individual's input systems will be impervious to whatever information is stored in the central system and thus to whatever she knows, believes or – for that matter – desires to be the case. In other words, to use Pylyshyn's (1984) term, the operations of input systems are cognitively impenetrable. As evidence of the informational encapsulation of input systems Fodor cites the familiar case of perceptual illusions that persist in the face of salient knowledge on the part of the deceived subject. The Müller–Lyer diagram comprises two parallel lines of equal length, one flanked by outward-pointing arrows and the other flanked by inward-pointing arrows. The line flanked by inward-pointing arrows will look longer to a perceiving human subject than the other line even if she knows that

the lines are of equivalent length. What this suggests is that the visual system is informationally encapsulated as there is a highly relevant piece of information stored in the central system that it does not have access to. If the visual system had access to the information that the lines are of equal length then the subject would hardly fall prey to the illusion. Incidentally, the informational encapsulation of the input systems goes some way towards explaining their speed: having to search the vast information store of the central system in order to garner relevant information would considerably slow down the processing of an input system.

6. *'Input systems have "shallow" outputs'* (1983: 86). In this context 'shallow' means constrained. Thus, input systems are constrained in terms of the information that they deliver as output. Input systems deliver their output to the central system and the central system subsequently comes to some conclusion about the nature of the external world (a process that involves the acquisition of a belief on the part of the subject). The conclusions that the central system arrives at in response to the deliverances of the input systems often go considerably beyond those deliverances in terms of its commitment to the nature of the external stimulus. For example, Fodor hypothesizes that the output of the language system represents such properties of heard utterances as their constituent words and their syntactic structure but not the communicative intentions of the speaker. Thus, it is not part of the function of the language system to determine whether the speaker was being ironic, sincere, threatening or whatever. The task of determining the communicative intentions of speakers is a task of the central system and involves the utilization of information that the language system has no access to. Thus, it is no objection to Fodor to assert that the language system cannot be informationally encapsulated as our judgements about the communicative intentions lying behind the utterances of our fellows are often significantly influenced by our beliefs about their personality, the context of utterance and so on. For Fodor will respond with the point that such judgements are the products of central processing and go considerably beyond the output of the language system. He would no doubt make an analogous point with respect to any claim to the effect that the judgements that we make on the basis of the use of our senses are sensitive to what we believe about the nature of the world.

7. *'Input systems are associated with a fixed neural architecture'* (1983: 98). That is, input systems are associated with localized structures in the brain.

8. '*Input systems exhibit characteristic and specific breakdown patterns*' (1983: 99). That is, input systems are prone to quite specific functioning problems as a result of damage to the brain or genetic impairment. The agnosias and aphasias are prominent examples of such breakdowns in functioning. A subject can suffer from such a condition whilst all her other input systems along with her central system function perfectly normally. The occurrence of such specific impairments to the functioning of input systems constitutes evidence for the neural localization of input systems.

9. '*The ontogeny of input systems exhibits a characteristic pace and sequencing*' (1983: 100). Fodor hypothesizes that input systems and the capacities associated with them develop at a rate and in an order that is uniform across the human species. Such development is genetically determined and is largely independent of the specifics of a subject's experiences and her general intelligence. With respect to the language system, evidence for such a claim has been garnered by Chomsky and used to motivate a nativist account of language acquisition. (See e.g. Chomsky 1986.) Thus, Fodor's modularity thesis involves a substantial nativist commitment as he conceives of the architecture of the mind and the development of its component modules as being innately determined. Moreover, following Chomsky, he is sympathetic to the idea that much of the task-specific information utilized by the input systems (particularly the language system) is innately specified.

For Fodor, the modularity of the input systems consists in their possession of all or most of the above properties. Hence, his account of the nature of a module is this: a module is a mental sub-system that is domain-specific, has a mandatory operation, is fast and so on. However, Fodor places special emphasis on domain specificity and informational encapsulation. For example, he writes: 'The informational encapsulation of the input systems is . . . the essence of their modularity' (1983: 70). Why does he place emphasis upon these two properties? As I stated above, the intuitive notion of a mental module is that of a specialized and relatively independent sub-system of the mind. Domain specificity is a salient form of specialization. As for the second property, I think that there is a more intimate relationship between informational encapsulation and the intuitive notion of a module than there is between that notion and, say, processing speed and having a mandatory operation. For, if a mental processor has its own specialized body of information to facilitate the performance of its function, and does not have access to other information stored within the mind, then there is a substantial respect in which it is a specialized, relatively independent sub-system of the mind.

Fodor claims inspiration for his claim that input systems are modules from the eighteenth–nineteenth-century faculty psychologist and phrenologist Franz Joseph Gall. However, Fodor's position has some prominent precedents in recent cognitive science. For example, Marr (1982) represents the visual system in such a way as to suggest that it is a Fodorian module. Indeed Marr's theory implies that the visual system itself decomposes into a number of more specialized modules, a possibility that Fodor explicitly entertains. In comparing the language system to an organ whose development is genetically determined and which utilizes a body of innately specified information (namely, Universal Grammar) Chomsky (1980) comes close to regarding the language system as a module.[3]

Are Input Systems Modules?

In 'Why Should the Mind be Modular?' (1989a) Fodor provides a teleological argument for his view that input systems are modules. In a nutshell, the argument is that given the function of perception one would expect perceptual systems to be modules; their being modular would bestow a distinct survival advantage upon us by facilitating the acquisition of true empirical beliefs. In other words, perception ought to be modular. In greater detail, the argument runs as follows. The function of perception is to infer the nature of the distal stimulus from the deliverances of the sensory transducers. This process plays an important role in the fixation of belief but the perceptual beliefs that an individual acquires will take into account not only the deliverances of perceptual processing but also her background beliefs. It is advantageous that the empirical beliefs that a creature acquires are true, as having and acting upon true beliefs will increase a creature's survival prospects. Empirical beliefs are generally acquired by means of non-demonstrative inference and to maximize the likelihood of producing true beliefs such a process must be governed by two constraints. On the one hand, it should be observationally adequate. That is, it should generate beliefs that fit as much of the observational data as possible. On the other hand, it should be conservative. That is, it should generate beliefs that square with the beliefs that one previously held so as not to require one to abandon one's firmly held prior commitments. These constraints can pull in opposite directions in the respect that unprejudiced observational data can sometimes conflict with prior commitments; in such cases a compromise must be reached. Now suppose for a moment that a creature's perceptual processes were not modular. Then how it perceived the world to be would be systematically affected by its background beliefs along with its expectations and desires regarding the nature of the external world. Consequently, there would be no constraint of observational adequacy operating on its belief acquisition process. The perceptual process would be so influenced by the creature's prior commitments that conservatism would rule the day; there would be no mechanism for generating unbiased, unprejudiced observational data. There would thus be no opportunity for the creature to take into account neutral observational data of the kind that could constitute an independent check on its commitments and facilitate it to alter those commitments when they are drastically at odds with reality. Assuming that a creature's beliefs will sometimes be at odds with reality, a non-modular perceptual system will be prone to misrepresenting the external world and so lead to the acquisition of false perceptual beliefs, something that does not aid the creature's chances of survival. Therefore, perceptual systems ought to be modular.

An important source of evidence for the thesis that input systems are modules comes from the study of individuals suffering from specific cognitive impairments as a result of genetic defect or brain damage. In *The Modularity of Mind* (1983) Fodor refers to such evidence but doesn't describe it in any detail. If the input systems are modules then the capacities associated with any given input system will be independent of the capacities associated with all the other input systems. More importantly, these capacities will be independent of capacities associated with the central system (such as general intelligence). Consequently, it will be possible (at least in principle) for an individual to suffer from a specific impairment to a particular input module whilst all her other capacities remain intact. Correlatively, it will be possible for an individual to have an impaired central system resulting in low general intelligence and difficulties in performing everyday tasks, whilst being perfectly normal with respect to the capacities associated with a particular input system. If, on the other hand, the mind is a uniform general-purpose processing system then such a double dissociation of perceptual and linguistic capacities and general intelligence will not be possible. In particular, if the central system is involved in perceptual and linguistic processing then severe damage to an individual's central system will have major across-the-board ramifications with respect to her perceptual and linguistic capacities. And, assuming that her sense organs are not damaged, if an individual displays a specific perceptual or linguistic impairment, that impairment must be due to a central processing problem that is likely to manifest itself in more widespread impairments.[4]

There is considerable evidence from the fields of cognitive neuropsychology and developmental psychology to suggest that input capacities and central capacities do doubly dissociate. Such evidence undermines the view that the mind is a uniform general-purpose processing system and is widely taken to support the modularity thesis. To get a flavour of this evidence, I will briefly describe some cases widely cited in the literature that suggest that linguistic capacities and general intelligence doubly dissociate.

William's syndrome[5] is a rare genetic disorder. Its subjects tend to have the following physical characteristics: 'elfin-like' faces, proneness to hypertension, below-average birthweight, poor muscle tone and premature ageing of the skin (Karmiloff-Smith *et al.* 1995). On the cognitive front, their general intelligence is severely impaired: they typically have an IQ in the 50–60 range and 'are incompetent at ordinary tasks like tying their shoes, finding their way, retrieving items from a cupboard, telling left from right, adding two numbers, drawing a bicycle, and suppressing their natural tendency to hug strangers' (Pinker 1994: 52). Nevertheless, William's syndrome subjects show evidence of significant linguistic capacities in the face of their general cognitive limitations. As Karmiloff-Smith *et al.* put it: 'Compared to their marked difficulties in simple arithmetic, some WS subjects are almost at ceiling on certain tasks measuring understanding of syntactically complex structures. . . . Also, in contrast to individuals with autism and Down Syndrome, they produce complex narratives that make extensive use of affective prosody' (1995: 200).

Another case that suggests that it is possible to have significant linguistic capacities whilst suffering from general cognitive defects and poor general intelligence is that of Christopher, a 'linguistic savant' whose condition is documented by N. V. Smith and Tsimpli (1995). Christopher suffers from brain damage and performs poorly in intelligence tests that do not involve verbal ability. Moreover, 'he is unable to look after himself; he has difficulty finding his way around; he has poor hand–eye co-ordination . . . but he can read, write and communicate in any of fifteen to twenty languages' (1995: 1). More specifically, in the case of English, his first language, Christopher's linguistic competence 'is as rich and as sophisticated as that of any native speaker' (1995: 78) whereas with respect to the other languages that he knows, his lexical knowledge outstrips his syntactic knowledge.

A case of individuals who suffer from an impairment of their linguistic capacities despite being of normal intelligence is constituted by a genetic disorder known as Specific Language Impairment (SLI). SLI individuals are prone to make grammatical errors in speech despite the fact that they grasp the associated concepts. For example, they have problems with tense despite the fact that they understand the temporal relations expressed by the words 'yesterday', 'today' and 'tomorrow' (Gopnik 1994). Thus, to borrow some examples cited by Smith (1999: 25), they are prone to utter such sentences as 'What did fell off the chair?', 'Which cat Mrs White stroked?' and 'Which coat was Professor Plum weared?'

In short William's syndrome and the case of Christopher, on the one hand, and SLI, on the other, would appear to suggest that language doubly dissociates from general intelligence and that, therefore, Fodor is correct in claiming that there exists a language module. However, a word of caution is needed. Although such cases provide an important source of evidence in support of Fodor's modularity thesis, they do not conclusively settle the issue. Shallice (1988) accepts that we should expect double dissociations to occur if the modularity thesis is true and that the existence of double dissociations is inconsistent with the view that the mind is a uniform general-purpose processor. However, he argues, it doesn't follow from the existence of double dissociations that the mind has a modular architecture. This is because there are possible architectures that are neither modular nor uniform general-processing systems that can experience dissociations when damaged. He cites the following as examples of such systems: systems based on a continuum of sub-processes; systems with overlapping processing regions; coupled systems; semi-modules; and multi-level systems. (See Shallice 1988, ch. 11 for details.) Another reason for caution is the fact that some researchers have questioned the legitimacy of the standard descriptions of William's syndrome and SLI proffered by advocates of the modularity thesis.[6]

The Central System

In addition to the claim that input systems are modules, there is a second important component of Fodor's modularity thesis. This is the claim that the central system, the domain of reasoning and belief fixation, does not have a modular structure. That is, the central system does not decompose into domain-specific and information-ally encapsulated sub-systems. Fodor thinks that this has a significant implication for cognitive science: cognitive science is unlikely to have much success in uncovering the workings of the central system; its successes are going to be limited to work on the input systems. Fodor describes his reasons for this pessimism in the following terms:

> The fact is that . . . global systems are per se bad domains for computational models, at least of the sort that cognitive scientists are accustomed to employ. The condition for successful science (in physics, by the way, as well as psychology) is that nature should have joints to carve it at: relatively simple subsystems which can be artificially isolated and which behave, in isolation, in something like the way that they behave *in situ*. Modules satisfy this condition; Quinean/isotropic–wholistic-systems by definition do not. If, as I have supposed, the central cognitive processes are nonmodular, that is very bad news for cognitive science. (1983: 128)

What are Fodor's reasons for concluding that the central system is non-modular? He thinks that it is close to self-evident that the central system is not domain-specific. For example, the process of fixing perceptual beliefs involves integrating data from various input modules and generating beliefs that square with the subject's general beliefs about the world. This involves taking input from a variety of distinct sources and is therefore not domain-specific. His argument for the informational unencapsulation of the central system is somewhat more complex and can be described in the following terms. For Fodor, belief fixation is typically a process of non-demonstrative (that is, non-deductive) inference and such a process involves framing hypotheses and then seeking to confirm them by considering data that bear upon their truth value. Hypothesis confirmation has two closely related properties that entail that it is not informationally encapsulated. The properties in question are those of being isotropic and being Quinean. Fodor's account of these properties along with his argument that hypothesis confirmation is isotropic and Quinean involves an appeal to confirmation in science.

Confirmation in science is isotropic in the respect that 'the facts relevant to the confirmation of scientific hypotheses may be drawn from anywhere in the field of previously established empirical (or, of course, demonstrative) truths' (Fodor 1983: 105). The scientific endeavour rests on the assumption that the world constitutes a complex causal system and that events in one part of this system can have significant causal ramifications elsewhere in the system. Given their acceptance that we are relatively ignorant of the workings of this causal network, when considering a scientific hypothesis scientists do not delimit the information that they consider relevant to the question at issue. On the contrary, the confirmation process may involve the consideration of any item of information at the scientist's disposal.

Confirmation in science is Quinean in that 'the degree of confirmation assigned to any given hypothesis is sensitive to properties of the entire belief system; as it were, the shape of our whole science bears on the epistemic status of each scientific hypothesis' (1983: 107). In viewing scientific confirmation in such terms, Fodor is endorsing Quine's (1953) attack on reductionism, the second dogma of empiricism. According to Quine, no empirical observation serves to refute conclusively any given scientific hypothesis (alternatively, no observation statement implies the falsity of a given scientific hypothesis). No matter how much pressure is placed on a scientific hypothesis by her observations, the scientist can consistently hold onto the hypothesis by making relevant adjustments to her belief system. Moreover, two competing hypotheses might both equally fit the empirical data and yet the scientific community prefer one to the other on the grounds that it is simpler, more conservative and better coheres with other widely accepted theories. In short, the process of confirming a scientific hypothesis is global and holistic as it takes into account the whole edifice of theories held by the scientist and the relationships that the hypothesis bears to that edifice.

Fodor argues that in virtue of being isotropic and Quinean, scientific confirmation is not informationally encapsulated. For the process involves not merely considering a limited body of data delivered by our input systems but the whole of the scientist's epistemic commitments.

This account of the nature of scientific confirmation provides Fodor with his main argument for the informational non-encapsulation (and, thus, non-modularity) of central processing.

He argues that as scientific confirmation is non-encapsulated then so is that paradigmatic central process of endorsing a scientific belief. And as the fixing of scientific beliefs is a form of non-demonstrative inference, there is good reason to think that non-demonstrative inference in general is non-encapsulated.

In *The Mind doesn't Work that Way* (2000) Fodor returns to the idea that central processing is typically global and holistic. Once again, he justifies this idea by considering scientific reasoning. When scientists choose between competing hypotheses, Fodor argues, they do so on the basis of considerations of simplicity and conservatism. Let us examine the nature of these considerations in turn.[7] It is a principle of science that when one is choosing between competing hypotheses one should, all else equal, choose the simplest. But the simplicity of a hypothesis is not one of its intrinsic properties; it is not, for example, a matter of its content or the number of words belonging to a sentence that expresses it. Suppose that a scientist is in the process of choosing between two competing hypotheses, namely, H and H*. Which is the simplest of these hypotheses will be relative to her belief system and will depend upon the nature of that belief system. Her belief system might be such that endorsing H would serve to simplify that system whereas endorsing H* would serve to complicate it. However, the belief system of one of her colleagues might be such that endorsing H* would serve to simplify his belief system whereas endorsing H would serve to complicate it. Consequently, choosing between competing hypotheses on the basis of considerations of simplicity involves taking into account the nature of one's belief system and for that reason it is a global and holistic process.

It is also a principle of science that when choosing between competing hypotheses one should choose the one that is, all else equal, the most conservative. Whenever we endorse a hypothesis, and so acquire a new belief, we are, on pain of irrationality, required to alter some of our prior epistemic commitments. The most conservative of two competing hypotheses is the one whose endorsement requires the least such modification. However, it is not merely a matter of numbers. Endorsing H might require a scientist to abandon a greater number of the beliefs that she previously held than would endorsing H* whilst, nevertheless, the principle of conservatism demand that she endorse H. For the beliefs that endorsing H would require her to abandon could be relatively peripheral whilst those that endorsing H* would require her to abandon could be central to her belief system. Consequently, choosing between competing hypotheses on the basis of considerations of conservatism involves determining the relative centrality of the beliefs that endorsing either of the hypotheses would require one to abandon. And doing that involves executing a global and holistic process as the relative centrality of a belief is a matter of its place in a belief system.

In *The Modularity of Mind* (1983) Fodor draws the sceptical conclusion that cognitive science has little hope of shedding light on the workings of the central system. In *The Mind doesn't Work that Way* (2000) he goes one step further and suggests that the global and holistic nature of central processing undermines the plausibility of CTM as a theory of such processing. For computers are very good at executing such local inferential processes as modus ponens and conjunction simplification but are ill suited to executing global and holistic inferential processes. In order to execute the kind of global and holistic process that we routinely perform, a computer would either have to search exhaustively a whole belief system or have to take a whole belief system as its input. But, thinks Fodor, it is implausible that the mind works in this kind of way. As he puts it:

> The totality of one's epistemic commitments is *vastly* too large a space to have to search through if all one's trying to do is figure out whether, since there are clouds, it would be wise to carry an umbrella. Indeed, the totality of one's epistemic commitments is vastly too large a space to have to search *whatever* it is that one is trying to figure out. (2000: 31)

Thus, he concludes, cognitive science is in need of a radical new idea as to how central processing works. However, he is still committed to CTM as a theory of intentional states as, unlike any of its competitors, it has the capacity to account for the productivity and systematicity of our intentional states along with the intensionality of sentences that ascribe intentional states to individuals.

Fodor's arguments for the global and holistic nature of central processing has received considerably less sympathy than his arguments for the modularity of input systems and I think there are several good reasons to be suspicious of his reasoning. First, I think that he exaggerates the extent to which the reasoning processes executed by individual scientists in the course of evaluating hypotheses are global and holistic. Consider the property of being isotropic. It is one thing for a scientist to be committed to the idea

that information relevant to the evaluation of a particular hypothesis could (at least in principle) come from any empirical domain
and quite another for her to consider all of her empirical knowledge
when engaged in the process of evaluating that hypothesis. The scientist will inevitably operate with a tacit understanding of what
information is relevant and what is not. Such a tacit understanding
will be dictated by the particular theories that she holds and will
serve to delimit or constrain the information she takes into account
when engaged in the process of scientific confirmation. Of course,
what information is delimited is not fixed once and for all; a scientist's theories could change and so bring about a change in the information that she would take into account in evaluating a particular
hypothesis. With respect to the property of being Quinean, it is
hardly plausible that individual scientists consider the whole
edifice of their theoretical commitments when evaluating a particular hypothesis. This is not to say that considerations of simplicity, conservatism, coherence and the like have no role to play in the
scientific process. It is just that the individual scientist's judgements
on such matters will be influenced by views held in the wider community and will not be based on her executing the global and holistic process that Fodor conceives.

At this point it is worth noting that scientists do not work in isolation but belong to a community. The members of this community
engage in an ongoing dialogue with their fellows that serves to
influence the theoretical commitments of individual scientists, their
conceptions of what information is relevant when evaluating
particular hypotheses, their judgements about the relations of
such hypotheses to well-established theories and so on. Moreover,
belonging to a community obviates the need of the individual to
consider all of the potentially relevant considerations when striving
to make rational and informed theoretical decisions. This implies
that what might be true of the scientific community as a whole –
that it executes a global and holistic process of hypothesis confirmation – may not be true of the processes executed by any of its
members. For a group of individuals each executing a non-global
and non-holistic process might interact in such a way as to generate a collective process that is holistic and global. Thus, Fodor
cannot legitimately draw conclusions about the nature of the psychological processes executed by individual scientists from pre-
misses concerning the nature of the scientific community and the
products of its activity.

I do not want to push the above points too far. At best they suggest that individual scientists do not reason in a manner that is entirely isotropic and Quinean. However, I have effectively conceded that in principle there is no information stored in the central system that such reasoning does not have access to. And that an individual's beliefs (in the form of her theoretical commitments) influence her reasoning about scientific matters in a way that they do not influence the processing behaviour of her input systems. It is plausible to claim that such concessions imply that there is a substantial respect in which scientific confirmation is not informationally encapsulated.

My second reason for scepticism with respect to Fodor's claim that central processing is global and holistic is as follows. Even if Fodor is correct in his claims about scientific reasoning, it does not follow that there are not certain central system processes that are neither domain-general nor informationally encapsulated. Scientific reasoning is a slow, self-conscious, demanding and highly intellectual process. It is engaged in by only a small proportion of the human population and such individuals are typically unusually curious and highly intelligent recipients of a lengthy period of specialist training. In all these respects scientific reasoning would appear to be quite unlike many familiar central system processes. Most people, regardless of their intelligence or educational background, are capable of effortlessly and unselfconsciously categorizing objects, recognizing faces, engaging in folk psychology, engaging in practical reasoning, acquiring spatial information and navigating their home environments, making moral judgements and appreciating music and other art forms. Given the apparent differences between such processes and scientific reasoning, one ought to be wary of making general claims about central system processing on the basis of an examination of scientific reasoning.

Third, all of the evidence that Fodor presents is entirely consistent with the central system's having a modular structure. For example, the central system could have the following architecture. The central system decomposes into several distinct sub-systems each of which has a distinctive function which it executes by running its own specialist program. One such system is the theoretical reasoning system. It is not a module in Fodor's sense as it can be used to reason about a wide variety of subject matters and has access to all of the individual's beliefs. The theoretical reasoning system exists alongside a number of Fodorian modules from which it takes its input but whose processing it is not involved in. There are distinct Fodorian modules for folk psychology, object recognition, face recognition, moral judgement, aesthetic appreciation, the acquisition of spatial information and navigation and so on. Indeed, one might think that the theoretical reasoning system is a module in an intuitively powerful respect, as it is a task-specific and relatively independent component of a larger system that runs according to a specialist program. I do not wish to argue that the central system has such an architecture. My point is that its having such a modular architecture is consistent with all of the evidence for the non-modularity of the central system that Fodor produces.

Before concluding this section I will sketch some reasons for taking seriously the view that, contrary to Fodor's position, the central system has a modular organization. First, there is considerable evidence from cognitive neuropsychology that there is a specialized face recognition module.[8] Normal human subjects can effortlessly recognize faces of individuals of their acquaintance and learn new faces. One might suspect that face recognition is performed by the very system that is concerned with object recognition in general. However, studies of individuals suffering from brain damage indicate that face recognition and general object recognition dissociate thus supporting the thesis that there is a specific module for face recognition. Prosopagnosia is an inability to recognize faces by visual means as a result of brain damage. Some prosopagnosics (for example LF described by Farah *et al.* 1995) display a close to normal ability when it comes to object recognition in general. Moreover, there are cases of associative visual agnosics who have problems with object recognition who are nevertheless close to normal when it comes to face recognition (for example CK as described in Farah 1995).

Such evidence for the existence of a face recognition module constitutes a problem only if face recognition is a central process. Indeed, Fodor refers to face recognition as a plausible candidate for a modular process in *The Modularity of Mind* (1983) but he clearly regards face recognition as an input process executed by the visual system (or a component of that system). But how plausible is it to regard face recognition as a product or component of early visual processing? Isn't it likely (or at least possible) that the face recognition process takes as input highly processed visual data rather than the deliverances of the retinal transducer? Moreover, Fodor characterizes the output of input systems as being shallow, but the product of the visual recognition process is hardly shallow. In his discussion of object recognition Fodor speculates that some object recognition is executed by the visual module. However, he goes on, the visual module only assigns distal stimuli to basic categories leaving the task of assigning stimuli to non-basic categories to the central system.[9] Parity of reasoning would suggest that the visual system categorizes faces as such but leaves the task of determining their precise identity to the central system.

Folk psychology constitutes another plausible candidate for a central system module.[10] Such a module would take its input from various input systems and would generate descriptions, explanations and predictions of the mental and behavioural life of our fellows utilizing largely innate information concerning human psychology. Given the centrality of folk psychology to human life there are good ecological reasons for the existence of a folk psychology module. There is substantial evidence that folk psychology is universal across all cultural groups and that the ability to engage in folk psychology develops at a uniform rate in normal humans regardless of their intelligence and without explicit instruction. It would appear that the normal child has acquired a mastery of the basics of folk psychology by the age of 4 – at which point she is able to appreciate that her fellows can have false beliefs (or beliefs at odds with her own) – and can predict behaviour on the basis of the attribution of false beliefs. (See Wellman 1990; Astington *et al.* 1988; and Perner 1991.) Along with the facts that engaging in folk psychology is usually effortless and mandatory (it is difficult to observe a human individual without interpreting her actions and state of mind and forming expectations about how she will behave), all this suggests that there exists a folk psychology module. Moreover, there are dissociations that further support this thesis. Autism is a condition characterized in terms of abnormal social behaviour, verbal and non-verbal communication difficulties and a tendency to engage in unimaginative and repetitive behaviour. Autists have limitations when it comes to engaging in folk psychology as is evidenced by the difficulties that they have in appreciating that their fellows can have false beliefs and in making behavioural predictions on the basis of the attribution of false beliefs. Such problems are unlikely to be the product of general intellectual limitations, for in terms of their ability to psychologize, autistic children are often outperformed by children with Down syndrome. On the other hand, children with William's syndrome (who, recall, have major intellectual limitations and great difficulties performing everyday practical tasks) are close to normal in terms of the development of folk-psychological abilities. (See Karmiloff-Smith *et al.* 1995.) In short, the cases of autism and William's syndrome suggest that folk psychology dissociates from general intelligence.

Nothing that I have said in this section conclusively establishes that the central system has a modular structure; to do that would be impossible given our current state of knowledge. But it does suggest that we should be wary of accepting Fodor's case for the non-modularity of the central system.

Philosophical Implications of the Modularity Thesis

Fodor is keen to emphasize that the question of the viability of the modularity thesis is an empirical question. However, he has argued that the modularity thesis has significant philosophical implications and that it bears a close relationship to his critique of holism. (With respect to the philosophical implications of the modularity thesis, see Fodor 1984b, 1985b. With respect to the relationship between the modularity thesis and the critique of holism, see Fodor 1990a, introduction.) In this section I will examine these reputed philosophical implications.

A naive and once widespread view of the nature of observation and its role in science can be described in the following terms. We have perceptual systems that enable us to observe the external world. The use of such systems issues in the having of a perceptual experience that represents its distal cause as being a particular way. In the normal course of things such experiences are veridical and will lead to the formation of a corresponding belief about the nature of the external world. We are also capable of describing the contents of our perceptual experiences and, therefore, of specifying how we observe the world to be. The statements that so specify the contents of our perceptual experiences (or of how we observe the world to be by means of perception) are known as observation statements. We often make inferences from how we observe the world to be to conclusions about facts that we do not directly observe. Here is an everyday example of such a process. I see the colour drain from your face as you are confronted by Fang and so conclude that you have a deep-seated fear of that beast. In making this inference I draw on background knowledge or beliefs that I have and in doing so acquire a new belief that goes beyond how I directly perceive or observe the world to be. Here is another example. I take a swig of wine, swill it round my mouth and have a rich, multi-layered gustatory experience. I turn to address the question of the variety of grape from which the wine is made. Reflecting on my gustatory experience and employing my knowledge of the characteristic taste of the major wine varietals, I conclude that the wine is a Pinot Noir. The statements that report the contents of the beliefs that we acquire by means of such inferences are to be sharply distinguished from observation statements.

Observation is theory-neutral in the respect that how an individual perceives the world to be when her perceptual systems are stimulated is not influenced by the particular theories that she holds or by her desires or expectations about the nature of the distal stimuli. In other words, observation is cognitively impenetrable or informationally encapsulated. In short, there is a distinction between observation and theoretical inference or between perception and cognition.

The theory-free nature of perception means that individuals who hold different theories concerning the nature of the world can still agree in how they observe or perceive the world to be. It is just that those observations may well prompt them to arrive at divergent conclusions about the nature of facts that they cannot directly observe. Indeed, distinct individuals with normally functioning perceptual systems will typically agree in how they observe the world to be when placed in the same perceptual situation no matter how much they differ in terms of the theories, desires and expectations that they hold. This fact makes an objective science a possibility. To command our respect a scientific theory must fit the observational data. Moreover, any given scientific theory will imply that in certain circumstances particular observable events will occur. This enables us to test scientific theories in a neutral and objective manner. For we can construct experimental situations and observe whether the observable events whose occurrence is implied by the theory under consideration actually take place. If the predicted event takes place then the theory is confirmed; if not it is proven to be false in virtue of being at odds with the observed facts. The crucial point is that scientists who disagree with respect to the truth value of a theory prior to an experiment designed to test that theory will nevertheless agree on which observable events took place in the experimental setting. Consequently, they will agree on whether the experiment confirms or disconfirms the theory. This enables scientific theories to be tested in a neutral manner and thus guarantees the objectivity of science.

From the late 1950s the view of the nature of observation and the neutrality and objectivity of science described in the preceding three paragraphs came under an increasingly influential attack within the philosophy of science. Writers such as Hanson (1958), Kuhn (1962) and Feyerabend (1975) argued that there is no observation–theory distinction: all observations are influenced by our theoretical commitments so that scientists in the grip of competing theories will diverge in terms of how they observe the world to be. Similarly, the observation statements that issue from a scientist will reflect her theoretical commitments. Consequently, experimentation and observation cannot be employed to test theories in a neutral manner and the scientific enterprise is not quite the objective business it was once portrayed to be.

Such views lead quite naturally to relativism, a position that Fodor is rabidly opposed to. In a characteristically humorous and indignant passage he expresses his hostility to relativism in the following terms:

'But look' you might ask, 'why do you care about modules so much? You've got tenure; why don't you take off and go sailing?' This is a perfectly reasonable question and one that I often ask myself. . . . [R]oughly, and by way of striking a closing note[.] The idea that cognition saturates perception belongs with (and is, indeed, historically connected with) the idea in the philosophy of science that one's observations are comprehensively determined by one's theories; with the idea in anthropology that one's values are comprehensively determined by one's culture; with the idea in sociology that one's epistemic commitments, including especially one's science, are comprehensively determined by one's class affiliations; and with the idea in linguistics that one's metaphysics is comprehensively determined by one's syntax. All these ideas imply a sort of relativistic holism: because perception is saturated by cognition, observation by theory, values by culture, science by class, and metaphysics by language, rational criticism of scientific theories, ethical values, metaphysical world-views, or whatever can take place only within the framework of assumptions that – as a matter of geographical, historical, or sociological accident – the interlocutors happen to share. What you can't do is criticize the framework.

   The thing is I *hate* relativism. I hate relativism more than I hate anything, excepting, maybe, fiberglass powerboats. More to the point, I think that relativism is very probably false. What it overlooks, to put it briefly and crudely, is the fixed structure of human nature. . . . Well, in cognitive psychology the claim that there is a fixed structure of human nature traditionally takes the form of an insistence on the heterogeneity of cognitive mechanisms and on the rigidity of the cognitive architecture that affects their encapsulation. If there are faculties and modules, then not everything affects everything else; not everything is plastic. Whatever the All is, at least there is more than One of it. (1985b: 205–6)

Fodor thinks that the modularity thesis resuscitates the observation–theory distinction and so goes some way towards securing the neutral and objective status of science and thereby undermines relativism. According to the modularity thesis, the distinct perceptual systems are input systems and input systems are in general modules. Thus, perceptual systems are informationally encapsulated so that perceptual processing is unaffected by the theories that we contingently hold as such theories are bodies of beliefs stored in the central system. As Fodor puts it in 'Observation Reconsidered':

> if perceptual processes are modular, then, by definition, bodies of theory that are inaccessible to the modules *do not affect the way the perceiver sees the world*. Specifically, perceivers who differ profoundly in their background theories – scientists with quite different axes to grind, for example – might nevertheless see the world in exactly the same way, so long as the bodies of theory they disagree about are inaccessible to their perceptual mechanisms. (1984b: 246)

Some advocates of the claim that observation is theory-loaded (for example, Kuhn) have made appeals to the psychological literature to support their position; in particular to the kinds of evidence presented by 'new look' theorists such as Bruner (1957) in support of their claims that perception involves higher-level processing. In challenging 'new look' accounts of perception the modularity thesis directly challenges an important premiss of the relativist's argument. However, there is another important argument for relativism that relies upon a commitment to semantic holism. Put briefly, this argument runs as follows. The content of a concept employed by a scientist is determined by the theory to which that concept belongs; that is, by the collection of beliefs involving the concept that she endorses. Consequently, there will be no overlap in the concepts employed by scientists who endorse competing theories. Even if such scientists share a term, that term will express a different concept or have a different meaning from one scientist to the next. In short, distinct scientific theories are incommensurable and their advocates, rather than disagreeing with one another on some substantial matter of fact, are simply talking past one another. And there couldn't be – not even in principle – the kind of crucial experiment that would enable the scientist to make a rationally based choice between two competing theories.

The above argument rests upon a holist premiss and so would collapse if holism were false. Therefore, Fodor's attack on holism and his arguments for an atomist alternative have bearings on the viability of an important argument for relativism just as his defence of the modularity thesis can be seen as an attack on another distinct argument for relativism. Thus, there is what he describes as a 'thematic' connection between his reflections on the nature of meaning and his investigations into the architecture of the mind. (See Fodor 1990a, introduction, for Fodor's discussion of this connection.)

We now come to the question whether the modularity thesis has the philosophical implications that Fodor takes it to have. Assuming that the modularity thesis is true, does it serve to secure the possibility of an objective science? I think that we must return a negative answer to this question for the following reasons.

First, Fodor is keen to emphasize that the output of perceptual modules is shallow. The output of such modules is not perceptual beliefs; rather, the beliefs that we acquire as a result of our perceptual experiences are the product of processes that also take into account the output of other perceptual modules along with whatever background beliefs we hold. Consequently, the perceptual modules of two scientists holding competing theories could deliver identical outputs in a given experimental setting whilst they nevertheless came to hold divergent perceptual beliefs. But to support Fodor's view of the role of observation in science it is necessary that scientists holding competing theories acquire identical perceptual beliefs when their perceptual systems receive a given input stimulation.

Second, even if it were the case that identical perceptual experiences generally lead to identical perceptual beliefs, Fodor would not be home and dry. In order for observation to settle disputes in science it is not enough that scientists agree in their observations. They must also agree in the significance that they bestow on any given piece of observational data and modularity alone does not guarantee any such agreement. Suppose that two scientists are engaged in a debate concerning the viability of theory T (one of them is sympathetic to the theory, the other not). In addition, suppose that this disagreement is not isolated and local; on the contrary, there is a whole battery of other scientific issues over which they disagree. Then they are hardly likely to agree on which observational data would settle the question of the truth value of theory T. It is difficult to see how Fodor could deny this point given his commitment to the claim that scientific confirmation is isotropic in the respect that in principle any empirical fact is relevant to the confirmation of a given scientific hypothesis. If scientific confirmation is isotropic then any scientist's conception of which empirical facts (and, thus, which observational data) are relevant to the confirmation of a given hypothesis will be sensitive to the whole network of theories and beliefs that she holds. In particular, they will be sensitive to her beliefs concerning the nature of the causal relationships that hold between disparate elements of the physical world. And the truth of the modularity thesis does not in itself rule out such disagreement.

Third, Fodor's view of the role of observation in science does not sit happily with his commitment to the idea that scientific confirmation is Quinean. If scientific confirmation is Quinean then the following scenario is a real possibility. Two scientists are sympathetic to a particular hypothesis and conduct an experiment to test that hypothesis. They agree on the observational data thrown up by this experiment. However, they respond in different ways to this data. One of them abandons his commitment to the hypothesis since to hold onto it in the light of his observations would require him to make adjustments to his background beliefs that are unacceptable to him. The background beliefs of his colleague are somewhat different; so much so that he can square his acceptance of the hypothesis in question with the observational data by executing some relatively minor changes in his background beliefs. He chooses to do this and so maintains his acceptance of the hypothesis despite the fact that he accepts the veracity of the very observational data that led his colleague to reject the hypothesis.

In reality, experimentation and observation do play an important role in settling scientific disputes and establishing consensus in the scientific community. Therefore, there must be mechanisms at work that limit the extent to which scientists diverge in the perceptual beliefs that they acquire in any given experimental situation, and in their views about the significance of any given item of observational data. The modularity thesis does not in itself explain such agreement and the problem for Fodor is that the relativist has an explanation close at hand. For, the relativist can point out that scientists are generally the products of a specific cultural background and tend to share a common educational history. Hence, it is no surprise that they agree so much of the time. But such agreement is no testament to the neutrality and objectivity afforded by the scientific method.

Conclusion

According to Fodor's modularity thesis, input systems are modules, that is, domain-specific, informationally encapsulated sub-systems of the mind. In this respect, input systems contrast with the central system, that is, that part of the mind that is concerned with belief fixation and general reasoning. The processes executed by the central system are global and holistic and for that reason they are not amenable to investigation by cognitive science. I have argued that there is considerable empirical evidence in support of Fodor's claim that perception and linguistic processing are modular. For studies of individuals suffering from brain damage and genetic disorders suggest that linguistic and perceptual capacities doubly dissociate from general intellectual capacities. However, I have been less enthusiastic about Fodor's reflections on the central system. Therefore, I conclude that his view of the prospects for a cognitive science of the central system and of the plausibility of CTM as a theory of central processing is unduly pessimistic.

Afterword

This afterword serves as a conclusion to the comprehensive account of Fodor's output that I have given in the preceding chapters.

Fodor's output consists of a number of interrelated views that together constitute an attempt to provide a substantial vindication of folk psychology within a physicalist framework. They do this by explaining how we humans could be as folk psychology represents us to be consonant with the fact that the world is at bottom physical in nature. We have seen how, in the course of constructing this vindication of folk psychology, Fodor has raised a number of fascinating questions. To recapitulate, these questions include the following.

- What is the relationship between folk psychology and scientific psychology?
- What is the relationship between psychology (both folk and scientific) and such lower-level sciences as neuroscience and physics?
- Is cognition a form of computation?
- What is the role of natural language in thought?
- To what extent are our concepts innate?
- Why do our intentional states have the contents that they have?
- From the perspective of scientific psychology, are the contents of our intentional states exhaustively determined by our intrinsic physical properties?

- What is the architecture of the mind? Is it a homogeneous processing system or does it comprise a number of independent sub-systems?

Fodor has provided bold and original answers to all of these questions that can be summarized in the following terms.

- Folk psychology consists of a large battery of causal generalizations that can be utilized for the purposes of describing, explaining and predicting human behaviour and episodes in our mental lives. Many of these generalizations refer to such intentional states as beliefs, desires, intentions and their kin. Scientific psychology is an intentional psychology; it recognizes the reality of beliefs, desires and the like, and endorses many of the generalizations of folk psychology. In short, scientific psychology is a refinement and extension of folk psychology.
- The relationship that psychology (both folk and scientific) bears to lower-level sciences and, ultimately, to physics, is that characteristic of a special science. Psychological phenomena are token-identical to, or constituted by, physical phenomena in the central nervous system. Psychological properties do not reduce to physical properties. Rather, they supervene upon such properties. Consequently, though psychological laws do not reduce to the laws of physics, they are underpinned by those laws.
- Intentional states are computational relations to sentences of the language of thought, a language that has a combinatorial syntax and semantics. Cognitive processes such as thinking are computational processes involving the manipulation of sentences of LOT.
- Although thinking involves the deployment of a language, that language is not a natural language. Rather than serving as the medium of thought, we use natural languages such as English to express and communicate our thoughts. Thus, thought is prior to language.
- For many years Fodor held that most of our concepts are innate. In other words, LOT is an innate language the possession of which is a prerequisite for learning the meanings of the words of any natural language. More recently he has attempted to retreat from this position of radical concept nativism by arguing that those concepts that express mind-

independent properties (of which there are many) are not innate.

- Content reduces to information so that the contents of our intentional states are determined by the nomic relations that the simple non-logical symbols of LOT bear to the properties that they express. Thus, content is atomistic, making it intelligible how distinct individuals, or time slices of the same individual, can share concepts and intentional states.

- For many years Fodor argued that scientific psychology must individuate intentional states in such a way as to respect the local supervenience of the psychological on the physical. Thus, unlike folk psychology, it must employ a notion of narrow content. More recently he has changed his stance on this issue. Due to the existence of contingent mechanisms that prevent the proliferation of twin and Frege cases, scientific psychology has no need to 'go narrow'.

- The mind is not a homogeneous processing system. Input systems are modules, that is, domain-specific, informationally encapsulated sub-systems. There are six such modular input systems; five corresponding to the senses as traditionally conceived along with a language module. The central system, the domain of belief fixation, does not have a modular architecture and the processes that it executes are global and holistic.

To what extent should we endorse Fodor's position? I have offered criticisms of several of Fodor's views. For example, I have objected to the details of his naturalistic theory of content, raised doubts about the success of his attempt to retreat from radical concept nativism, and questioned the power of his attack on connectionism. Moreover, I have opposed his arguments for the claim that scientific psychology should be narrow and expressed scepticism with respect to his view that central processing is global and holistic and that there cannot be (at least in the foreseeable future) a successful cognitive science of such processing. However, such disagreement has been presented against a general background of enthusiasm for Fodor's work. In particular, I have considerable sympathy for his physicalism, his enthusiasm for folk psychology and a closely related scientific psychology, his account of the structure of science, his view of the role of natural language in thinking, his atomism, his recent endorsement of broad psychology and his claim that input systems are modules.

What about CTM, the centrepiece of Fodor's output? There is a lot to be said in favour of CTM, for example, its ability to account for the rational coherence, the productivity and the systematicity of thought. Moreover, I have yet to encounter a convincing refutation of CTM and find the worries that Fodor himself raises in *The Modularity of Mind* (1983) and *The Mind Doesn't Work That Way* (2000) unduly pessimistic. Nevertheless, I choose to adopt an agnostic stance. Fodor never claimed to have any demonstrative arguments for CTM. Rather, he explicitly characterized it as being a product of speculative psychology whose truth value is ultimately an empirical matter. At this point in our intellectual history we do not have sufficient knowledge of the workings of the human mind to determine whether or not CTM is true. In the long run CTM might be vindicated. Then again, it might turn out to be a stimulating and historically important but false hypothesis.

Fodor has done much to set the agenda in the philosophy of mind over the last forty years. Time and time again he raised an issue that has subsequently become the burning issue of the day. Given their provocative nature, his views have not won universal acceptance. Nevertheless, few philosophers would question the interest or significance of Fodor's work and even the most fervent of his opponents typically feel the need to discuss his pronouncements and characterize their own position in terms of its relationship to Fodor's. In short, Fodor has made a major contribution to the philosophy of mind and he is arguably its most important contemporary practitioner.

Notes

Chapter 1   The Fodorian Project

1   It is worth noting that there are several terms widely used in the philosophical literature that are roughly synonymous with the term 'intentional state'. The most widely used is 'propositional attitude' (or 'attitude' or 'PA' for short) as having an intentional state involves having an attitude (for example, the belief attitude or the desire attitude) towards a proposition. Other synonyms are 'thought', and 'representational state'. What I have referred to as 'content' is often labelled 'propositional content' or 'representational content'.

2   I can now explain why intentional states are so called. Scholastic philosophers used the term 'intentionality' to refer to the property of aboutness, a usage that was revived by Franz Brentano in the 19th century. Beliefs, desires and the like have intentionality as, being meaningful, they are about objects and possible states of affairs. Hence, they have come to be known as intentional states.

3   Suppose that the statement that all the occupants of the room are bearded is true. It doesn't follow that (contrary to fact) had Bill Clinton entered the room he would have been bearded. Neither does it follow that the next person who enters the room will be bearded. In other words, the statement expresses an accidental generalization. Now consider the lawful generalization that all water expands when frozen. This implies that had the sample of water that I have just drunk been frozen then it would have expanded. Moreover, it implies that if I freeze the water in the glass before me then it will expand. It is widely held that scientific laws differ from accidental generalizations in that they imply counterfactual and hypothetical statements and that they are supported by their instances. In this respect, the causal generalizations in which intentional states feature are like scientific laws.

4   Intensionality should not be confused with intentionality. In order to avoid any confusion between the two, John Searle (1983) has coined the terms intentionality-with-a-t and intensionality-with-an-s.

5   See e.g. Gordon (1986), Heal (1986) and Goldman (1989).

6   Thus, he will have no truck with the eliminativism of Quine (1966), Feyerabend (1963), Rorty (1965), P. M. Churchland (1979, 1981) and P. S. Churchland (1986).

7   This is not to say that there is no overlap in the properties that figure in the explanations and descriptions of distinct sciences. For example, a biologist might describe a species of plant as being well adapted to a mountainous terrain or a species of animal as being wiped out by a volcanic eruption. And all sciences attribute physical dimensions to objects and talk about the spatial and temporal relationships holding between phenomena.

8   It might be objected that there are certain perfectly respectable special science states that are clearly not identical to, or constituted by, physical states. For example, consider the state of being soluble. The solubility of a sugar cube cannot be identified with anything physical (for example, the molecular structure of the sugar cube) unlike a rusty knife's state of being rusty (that can be identified with a collection of molecules of iron oxide lying on the knife's surface). This is because solubility is a dispositional state: for the sugar cube to be soluble just is for it to be the case that if it were submerged in water it would dissolve. In response, an advocate of the above described account of the structure of science might – reasonably – respond by pointing out that her claims only require a slight modification in the light of this objection. For it is only physical objects that are soluble and the solubility of a soluble object will be a product of its physical nature and the laws of physics. Moreover, instances of the events in terms of which solubility is defined (being submerged in water and dissolving) are always identical to, or constituted by, physical events.

9   I am assuming that if, for example, there are no biological laws then biology does not count as a legitimate science.

10 For discussion of the nature of supervenience, see Kim (1980, 1984) and Horgan (1993).

11 Lewis (1966) and Davidson (1970) are important examples of arguments for physicalism that also appeal to causal considerations. For a spirited reply to his genre of physicalist reasoning, see Crane (1995).

Chapter 2   Philosophical and Scientific Background

1   This conception of the nature of philosophy is clearly evident in Ryle (1949).

2   For a good example, see Norman Malcolm's comments on scientific research into dreaming in Malcolm (1959).

3   Quine is the figure most responsible for this development. In particu-
    lar, see Quine (1951).
4   All these objections are prominent in the work of Skinner. In particu-
    lar, see Skinner (1953, 1964). For a sympathetic reconstruction of
    Skinner's reasoning, see Dennett (1978*d*).
5   Chomsky (1959) is of particular importance.
6   Although the position I am about to describe is closely associated with
    Ryle in the respect in which it was endorsed by many philosophers
    who were influenced by his writings, it is arguable that it is not Ryle's
    actual position. For Ryle was probably not as blatantly reductionist as
    many have taken him to be.
7   Ryle develops similar objections to what he calls 'intellectualist'
    accounts of intelligent performances. For example, he objects to expla-
    nations of a clown's clever clowning that appeal to a prior mental
    process of planning. For processes of planning themselves require
    intelligence and are thus too closely related to the act that they are
    invoked to explain to give us any explanatory purchase. Fodor (1975)
    misdiagnoses Ryle's objection to 'intellectualist' explanations of the
    clown's clever clowning. He accuses Ryle of failing to see that there is
    a distinction between conceptual and causal questions and argues that
    appeals to mental processes can legitimately figure in answers to the
    question 'what makes the clown's clowning clever?' when understood
    as a causal question. Ryle would argue that he fully appreciates the
    distinction between causal and conceptual questions and that 'intel-
    lectualist' causal explanations of intelligent acts get us nowhere as they
    are either circular or lead to infinite regress.
8   Important early champions of the type identity theory include Place
    (1956) and Smart (1959).
9   Or, alternatively, to be in pain is to have one's C-fibres firing or that
    what all creatures that are in pain have in common in virtue of which
    they are in pain is that their C-fibres are firing.
10 See Davidson (1970) for an important defence of the token identity
    theory.
11 Thus 'function' in 'functionalism' should be understood in causal
    rather than teleological terms.
12 A Turing machine is a simple computing device whose states are char-
    acterized in terms of their relations to inputs, outputs and other states.
    See Block (1980a) and Kim (1996, ch. 4) for helpful discussions of the
    nature of Turing machines and of their role in early formulations of
    functionalism.
13 Chomsky's ongoing work concerning our knowledge of language and
    the acquisition of that knowledge constitutes one of the most promi-
    nent achievements in the history of cognitive science. For accessible
    accounts of Chomsky's output, see McGilvray (1999) and N. V. Smith
    (1999).

Chapter 3   The Computational Theory of Mind

1   LOT is sometimes called 'mentalese'.

2   Fodor uses the term 'CTM' but he more frequently uses the term 'the Representational Theory of Mind' (RTM for short) to label his position. I prefer the former label as it is much more specific than the latter: CTM is a version of RTM but not every variant of RTM is a version of CTM.

3   Descartes (1985), Locke (1975), Hume (1975) and Kant (1961) are all prominent advocates of RTM.

4   For ease of exposition, from this point on I will abbreviate 'identical to or constituted by' as 'identical to'.

5   An example of a syntactic similarity would be one that holds between the English sentences 'the dog chased the runner' and 'the cat ate the mouse'.

6   The most prominent recent advocate of the idea that natural language meaning is to be explained in terms of the content of our underlying intentional states is Grice (1957).

7   In this respect Fodor's views contrast with those of Davidson (1975).

8   In this respect Fodor differs from his colleague and sympathizer Zenon Pylyshyn (1984).

9   In general, the functional role of a state within a system is not merely a matter of the causal ramifications that it actually has within the system. Rather, it is a matter of the ramifications that it would have in conjunction with other states were those states tokened. That is why it is necessary to specify generalizations concerning how S is processed in order to describe its functional role.

10   This objection to Fodor's CTM is advanced by Dennett (1975).

11   See e.g. Chomsky (1986).

12   Fodor has expressed enthusiasm both for the Chomskian claim that Universal Grammar is innate (see e.g. Fodor 1983, pt 1) and for the claim that folk psychology is innate (see e.g. Fodor 1978b).

13   Fodor identifies 17th- and 18th-century empiricists as advocates of such a viewpoint. For them, all non-sensory concepts are definable in terms of sensory concepts that are themselves innate.

14   Such concepts are known as lexical concepts.

15   Important advocates of the prototype theory include Rosch (1973, 1975, 1978), Smith and Medin (1981) and Lakoff (1987).

16   He tends to call the prototype theory 'the stereotype theory'.

17   Such an account isn't circular as the doorknob prototype can be described without invoking the property of being a doorknob. Describing the doorknob prototype will involve specifying such things as the shape, size, material constitution (and so on) that doorknobs typically have.

18   A cognitivist theory of concept acquisition is one according to which acquiring a concept involves forming beliefs about the items that fall

in the extension of the target concept. The idea that concept-learning is a species of hypothesis-testing and confirmation is a paradigmatic cognitivist theory.

Chapter 4   Challenges to the Computational Theory of Mind

1   Accessible discussions of these objections can be found in Sterelny (1990), Glymour (1992), Crane (1996) and Rey (1997).

2   The relevant writings of Davidson include Davidson (1970, 1973a,b, 1974, 1987). Helpful accounts of Davidson's philosophy of mind can be found in Kim (1985), Evnine (1991), Child (1994) and Heil (1998).

3   A second rare example of Fodor engaging with Davidson appears in Fodor and LePore (1992), in which the authors devote a chapter to some of Davidson's work in the philosophy of language with a view to undermining his arguments for semantic holism. However, Fodor and LePore's reflections do not constitute a full-blooded engagement with Davidson's philosophy of mind.

4   The most relevant writings of Dennett are Dennett (1978b,c, 1979, 1981, 1991).

5   Fodor once held that explaining a cognitive capacity involves decomposing the mind–brain into a team of homunculi. See Fodor (1968a).

6   I will reserve direct discussion of semantic holism until ch. 5, where Fodor's objections to holism and his attempt to vindicate an atomistic alternative are considered in some detail.

7   Strictly speaking, the conclusion is that no computer, *qua* computer or in virtue of its computational activity, is capable of understanding natural language.

8   This response draws on Sterelny (1990) and Rey (1997).

9   Connectionism is also known as parallel distributed processing (PDP for short).

10   For book-length introductions to connectionism, see Bechtel and Abrahamsen (1991) and Clark (1989). For a classic collection of connectionist articles, see Rumelhart *et al.* (1986).

11   It is sometimes said that connectionist systems are a species of computer so that, strictly speaking, connectionism is a variant of the computational theory of mind. However, the reader should bear in mind that, in keeping with my use of the term throughout this book, I mean 'CTM' to refer only to Fodor's specific version of the computational theory of mind in what follows.

12   The system underwent a training process that involved being repeatedly presented with descriptions of members of a particular collection of individuals and having its connection weights altered until, in response to a description of any given individual in the collection, it would give a correct identification of their identity as its output. See

Bechtel and Abrahamsen (1991, ch. 3) for an account of learning in connectionist systems.

13 The papers in question are Fodor and Pylyshyn (1988); Fodor and McLaughlin (1990); Fodor (1996).

14 In the context of this debate, CTM is generally known as classicism and computers that manipulate syntactically structured symbols are known as classical systems.

Chapter 5   Explaining Mental Content

1 For a collection of papers largely focused upon Fodor's theory of content, see Loewer and Rey (1991).

2 I shall follow the standard convention of referring to symbols of LOT by means of capitalized words and expressions, meanings by means of italicized words and expressions and natural language symbols by means of words and expressions flanked by inverted commas.

3 Teleological theories of a biological, evolutionary form have been advanced by a number of philosophers in recent years. Some notable examples are: Millikan (1984, 1989), Papineau (1987, 1993), Dretske (1986) and Dennett (1978b). Indeed, Fodor briefly flirted with a version of the teleological theory. See his long-suppressed paper 'Psychosemantics, or Where do Truth Conditions Come From?' (1990d). It should be noted that the version of the teleological theory described above is the one that Fodor considers and does not completely coincide with theories championed by any of the philosophers just cited. However, it is arguable that Fodor's primary objection to the teleological theory that he discusses causes problems for all teleological theories.

4 It should be noted that in 'A Theory of Content, II' (1990c) Fodor expresses reservations about cashing out the notion of asymmetric dependence in terms of possible worlds.

5 Alternative names for CRS to be found in the literature include functional role semantics and inferential role semantics.

6 It should be noted that though Quine's arguments are hugely influential, not all philosophers accept that there is no analytic–synthetic distinction. For example, see Wright (1984).

7 Recall Fodor's arguments for CTM and Fodor and Pylyshyn's related objection to connectionism described, respectively, in chs 3 and 4.

8 See ch. 3 for the details of this argument.

9 One point in favour of CRS is that it avoids this problem as WATER and H_2O enter into different inferential connections.

10 This accusation is made by Stich (1983) and Devitt (1991).

11 Fodor asserts that the possible world where we can distinguish between water and XYZ but do not intend to use WATER as a kind concept is more distant than the world where we can distinguish between water and XYZ and do intend to use WATER as a kind concept.

12 The unamended version of Fodor's theory can explain why, for example, UNICORN expresses the property of being a unicorn despite the fact that, as that property is uninstantiated, a unicorn has never actually caused a tokening of UNICORN. For, the uninstantiation of the property of being a unicorn is entirely consistent with it being a law that unicorns cause tokenings of UNICORN. For all that law requires is that had there been unicorns, they would have caused tokenings of UNICORN.

13 This line of thought is closely associated with Kripke's Wittgenstein (Kripke 1982) and with the work of John McDowell (see e.g. McDowell 1986, 1994; McCulloch 1995).

14 For a more detailed version of this argument, see Cain (1999).

15 McGinn (1989) and Segal (1991) make a similar point about the relationship between the content of visual states and the behaviour that they cause.

Chapter 6 Individualism and Narrow Content

1 A terminological note. Individualism also goes by the name 'internalism' and externalism is sometimes labelled 'anti-individualism' and 'contextualism'. I will employ the terms 'individualism' and 'externalism' as they are the most widely used in the literature.

2 To say this is not to deny that the external world can causally influence the intrinsic physical properties of the coin or that its intrinsic physical properties can change over time as a result of impingements by the external world.

3 Recall that supervenience is a relation of synchronous non-causal determination holding between distinct families of properties. Generally, A properties supervene upon B properties if and only if the A properties that an object has are exhaustively determined by its B properties so that no two objects could differ with respect to their A properties without differing with respect to their B properties. See ch. 1 for further details.

4 To show that this is not an isolated case Burge presents a whole battery of parallel cases. These cases feature the following terms: 'sofa', 'contract', 'brisket', 'clavichord' and 'red'.

5 However, they are not universally accepted. For a recent argument against Putnam and Burge's conclusions, see Segal (2000).

6 In *The Elm and the Expert* (1994a) Fodor attempts to undermine this argument. However, he points out that for a long time it held a great power over him and motivated his commitment to the individualistic idea that scientific psychology must employ a notion of narrow content.

7 Burge's (1986) consideration of Marr's theory of vision is a classic example of this kind of argument.

8 Fodor is effectively endorsing the deductive–nomological theory of explanation championed by Hempel (1965).
9 For example, Burge (1986), van Gullick (1989), Egan (1991) and Wilson (1995) all express reservations.
10 Perhaps there is something mysterious about how a change in an individual's environment can cause a change in the causal powers of her intentional states, as there is no physical event constituting the latter change that is clearly distinct (spatially and/or temporally) from its putative cause. However, this is no problem for the externalist as it suggests that the relationship between the environmental change and the change in the causal powers of the individual's intentional states is not causal after all.
11 A qualification is needed here. Fodor thinks that there are some instances of S that are bona fide despite the fact that they do not satisfy his position. These are cases where 'the property that distinguishes the causes is itself the property of having a certain causal power' (1991a: 15). An example of such a property is that of being soluble; to be soluble *just is* to have the power to dissolve when placed in water. The twin case does not fall into this category: the property of being a water thought is not the property of having a particular causal power.
12 For example, consider the following conceivable species of creature. Members of this species are allergic to water and are hard-wired in such a way that whenever they form a belief that the stuff before them is water, that belief, unmediated by any desires that they have, causes them to turn and flee. And, whenever they form a desire to drink water, this desire causes them to feel shame and revulsion.
13 Thus, there is a key difference between the property of being a water thought and that of being an H-particle that could be appealed to in order to account for the fact that the former affects causal powers whereas the latter does not.
14 This account is inspired by Kaplan (1977).
15 See Block (1991) for an argument of this type.
16 This objection to broad psychology is closely tied to Fodor's point in 'Methodological Solipsism' (1980) that how an individual acts on the basis of a thought crucially depends on how she represents the referent of the thought. Therefore, to be of explanatory and predictive value, psychology must concern itself with modes of presentations, that is (assuming CTM) with the syntax of the LOT sentences that express the broad contents of our thoughts.

Chapter 7   The Modularity Thesis

1 Examples of psychological works that contain extensive discussions of the central claims of *The Modularity of Mind* include Garfield (1987), Shallice (1988), Karmiloff-Smith (1992) and N. V. Smith and Tsimpli (1995).

2   With respect to output systems Fodor writes: 'It would please me if
    the kinds of arguments that I shall give for the modularity of input
    systems proved to have application to motor systems as well. But I
    don't propose to investigate that possibility here' (1983: 42).
3   As N. V. Smith (1999, ch. 1) notes, there are some key differences
    between Fodor and Chomsky's views of the language system. First,
    Chomsky conceives of the language system as being as much an
    output as an input system: the language system is as much concerned
    with language production as it is with language comprehension. One
    cannot legitimately conceive of a distinct input and output system for
    language as one never finds individuals who can speak only English
    and understand only Japanese. (See Chomsky 1986, ch. 1.) Second, the
    language system is not domain-specific in the respect that it is only
    sensitive to sounds that constitute utterances. On the contrary, it
    processes such non-linguistic sounds as door squeaks. (Chomsky
    1987.)
4   A qualification is needed here. Strictly speaking, it is consistent with
    the view that the mind is a uniform general-purpose processing
    system that damage to the central system can impair a particular
    capacity whilst leaving most other capacities intact. For the capacity
    in question might be unusually hard, placing demands of the central
    system (in terms of attention, processing power, memory capacity and
    the like) in excess of those placed on it by other tasks.
5   William's syndrome is also known as Beuren's syndrome and infan-
    tile hypercalcaemia.
6   Cowie (1999, ch. 11) provides a review of this sceptical literature and
    concludes that our current knowledge of such disorders as SLI and
    William's syndrome is not such as to legitimize a confident assertion
    that language dissociates from general intelligence.
7   As Quine emphasizes the importance of the role that considerations
    of simplicity and conservatism play in science, Fodor is, in effect,
    merely reaffirming his commitment to the idea that scientific reason-
    ing is Quinean.
8   See Farah (1995) for an overview of this data.
9   DOG is an example of a basic category unlike the more general ANIMAL
    and the more specific POODLE.
10 Prominent champions of the idea that there is a folk psychology
    module include Leslie (1991) and Baron-Cohen (1995).

References

Aizawa, K. (1997) 'Explaining Systematicity'. *Mind and Language*, 13: 115–36.

Astington, J. W., Harris, P. L., and Olson, D. R. (eds) (1998), *Developing Theories of the Mind*. Cambridge: Cambridge University Press.

Baron-Cohen, S. (1995) *Mindblindedness*. Cambridge, Mass.: MIT Press.

Baumgartner, P., and Payr, S. (eds) (1995) *Speaking Minds: Interviews with Twenty Eminent Cognitive Scientists*. Princeton: Princeton University Press.

Bechtel, W., and Abrahamsen, A. (1991) *Connectionism and the Mind*. Oxford: Blackwell.

Block, N. (ed.) (1980a) *Readings in Philosophy of Psychology*, vol. I. Cambridge, Mass.: Harvard University Press.

Block, N. (1980b) 'What is Functionalism?' In Block (1980a).

Block, N. (ed.) (1981) *Readings in Philosophy of Psychology*, vol. II. Cambridge, Mass.: Harvard University Press.

Block, N. (1986) 'Advertisement for a Semantics in Psychology'. *Midwest Studies in Philosophy*, 10: 257–74. Reprinted in Stich and Warfield (1994).

Block, N. (1990) 'Can the Mind Change the World?' In Boolos (1990).

Block, N. (1991) 'What Narrow Content is Not'. In Loewer and Rey (1991).

Boden, M. (ed.) (1990) *The Philosophy of Artificial Intelligence*. Oxford: Oxford University Press.

Boolos, G. (ed.) (1990) *Meaning and Method: Essays in Honor of Hilary Putnam*. Cambridge: Cambridge University Press.

Botterill, G., and Carruthers, P. (1999) *Philosophy of Psychology*. Cambridge: Cambridge University Press.

Bruner, J. (1957) 'On Perceptual Readiness'. *Psychological Review*, 64: 123–52.

Burge, T. (1979) 'Individualism and the Mental'. *Midwest Studies in Philosophy*, 5: 73–122.

Burge, T. (1986) 'Individualism and Psychology'. *Philosophical Review*, 95: 3–46.

Cain, M. J. (1999) 'Fodor's Attempt to Explain Mental Content'. *Philosophical Quarterly*, 49: 520–6.

Cain, M. J. (2000) 'Individualism, Twin Scenarios and Visual Content'. *Philosophical Psychology*, 13: 441–63.

Carruthers, P. (1992) *Human Knowledge and Human Nature*. Oxford: Oxford University Press.

Carruthers, P. (1996) *Language, Thought, and Consciousness*. Cambridge: Cambridge University Press.

Child, W. (1994) *Causality, Interpretation and the Mind*. Oxford: Oxford University Press.

Chisholm, R. M. (1957) *Perceiving*. Ithaca, NY: Cornell University Press.

Chomsky, N. (1959) 'Review of Skinner's *Verbal Behavior*'. *Language*, 35: 26–58. Reprinted in Block (1980a).

Chomsky, N. (1980) *Rules and Representations*. Oxford: Blackwell.

Chomsky, N. (1986) *Knowledge of Language: Its Nature, Origin, and Use*. New York: Praeger.

Chomsky, N. (1987) *Language in a Psychological Setting*. Special issue of *Sophia Linguistica*, 22, Sophia University, Tokyo.

Churchland, P. M. (1979) *Scientific Realism and the Plasticity of Mind*. Cambridge: Cambridge University Press.

Churchland, P. M. (1981) 'Eliminative Materialism and the Propositional Attitudes'. *Journal of Philosophy*, 78: 67–90.

Churchland, P. S. (1986) *Neurophilosophy*. Cambridge, Mass.: MIT Press.

Clark, A. (1989) *Microcognition*. Cambridge, Mass.: MIT Press.

Cowie, F. (1999) *What's Within: Nativism Reconsidered*. Oxford: Oxford University Press.

Crane, T. (1995) 'The Mental Causation Debate'. *Proceedings of the Aristotelian Society*, suppl. vol. 69: 211–36.

Crane, T. (1996) *The Mechanical Mind*. Harmondsworth: Penguin.

Crane, T., and Mellor, D. H. (1990) 'There is No Question of Physicalism'. *Mind*, 99: 185–206.

Cummins, R. (1989) *Meaning and Mental Representation*. Cambridge, Mass.: MIT Press.

Davidson, D. (1963) 'Actions, Reasons, and Causes'. *Journal of Philosophy*, 60: 685–700. Reprinted in Davidson (1980).

Davidson, D. (1967) 'Causal Relations'. *Journal of Philosophy*, 64: 691–703. Reprinted in Davidson (1980).

Davidson, D. (1970) 'Mental Events'. In L. Foster and J. W. Swanson (eds) *Experience and Theory*. Amherst, Mass.: University of Massachusetts Press. Reprinted in Davidson (1980). References to reprinted version.

Davidson, D. (1973a) 'The Material Mind'. In P. Suppes, L. Henkin, G. C. Moisil, and A. Joja (eds) *Proceedings of the Fourth International Congress for Logic, Methodology, and Philosophy of Science, Bucharest, 1971*. Amsterdam: North Holland. Reprinted in Davidson (1980).

Davidson, D. (1973b) 'Radical Interpretation', *Dialectica*, 27: 125–39. Reprinted in Davidson (1984).

Davidson, D. (1974) 'Psychology as Philosophy'. In S. C. Brown (ed.) *Philosophy of Psychology*. London: Macmillan. Reprinted in Davidson (1980).

Davidson, D. (1975) 'Thought and Talk'. In S. Guttenplan (ed.) *Mind and Language*. Oxford: Oxford University Press. Reprinted in Davidson (1984).

Davidson, D. (1980) *Essays on Actions and Events*. Oxford: Oxford University Press.

Davidson, D. (1984) *Inquiries into Truth and Interpretation*. Oxford: Oxford University Press.

Davidson, D. (1987) 'Problems in the Explanation of Action'. In P. Pettit, R. Sylvan, and J. Norman (eds) *Metaphysics and Morality: Essays in Honour of J. J. C. Smart*. Oxford: Blackwell.

Davies, M. (1986) 'Externality, Psychological Explanation, and Narrow Content'. *Proceedings of the Aristotelian Society*, suppl. vol. 60: 263–83.

Dennett, D. C. (1975) 'Brain Writing and Mind Reading'. In K. Gunderson (ed.) *Language, Mind and Meaning*. Minnesota Studies in the Philosophy of Science, vii. Minneapolis: University of Minnesota Press. Reprinted in Dennett (1978a).

Dennett, D. C. (1978a) *Brainstorms: Philosophical Essays on Mind and Psychology*. Montgomery, Vt.: Bradford Books.

Dennett, D. C. (1978b) 'Artificial Intelligence as Philosophy and as Psychology'. In M. Ringle (ed.) *Philosophical Perspectives on Artificial Intelligence*. New York: Humanities Press. Reprinted in Dennett (1978a).

Dennett, D. C. (1978c) 'A Cure for the Common Code?' In Dennett (1978a).

Dennett, D. C. (1978d) 'Skinner Skinned'. In Dennett (1978a).

Dennett, D. C. (1979) 'True Believers: The Intentional Strategy and why it Works'. In A. Heath (ed.) *Scientific Explanation*. Oxford: Oxford University Press. Reprinted in Dennett (1987a).

Dennett, D. C. (1981) 'Three Kinds of Intentional Psychology'. In R. Healy (ed.) *Reduction, Time and Reality*. Cambridge: Cambridge University Press. Reprinted in Dennett (1987a).

Dennett, D. C. (1982) 'Styles of Mental Representation'. *Proceedings of the Aristotelian Society*, 83: 213–16. Reprinted in Dennett (1987a).

Dennett, D. C. (1987a) *The Intentional Stance*. Cambridge, Mass.: MIT Press.

Dennett, D. C. (1987b) 'Evolution, Error and Intentionality'. In Y. Wilks and D. Partridge (eds) *Source Book on the Foundations of Artificial Intelligence*. Cambridge: Cambridge University Press. Reprinted in Dennett (1987a).

Dennett, D. C. (1991) 'Real Patterns', *Journal of Philosophy*, 87: 27–51.

Descartes, R. (1985) *The Philosophical Writings of Descartes*, trans. J. Cottingham, R. Stoothoff, and P. Murdoch. Cambridge: Cambridge University Press.

Devitt, M. (1989) 'A Narrow Representational Theory of Mind'. In Silvers (1989).

Devitt, M. (1991) 'Why Fodor can't Have it Both Ways'. In Loewer and Rey (1991).

Dretske, F. I. (1981) *Knowledge and the Flow of Information*. Cambridge, Mass.: MIT Press.

Dretske, F. I. (1986) 'Misrepresentation'. In R. Bogdan (ed.) *Belief*. Oxford: Oxford University Press.

Dreyfus, H. L. (1979) *What Computers can't Do*. New York: Harper & Row.

Dreyfus, H. L., and Dreyfus, R. (1987) 'The Frame Problem'. In Pylyshyn (1987).

Egan, F. (1991) 'Must Psychology be Individualistic?' *Philosophical Review*, 100: 179–203.

Evnine, S. (1991) *Donald Davidson*. Cambridge: Polity Press.

Farah, M. J. (1995) 'Dissociable Systems of Recognition: A Cognitive Neuropsychology Approach'. In S. Kosslyn and D. Osherson (eds) *An Invitation to Cognitive Science*, 2nd edn, vol. ii: *Visual Cognition*. Cambridge, Mass.: MIT Press.

Farah, M. J., Klein, K. L., and Levinson, K. L. (1995) 'Face Perception and Within-Category Discrimination in Prosopagnosia'. *Neuropsychologia*, 33: 661–74.

Feyerabend, P. (1963) 'Materialism and the Mind Body Problem'. *Review of Metaphysics*, 17: 49–67.

Feyerabend, P. (1975) *Against Method*. London: Verso.

Field, H. (1977) 'Logic, Meaning and Conceptual Role'. *Journal of Philosophy*, 74: 379–409.

Field, H. (1978) 'Mental Representation'. *Erkenntnis*, 13: 9–61. Reprinted in Block (1981).

Fodor, J. A. (1968a) 'The Appeal to Tacit Knowledge in Psychological Explanation'. *Journal of Philosophy*, 65: 627–40. Reprinted in Fodor (1981a).

Fodor, J. A. (1968b) *Psychological Explanation*. New York: Random House.

Fodor, J. A. (1974) 'Special Sciences'. *Synthese*, 28: 97–115. Reprinted in Fodor (1981a). Reference to reprinted version.

Fodor, J. A. (1975) *The Language of Thought*. New York: Thomas Y. Crowell.

Fodor, J. A. (1978a) 'Tom Swift and his Procedural Grandmother'. *Cognition*, 6: 229–47.

Fodor, J. A. (1978b) 'Three Cheers for Propositional Attitudes'. In E. Cooper and E. Walker (eds) *Sentence Processing*. Hillsdale, NJ: Erlbaum. Reprinted in Fodor (1981a).

Fodor, J. A. (1978c) 'Propositional Attitudes'. *The Monist*, 61: 501–23. Reprinted in Fodor (1981a).

Fodor, J. A. (1980) 'Methodological Solipsism Considered as a Research Strategy in Cognitive Psychology'. *Behavioural and Brain Sciences*, 3: 63–109. Reprinted in Fodor (1981a). Reference to reprinted version.

Fodor, J. A. (1981a) *RePresentations*. Cambridge, Mass.: MIT Press.

Fodor, J. A. (1981b) 'The Present Status of the Innateness Controversy'. In Fodor (1981a).

Fodor, J. A. (1981c) 'Imagistic Representation'. In N. Block (ed.) *Imagery*. Cambridge, Mass.: MIT Press.

Fodor, J. A. (1983) *The Modularity of Mind*. Cambridge, Mass.: MIT Press.

Fodor, J. A. (1984a) 'Semantics Wisconsin Style'. *Synthese*, 59: 231–50. Reprinted in Fodor (1990a). Reference to reprinted version.

Fodor, J. A. (1984b) 'Observation Reconsidered'. *Philosophy of Science*, 51: 23–43. Reprinted in Fodor (1990a). Reference to reprinted version.

Fodor, J. A. (1985a) 'Fodor's Guide to Mental Representation'. *Mind*, 94: 66–100.

Fodor, J. A. (1985b) 'Precis of *Modularity of Mind*'. *Behavioural and Brain Sciences*, 8: 1–42. Reprinted in Fodor (1990a). Reference to reprinted version.

Fodor, J. A. (1987) *Psychosemantics*. Cambridge, Mass.: MIT Press.

Fodor, J. A. (1989a) 'Why should the Mind be Modular?' In George (1989). Reprinted in Fodor (1990a). Reference to reprinted version.

Fodor, J. A. (1989b) 'Making Mind Matter More'. *Philosophical Topics*, 67: 59–79. Reprinted in Fodor (1990a).

Fodor, J. A. (1989c) 'Substitution Arguments and the Individuation of Belief'. In G. Boolos (1989). Reprinted in Fodor (1990a).

Fodor, J. A. (1990a) *A Theory of Content and Other Essays*. Cambridge, Mass.: MIT Press.

Fodor, J. A. (1990b) 'A Theory of Content, I: The Problem'. In Fodor (1990a).

Fodor, J. A. (1990c) 'A Theory of Content, II: The Theory'. In Fodor (1990a).

Fodor, J. A. (1990d) 'Psychosemantics, or Where do Truth Conditions Come From?' In Lycan (1990).

Fodor, J. A. (1991a) 'A Modal Argument for Narrow Content'. *Journal of Philosophy*, 88: 5–26.

Fodor, J. A. (1991b) 'You can Fool Some of the People All of the Time, Everything Else being Equal: Hedged Laws and Psychological Explanation'. *Mind*, 100: 19–34.

Fodor, J. A. (1991c) 'Replies'. In Loewer and Rey (1991).

Fodor, J. A. (1994a) *The Elm and the Expert*. Cambridge, Mass.: MIT Press.

Fodor, J. A. (1994b) 'Fodor, Jerry, A.' In Guttenplan (1994).

Fodor, J. A. (1996) 'Connectionism and the Problem of Systematicity (continued): Why Smolensky's Solution *Still* doesn't Work'. *Cognition*, 62: 109–19. Reprinted in Fodor (1998b). Reference to reprinted version.

Fodor, J. A. (1998a) *Concepts: Where Cognitive Science Went Wrong*. Oxford: Oxford University Press.

Fodor, J. A. (1998b) *In Critical Condition: Polemical Essays in Cognitive Science and the Philosophy of Mind*. Cambridge, Mass.: MIT Press.

Fodor, J. A. (2000) *The Mind doesn't Work that Way*. Cambridge, Mass.: MIT Press.

Fodor, J. A., and Chihara, C. (1965) 'Operationalism and Ordinary Language'. *American Philosophical Quarterly*, 2: 281–95. Reprinted in Fodor (1981a).

Fodor, J. A., and Katz, J. J. (eds) (1964) *The Structure of Language: Readings in the Philosophy of Language*. Englewood Cliffs, NJ: Prentice-Hall.

Fodor, J. A., and LePore, E. (1992) *Holism: A Shopper's Guide*. Oxford: Blackwell.

Fodor, J. A., and LePore, E. (1994) 'The Red Herring and the Pet Fish: Why Concepts Still can't be Prototypes'. *Cognition*, 58: 253–70.

Fodor, J. A., and McLaughlin, B. (1990) 'Connectionism and the Problem of Systematicity: Why Smolensky's Solution doesn't Work'. *Cognition*, 35: 183–204. Reprinted in Fodor (1998b). Reference to reprinted version.

Fodor, J. A., and Pylyshyn, Z. (1988) 'Connectionism and Cognitive Architecture: A Critical Analysis'. *Cognition*, 28: 3–71. Reprinted in Haugeland (1997). Reference to reprinted version.

Fodor, J. A., Bever, T., and Garrett, M. (1974) *The Psychology of Language*. New York: McGraw Hill.

Frege, G. (1952) 'On Sense and Reference'. In M. Black and P. Geach (eds) *Translations from the Philosophical Writings of Gottlob Frege*. Oxford: Blackwell.

Garfield, J. (ed.) (1987) *Modularity in Knowledge Representation and Natural-Language Understanding*. Cambridge, Mass.: MIT Press.

Geach, P. (1957) *Mental Acts*. London: Routledge & Kegan Paul.

George, A. (ed.) (1989) *Reflections on Chomsky*. Oxford: Blackwell.

Glymour, C. (1992) *Thinking Things Through*. Cambridge, Mass.: MIT Press.

Goldman, A. (1989) 'Interpretation Psychologised'. *Mind and Language*, 4: 161–85.

Gopnik, M. (1994) 'Impairments of Tense in a Familial Language Disorder'. *Journal of Neurolinguistics*, 8: 109–33.

Gordon, R. (1986) 'Folk Psychology as Simulation'. *Mind and Language*, 1: 158–71.

Grice, H. P. (1957) 'Meaning'. *Philosophical Review*, 66: 377–88.

Grimm, R., and Merrill, D. (eds) (1988). *Contents of Thought*. Tucson: University of Arizona Press.

Guttenplan, S. (ed.) (1994) *A Companion to the Philosophy of Mind*. Oxford: Blackwell.

Hanson, N. R. (1958) *Patterns of Discovery*. Cambridge: Cambridge University Press.

Harman, G. (1982) 'Conceptual Role Semantics', *Notre Dame Journal of Formal Logic*, 23: 242–56.

Haugeland, J. (1978) 'The Nature and Plausibility of Cognitivism'. *Behavioral and Brain Sciences*, 1: 215–26. Reprinted in Haugeland (1981).

Haugeland, J. (1981) *Mind Design*. Cambridge, Mass.: MIT Press.

Haugeland, J. (1997) *Mind Design* II. Cambridge, Mass.: MIT Press.

Heal, J. (1986) 'Replication and Functionalism'. In J. Butterfield (ed.) *Language, Mind and Logic*. Cambridge: Cambridge University Press.

Heil, J. (1998) *Philosophy of Mind: A Contemporary Introduction*. London: Routledge.

Hempel, C. (1965) *Aspects of Scientific Explanation*. New York: Free Press.

Horgan, T. (1993) 'From Supervenience to Superdupervenience: Meeting the Demands of a Material World'. *Mind*, 102: 555–86.

Hume, D. (1975) *A Treatise of Human Nature*, ed. L. A. Selby-Bigge. Oxford: Oxford University Press.

Kant, I. (1961) *Critique of Pure Reason*, trans. N. Kemp Smith. London: Macmillan.

Kaplan, D. (1977) 'Demonstratives'. In J. Almog, J. Perry, and H. Wettstein (eds) (1989) *Themes from Kaplan*. Oxford: Oxford University Press.

Karmiloff-Smith, A. (1992) *Beyond Modularity*. Cambridge, Mass.: MIT Press.

Karmiloff-Smith, A., Klima, E., Grant, J., and Baron-Cohen, S. (1995) 'Is there a Social Module? Language, Face Processing and Theory of Mind in Individuals with Williams Syndrome'. *Journal of Cognitive Neuroscience*, 7: 196–208.

Kim, J. (1980) 'Supervenience as a Philosophical Concept'. *Metaphilosophy*, 21: 1–27. Reprinted in Kim (1993).

Kim, J. (1984) 'Concepts of Supervenience'. *Philosophy and Phenomenological Research*, 65: 153–76. Reprinted in Kim (1993).

Kim, J. (1985) 'Psychophysical Laws'. In E. LePore and B. McLaughlin (eds) *Actions and Events: Perspectives on the Philosophy of Donald Davidson*. Oxford: Blackwell.

Kim, J. (1993) *Supervenience and Mind*. Cambridge: Cambridge University Press.

Kim, J. (1996) *Philosophy of Mind*. Oxford: Westview Press.

Kripke, S. (1980) *Naming and Necessity*. Oxford: Blackwell.

Kripke, S. (1982) *Wittgenstein: On Rules and Private Language*. Oxford: Blackwell.

Kuhn, T. S. (1962) *The Structure of Scientific Revolutions*. Chicago, Ill.: University of Chicago Press.

Lakoff, G. (1987) *Women, Fire and Dangerous Things*. Cambridge: Cambridge University Press.

Leslie, A. (1991) 'The Theory of Mind Impairment in Autism: Evidence for a Modular Mechanism of Development?' In A. Whiten (ed.) *Natural Theories of Mind: Evolution, Development and Simulation of Everyday Mindreading*. Oxford: Blackwell.

Lewis, D. (1966) 'An Argument for the Identity Theory'. *Journal of Philosophy*, 63: 17–25.

Lewis, D. (1970) 'How to Define Theoretical Terms'. *Journal of Philosophy*, 67: 427–46.

Lewis, D. (1973) *Counterfactuals*. Cambridge, Mass.: Harvard University Press.

Loar, B. (1981) *Mind and Meaning*. Cambridge: Cambridge University Press.

Locke, J. (1975) *An Essay concerning Human Understanding*, ed. P. H. Nidditch. Oxford: Oxford University Press.

Loewer, B., and Rey, G. (eds) (1991) *Meaning in Mind: Fodor and his Critics*. Oxford: Blackwell.

Lucas, J. R. (1964) 'Minds, Machines, and Gödel'. In A. R. Anderson (ed.) *Minds and Machines*. Englewood Cliffs, NJ: Prentice-Hall.

Lycan, W. G. (1984) *Logical Form in Natural Language*. Cambridge, Mass.: MIT Press.

Lycan, W. G. (ed.) (1990) *Mind and Cognition: A Reader*. Oxford: Blackwell.

McCulloch, G. (1995) *The Mind and its World*. London: Routledge.

McDowell, J. (1986) 'Singular Thought and the Extent of Inner Space'. In P. Pettit and J. McDowell (eds) *Subject, Thought and Context*. Oxford: Oxford University Press.

McDowell, J. (1994) *Mind and World*. Cambridge, Mass.: Harvard University Press.

McGilvray, J. (1999) *Chomsky: Language, Mind and Politics*. Cambridge: Polity Press.

McGinn, C. (1989) *Mental Content*. Oxford: Blackwell.

Malcolm, N. (1959) *Dreaming*. London: Routledge & Kegan Paul.

Marr, D. (1982) *Vision*. San Francisco: Freeman.

Matthews, R. (1997) 'Can Connectionists Explain Systematicity?' *Mind and Language*, 12: 154–77.

Millikan, R. G. (1984) *Language, Thought and Other Biological Categories*. Cambridge, Mass.: MIT Press.

Millikan, R. G. (1989) 'Biosemantics'. *Journal of Philosophy*, 86: 281–97. Reprinted in Stich and Warfield (1994).

Morton, A. (1980) *Frames of Mind*. Oxford: Oxford University Press.

Nagel, T. (1974) 'What is it Like to be a Bat?'. *Philosophical Review*, 83: 435–50.

Papineau, D. (1987) *Reality and Representation*. Oxford: Blackwell.

Papineau, D. (1993) *Philosophical Naturalism*. Oxford: Blackwell.

Penrose, R. (1989) *The Emperor's New Mind: Concerning Computers, Minds and the Laws of Physics*. Oxford: Oxford University Press.

Perner, J. (1991) *Understanding the Representational Mind*. Cambridge, Mass.: MIT Press.

Pinker, S. (1994) *The Language Instinct*. Harmondsworth: Penguin.

Place, U. T. (1956) 'Is Consciousness a Brain Process'. *British Journal of Psychology*, 47: 44–50.

Popper, K. (1962) *Conjectures and Refutations: The Growth of Scientific Knowledge*. New York: Harper & Row.

Putnam, H. (1965) 'Brains and Behaviour'. In R. J. Butler (ed.) *Analytical Philosophy*, vol. ii. Oxford: Oxford University Press. Reprinted in Block (1980a).

Putnam, H. (1967) 'Psychological Predicates'. In W. H. Capitan and D. D. Merrill (eds) *Art, Mind and Religion*. Pittsburgh, Pa.: University of Pittsburgh Press. Reprinted in Block (1980a) as 'The Nature of Mental States'.

Putnam, H. (1975a) *Mind, Language and Reality: Philosophical Papers*, vol. ii. Cambridge: Cambridge University Press.

Putnam, H. (1975b) 'The Meaning of "Meaning"'. In K. Gunderson (ed.) *Minnesota Studies in the Philosophy of Science*, vol. vii. Minneapolis: University of Minnesota Press. Reprinted in Putnam (1975a).

Putnam, H. (1992) *Renewing Philosophy*. Cambridge, Mass.: Harvard University Press.

Pylyshyn, Z. (1984) *Computation and Cognition*. Cambridge, Mass.: MIT Press.

Pylyshyn, Z. (1987) *The Robot's Dilemma: The Frame Problem in Artificial Intelligence*. Norwood, NJ: Ablex.

Quine, W. V. O. (1951) 'Two Dogmas of Empiricism'. *Philosophical Review*, 60: 20–43. Reprinted in Quine (1953).

Quine, W. V. O. (1953) *From a Logical Point of View*. Cambridge, Mass.: Harvard University Press.

Quine, W. V. O. (1960) *Word and Object*. Cambridge, Mass.: MIT Press.

Quine, W. V. O. (1966) 'On Mental Entities'. In his *The Ways of Paradox and Other Essays*. New York: Random House.

Rey, G. (1997) *Contemporary Philosophy of Mind*. Oxford: Blackwell.

Rorty, R. (1965) 'Mind–Body Identity, Privacy, and Categories'. *Review of Metaphysics*, 19: 24–54.

Rosch, E. (1973) 'On the Internal Structure of Perceptual and Semantic Categories'. In T. E. Moore (ed.) *Cognitive Development and the Acquisition of Language*. New York: Academic Press.

Rosch, E. (1975) 'Cognitive Representations of Semantic Categories'. *Journal of Experimental Psychology: General*, 104: 192–233.

Rosch, E. (1978) 'Principles of Categorization'. In E. Rosch and B. Lloyd (eds) *Cognition and Categorization*. Hillsdale, NJ: Erlbaum.

Rumelhart, D. E., McClelland, J. E., and the PDP Research Group (1986) *Parallel Distributed Processing: Explorations in the Microstructure of Cognition*, vol. i: *Foundations*. Cambridge, Mass.: MIT Press.

Ryle, G. (1949) *The Concept of Mind*. Harmondsworth: Peregrine.

Schiffer, S. (1987) *Remnants of Meaning*. Cambridge, Mass.: MIT Press.

Searle, J. R. (1980) 'Minds, Brains and Programs'. *Behavioral and Brain Sciences*, 3: 63–73. Reprinted in Haugeland (1981).

Searle, J. R. (1983) *Intentionality*. Cambridge, Mass.: MIT Press.

Searle, J. R. (1992) *The Rediscovery of Mind*. Cambridge, Mass.: MIT Press.

Segal, G. (1991) 'Defence of a Reasonable Individualism'. *Mind*, 100: 485–94.

Segal, G. (2000) *A Slim Book about Narrow Content*. Cambridge, Mass.: MIT Press.

Sellars, W. (1956) 'Empiricism and the Philosophy of Mind'. In H. Feigl and M. Scriven (eds) *The Foundations of Science and the Concepts of Psychology and Psychoanalysis*, Minnesota Studies in the Philosophy of Science, vol. i. Minneapolis: University of Minnesota Press. Reprinted in Sellars (1963).

Sellars, W. (1963) *Science, Perception and Reality*. London: Routledge & Kegan Paul.

Shallice, T. (1988) *From Neuropsychology to Cognitive Structure*. Cambridge: Cambridge University Press.

Silvers, S. (ed.) (1989) *Re-Representations: Readings in the Philosophy of Mental Representation*. Dordrecht: Kluwer Academic Publishers.

Skinner, B. F. (1953) *Science and Human Behavior*. New York: Macmillan.

Skinner, B. F. (1957) *Verbal Behavior*. New York: Appleton-Century-Crofts.

Skinner, B. F. (1964) 'Behaviorism at Fifty'. In T. W. Wann (ed.) *Behaviorism and Phenomenology*. Chicago, Ill.: University of Chicago Press.

Smart, J. C. C. (1959) 'Sensations and Brain Processes'. *Philosophical Review*, 68: 141–56.

Smith, E., and Medin, D. (1981) *Categories and Concepts*. Cambridge, Mass.: Harvard University Press.

Smith, N. V. (1999) *Chomsky: Ideas and Ideals*. Cambridge: Cambridge University Press.

Smith, N. V., and Tsimpli, I.-M. (1995) *The Mind of a Savant: Language Learning and Modularity*. Oxford: Blackwell.

Stalnaker, R. (1984) *Inquiry*. Cambridge, Mass.: MIT Press.

Stampe, D. (1977) 'Towards a Causal Theory of Linguistic Representation'. *Midwest Studies in Philosophy*, 2: 42–63.

Sterelny, K. (1990) *The Representational Theory of Mind*. Oxford: Blackwell.

Stich, S. P. (1978) 'Autonomous Psychology and the Belief–Desire Thesis'. *The Monist*, 61: 573–91.

Stich, S. P. (1983) *From Folk Psychology to Cognitive Science*. Cambridge, Mass.: MIT Press.

Stich, S. P., and Warfield, T. (eds) (1994) *Mental Representation*. Oxford: Blackwell.

van Gullick, R. (1989) 'Metaphysical Arguments for Internalism and why they don't Work'. In Silvers (1989).

Wellman, H. M. (1990) *The Child's Theory of Mind*. Cambridge, Mass.: MIT Press.

Wilson, R. A. (1995) *Cartesian Psychology and Physical Minds: Individualism and the Sciences of the Mind*. Cambridge: Cambridge University Press.

Wittgenstein, L. (1953) *Philosophical Investigations*, trans. G. E. M. Anscombe. Oxford: Blackwell.

Wittgenstein, L. (1958) *The Blue and the Brown Books*. Oxford: Blackwell.

Wright, C. (1984) 'Inventing Logical Necessity'. In J. Butterfield (ed.) *Mind, Language and Logic*. Cambridge: Cambridge University Press.

Index